COMMODORE
THE INSIDE STORY

COMMODORE
THE INSIDE STORY

THE UNTOLD TALE OF A COMPUTER GIANT

DAVID JOHN PLEASANCE

UNICORN

This edition first published in 2021 by
Unicorn, an imprint of Unicorn Publishing Group
5 Newburgh Street
London
W1F 7RG
www.unicornpublishing.org

First published in 2018 by Downtime Publishing

ISBN 978-1-913491-65-9

10 9 8 7 6 5 4 3 2 1

Edited and designed by Simon Busby
Cover idea by Marcel Franquinet
Cover design by Paul Kitching and Wayne Ashworth

Printed in Turkey

This book is dedicated to:

My first wife Sheila Floyd and our sons Marcel and Emile; my sister Susan and her husband Rob Mullin; my siblings, Christopher, Shane and Sandra; and my second wife Francia Mercedes Gomez and our daughter Lucidely.

My team at Commodore UK: Dawn Levack, John Smith, Kieron Sumner, Jonathan Anderson, Pauline Wakefield, Kelly Sumner, Bob Burridge and the late Nigel Jones.

And in loving memory of my parents June and Eddy, and my younger sister Stephanie.

CONTENTS

PART 2: COMMODORE MEMORIES

PART 3: APPENDIX

FOREWORD

I've had an almost symbiotic relationship with Commodore and Amiga computers.

My first computer was a Commodore PET CBM 4032, which arrived the same week as my eldest daughter, Emma. At the time, I was the technical applications manager at the company I worked for and was tasked with supervising the hardware and software development team as we added real-time data acquisition minicomputer systems to our well-site geological and engineering services.

I knew virtually nothing about the evolving microcomputer craze, so I decided to build my own Sinclair ZX80 and teach myself the rudiments of computing. Fortunately, one of my hardware engineers convinced me to look at a real computer like the Commodore PET or Apple II, and after reviewing all the microcomputer magazines of the day, I rejected the Apple II and chose the Commodore PET. Commodore was very well supported in the UK at the time and I was soon writing BASIC programs and PEEK-ing and POKE-ing with the best of them. It was the start of my Commodore addiction.

The PET was replaced by a Commodore 64, which I bought in 1983 having seen a demo of *International Soccer* playing in the window of a computer store in Aberdeen, Scotland. (This also coincided with the birth of my second daughter, Rachel. Fortunately, the link between my acquisition of new computers and the birth of children stopped at this point!) I then upgraded the C64 to a Commodore 128 and, in early 1986, I was transferred to Houston, Texas, to restructure a failing division of our parent company. After the relocation, I replaced the C128 with a Commodore 128D.

My transfer to Texas also resulted in my move to the Amiga,

although not quite in the manner you might expect.

During a particularly violent late-summer storm in 1988, my Commodore 128D, which was connected to the phone line by a 1200 baud modem, was zapped by a lightning strike. With the insurance cheque, I purchased an Amiga 2000.

Shortly afterwards, I started my own company and relocated to Cyprus. From that time onwards, I used a series of big-box Amigas in my business for video and graphics work, and to create technical manuals and sales brochures for our growing international business. In 1990, I added the newly released Amiga 3000.

When I moved back to the UK in 1992, I purchased several Amiga 4000s for my business from Commodore UK, and in 1994, I bought a couple of Amiga CD32s for my children (honest). Actually, I had a running joke with my daughters that I really wanted an Amiga 5000 – but, as history shows, it was not to be. Commodore International was in a death spiral and, despite releasing the Amiga CD32, declared bankruptcy that April.

After the bankruptcy, David Pleasance and Colin Proudfoot kept the UK business afloat and put together a creditable but ultimately failed bid to purchase Commodore's assets in a management buyout attempt. Like most Amigans, I had followed the Amiga's fate after Commodore's fall and crossed my fingers that the buyout would be successful. Unbelievably, under their joint stewardship, CBM UK survived for 14 months after the parent company went under; but after ESCOM acquired most of the Commodore and Amiga assets in 1995, they both left the Commodore and Amiga scene for good. Despite Commodore's demise, my company continued to use Amiga computers for all our technical manual and publicity needs up until the turn of the century.

Eventually, I sold my business in 2004, and after 30 years' working and travelling around the world, I was looking forward to a relaxing break. I reacquainted myself with the Amiga scene and discovered the Amiga next-generation evolution.

I purchased a Micro-A1-C (µA1-c) and Pegasos II in 2005 and began collecting Commodore and Amiga computers. In 2007, I started writing the 'Amiga Retrospective' series of articles for *Total Amiga* magazine, which later transferred to *Amiga Future* magazine.

The articles ran for 20 issues until 2010, by which time I had co-founded A-EON Technology to develop a new range of next-generation AmigaOne computers. The first model, the AmigaOne X1000, was released at the end of 2011, and I finally got my A5000 wish when the AmigaOne X5000 was commercially released in 2016.

Keeping it in the family, my youngest daughter Rachel wrote the boot sound for the AmigaOne X1000 and X5000, as well as the music and sound effects to several AmigaOS 4 animations and demos, while my oldest daughter Emma produced artworks for an Amiga graphics package. It's really no surprise as both my daughters were brought up using Amiga computers. At the time of writing, a new entry level machine, the AmigaOne A1222, is currently under beta test.

I met David in person for the first time in 2015 at the Amiga30 event in Amsterdam, celebrating 30 years of the Amiga. Since then, we have met up at several Amiga shows around the world, including in the UK, Germany and Poland, and have become good friends and business partners through our shared interest in FriendUP. He has shared many of his personal inside stories about his time at Commodore while chatting over a few drinks into the early hours of the morning – stories such as dealing with Irving Gould and Mehdi Ali, the failed buyout attempt, and what really caused the decline and fall of a company which even in 1992 had almost $1 billion in sales.

I found David's tales about the inner workings at Commodore fascinating and managed to convince him and Colin to let me interview them both for an *Amiga Future* article, which was published in two parts in 2016. As an executive producer for both Zach Weddington's *Viva Amiga* movie and *The Commodore Story* documentary by Steven Fletcher, I knew David's Commodore revelations would appeal to a wider audience, and when he told me he was thinking of writing a book about his experience I encouraged him to put pen to paper.

Most books written about Commodore and the Amiga naturally tend to focus on the groundbreaking hardware and the talented young developers who underpinned Commodore's contribution to the microcomputer revolution. Since the Amiga 30th anniversary celebrations, I have been fortunate enough to spend time with many Commodore legends such as RJ Mical, Carl Sassenrath, Dale Luck,

Glenn Keller, Dave Haynie and the late, great Dave Needle, among many others. Their stories have become folklore among Commodore and Amiga enthusiasts; however, little has been written from an insider's perspective about the company itself, which during the 1980s was more successful than Apple, creating the best-selling personal computer of all time with the Commodore 64, and going on to release the pioneering Amiga, with its custom chipset and pre-emptive multitasking operating system.

David Pleasance is very much a Commodore insider. He spent over 12 years with Commodore and served in several senior managerial positions in the UK, Switzerland and the US, before returning to the UK as the joint managing director of Commodore Business Machines UK Ltd. Under his leadership, the UK division became one of Commodore's most successful business units, selling more Amiga computers than any other.

So, if you really want to know the inside story of the rise and fall of Commodore and the dark secrets behind the company that dominated the 8-bit computer revolution and introduced the world to multimedia computing, you need to read this book. I don't think you will be disappointed.

TREVOR DICKINSON
Co-Founder of A-EON Technology Ltd
AANZ Arch Angel 2016
Wellington, New Zealand

INTRODUCTION

Hello and a warm welcome to *Commodore: The Inside Story* – my personal look back at this once-epic yet still much-loved company and its incredible line-up of products.

Since its declaration of bankruptcy on the 19th of April 1994, there has been much conjecture as to the truth behind what happened at Commodore and who was responsible. My intention here is to recount as many of the myriad incidents, stories, upsets, triumphs and downright outrageous events as I can recall, with the sole objective of ensuring that you, our loyal fans, gain a much better understanding of what went on within the company's hierarchy and what contributed to its eventual downfall.

With the addition of expansive accounts, short stories, technical research and personal quotes, generously submitted by fellow Commodore staff, significant industry figureheads and even self-confessed mega fans, I am proud to present this broad yet intimate perspective of a company that changed – and continues to change – so many people's lives.

So grab a hot (or chilled) drink, make yourself comfortable and enjoy this nostalgic trip back in time.

DAVID PLEASANCE
Peterborough, May 2018

PART 1
THE INSIDE STORY

-1-

IN THE BEGINNING...

I was born on the 28th of December 1948 in the seaside resort of Great Yarmouth, Norfolk, where I grew up with my parents, my older sister and brother, Sandra and Christopher, and two younger sisters, Stephanie and Susan. Thinking on it now, one of my earliest memories clearly shows I was destined to become a professional salesman.

My father had built me a 'push-and-go' cart, which he would take me to the seafront in to visit the makers of Great Yarmouth Rock, a crunchy candy made entirely of sugar, the core of which is run through with the words 'Gt. Yarmouth'.

But the candy had one problem – after a few days it would become soft and chewy. So I would buy the 'soft' candy for perhaps two pence per stick and go from door to door in my pushcart selling it for four pence each. It was primitive but entrepreneurial nonetheless!

My first overseas trip was on a family holiday to Holland at 14 years old, which spawned in me a massive desire to travel, and the following year I spent my summer holiday hitch-hiking around Europe.

I subsequently undertook an apprenticeship in sheet metalwork and welding – a job I hated – and became so restless I made the decision aged 17 to emigrate to Australia in search of adventure, and did so shortly after my younger brother, Shane, was born.

A view of Great Yarmouth's
Golden Mile from the top of the
Atlantis Tower, as it looks today

Living in Sydney during the late sixties was like living in paradise –
everything British was in vogue, and the Australian girls loved British
guys. My favourite place was The Union Jack Club, where only British
guys – with a passport and birth certificate to prove it – could be
members, but girls of any nationality could join. Total bliss!

At 20, a chance encounter with some British Navy sailors at a party
in Brisbane led me to The Folk Centre, a famous music institution, and
it was there that I heard Peter Williamson playing flamenco guitar, an
event that changed my life forever.

Peter was performing with his own flamenco group alongside his
wife Robin, a flamenco dancer, and Jan de Zwan, who would either
play second guitar or sing. (Jan could not play guitar and sing at the
same time – flamenco singing is a very different form of singing, and
the guitar rhythms are extremely difficult.)

I became a student of Peter's and was obsessed with becoming
a proficient performer myself, practising as much as 12 hours a day
during the working week and 16 hours a day at weekends.

David with his guitar

One Saturday afternoon at Peter's house, after my usual lesson had finished, he and his wife Robin were getting ready to go out, so to kill some time before leaving I began practising a flamenco rhythm called 'tientos'.

After a couple of minutes, Peter came flying into the room and asked frantically: 'Where did you learn that? I never taught you that!'

'Peter, I learned it from watching you and Jan,' I replied.

'You're not playing it quite right!' he said, and proceeded to correct me before leaving to finish getting ready. I kept on playing and eventually it sounded correct.

After a few minutes, Peter returned to the room. 'Have you got a white shirt and some black trousers?' he asked.

'One of the Jaléo Flamenco flyers we used for
our many promotional activities. We preferred
the more serious impact of black and white
images – even though as a flamenco quadro
we were very colourful in performance.'

I said yes.

'Right, go home and get changed – you are playing your first ever
live performance with us this afternoon.'

I was very, very nervous just at the thought of performing in front
of an audience, but still I rushed home to get ready.

They were due to give a performance as a group that afternoon, and
once Peter realised I could play the second guitar part for *tientos* it
meant Jan could sing while I provided the rhythm, which was needed
for Robin's footwork.

What they did not tell me was that my first-ever live performance
was to be on Queensland television in the Brisbane version of *New
Faces*! Talk about instant courage.

The best bit was we won the competition and went on to come second in the national heat in Sydney. Being flown to Sydney, met with

THE PANCAKE INN
CHARLOTTE ST. ENTRANCE
ELIZABETH ARCADE
BRISBANE

Tortilla

PHONE 21 4168

A contact card for The
Tortilla restaurant

a limo and taken to a five-star hotel by the television company was a real eye-opener, and I realised I could certainly get used to a lifestyle like this! So it spurred me on to even greater levels of practice.

After that, I would often play second rhythm guitar for Peter at local restaurant The Tortilla, where Peter performed every Friday, Saturday and Sunday evening.

After studying flamenco for just 14 months, I turned professional and became the resident guitarist at The Tortilla, as well as establishing and performing with my own flamenco *cuadro*,[1] Jaléo Flamenco, at many venues and concerts across Australia. I also played guitar and sang in a trio I formed with David Beresford (guitar and vocals) and Robbie Robinson (banjo, guitar and vocals), performing a variety of flamenco, contemporary-folk and comedy songs. Based on our initials, we called ourselves The DR. D Review.

I returned to the UK with the intention of making enough money to study flamenco in Spain. I stayed with my parents at their new house in Shrewsbury, Shropshire, where my father Edward, an electronics engineer, had bought a retail business called Telelectrics. From there he sold, rented and repaired consumer electronics – especially colour televisions, which had recently been launched onto the UK market (and were notoriously unreliable).

1   A *cuadro* is the name for a flamenco group usually comprising at least a guitarist, a dancer and a singer.

— A Salopian olé. . .

The excitement of the flamenco has been brought to Shropshire by four local people who have formed the first group of this kind in the county.

Los Duendos, which translated basically means spirit of flamenco, was the idea of professional flamenco guitarist, Dave Pleasance, Victoria Road, Shrewsbury

He is pictured with the other members, Phil Hayward, Bomere Heath, the other guitarist, and dancers Tina Ellis, Shrewsbury, and Eileen Enright, Wellington.

Dave learned the guitar as a hobby when he was in Australia. He got through to the final of a television talent contest and, after that, appeared several times on television. He returned to Spain to continue his study of the guitar.

Phil was one of his students and Tina became interested in flamenco when she was living in Seville teaching English. Eileen was a student at the Royal Academy of Dancing in London and is a qualified ballet teacher.

An article from a
Shropshire newspaper
about Los Duendos

Shropshire is well known for the highly regarded Shrewsbury School, a public school where the sons of many high-profile and wealthy celebrities and business moguls receive their education. I was approached by the school and subsequently appointed guitar tutor, teaching there from two to two-and-a-half days a week.

At one point I was teaching approximately 30 private students, taking weekly trips to London for guitar lessons, playing in a restaurant at the Prince Rupert Hotel two nights a week and performing in a cabaret with my flamenco group Los Duendos.

(I recall at a gig one night being announced by famous comedian Bernard Manning, who said: 'I am now going to introduce you to somebody who reckons he can play the guitar – if this guy can play guitar, I will show my arse to the Vatican!')

Around that time, I met and married my first wife, Sheila. Together we travelled to Spain, but due to economic and language difficulties we returned to the UK fairly quickly.

When we got back I began to help my dad in his shop, and I was soon offered a position as assistant manager at the Shrewsbury branch of Practical Credit Services, a subsidiary of the Provident Group, through whom Telelectrics offered credit terms to customers wanting to buy goods.

This career move provided a great opportunity for me and I thrived. Soon I was a manager-in-training and given the task of opening several new branches of Practical Credit Services, as Provident had determined they wanted an office of their subsidiary in every town that already had a Provident, their strategy being to own their own opposition. Ultimately, I was promoted to area manager and operated out of the Sheffield branch office.

In 1974, just a few days prior to the country changing its immigration laws, I returned to Australia, this time with Sheila by my side.

I joined Charge Card Services Limited, the first mass-market credit card in Australia, which was set up by 11 major banks. I was one of four permanent employees and oversaw a substantial number of staff lent by the various banks to launch Bankcard, the country's first mass-market credit card.

Left: Sheila and David on their wedding day

Below: Together in Australia

3M's Scotch Metafine
tape cassette

After a very successful launch, I was appointed state sales manager for Queensland and made responsible for all the major retail stores – a position I held for over four years.

I decided I wanted to move on in my career, so I moved into selling tangibles and joined 3M Company as Queensland sales manager in the consumer products division. It was an exciting role – I was given the freedom to access any of the massive portfolio of 87,000 products within any 3M division, devise marketing plans to offer selected items as consumer products and then sell them into the major retailers.

One of my most successful campaigns was the relaunch of the Scotch brand recording cassette range – Magnetic Tape – which included the world's first-ever metal particle tape, Metafine. I had the image for the whole range redesigned and wrote and produced a consumer-oriented user guide entitled, 'Scotch Brand Recording Tapes – The Truth Comes Out'.

But my real master stroke was to team up with hi-fi hardware manufacturers (Toshiba, Sony, Hitachi, etc) and retailers and collectively run marketing promotions, funded equally by all participants, that resulted in successful and incredibly cost-effective campaigns from which everyone benefited. As a direct result of this success,

I was headhunted by Pioneer Electronics and appointed state sales manager.[2]

In 1981, Sheila and I had our first son, Marcel, and two years later I decided to move back to the UK, where I believed I would be more likely to achieve my goal of attaining a more international role in business.

But before I returned, I decided to spend seven weeks travelling the world to discover the next big thing. It became obvious to me that computers – and particularly home computers – were destined to become a huge market. And I wanted in!

---

2   I learnt a very poignant lesson during my time at 3M. They had hired marketing consultants to review and change their branding with a view to giving 3M a higher profile (to the tune, I was told, of $3 million). What they came up with – after huge amounts of research – was to change the 3M logo from blue to red. Nothing more! One can only begin to imagine the cost incurred in changing the packaging of 87,000 products when it was simply a change of colour. Mind-blowing decision-making. There's little point paying huge sums of money and putting yourself in the hands of so-called 'experts' if an 11-year-old could have produced a better (or at least more justifiable) concept.

–2–

COMMODORE UK – THE FIRST FIVE MONTHS

MAY 1983 – SEPTEMBER 1983

Having just returned to England from Australia in May 1983, I started looking for a position somewhere in the then very nascent computer industry.

Of course, in those days there was no internet, so we had to rely on newspapers – particularly on Thursdays and Sundays – where all the advertisements for decent jobs were placed. I scoured them for a week or two looking for something that interested me in the computer field, though in truth I had no idea what might suit me or in which direction I should look.

Eventually, I found a position advertised through an agency in London who were recruiting for a company selling computer-based business services to businesses. I phoned the agency and after about 40 minutes of persuasive talking I managed to convince the recruitment agent to meet with me, despite my lack of experience with computers. The next thing I knew I was off to London via train for my interview.

I remember very clearly walking into the agency: it was a typical early-eighties central London boutique office with Conran furniture, decorated in shades of orange and lime green, as was the trend in those days.

As I entered, I held the door open for an attractive lady in her late twenties/early thirties who was just leaving. We exchanged pleasantries, as you do, and then I went through, sat down and met with the agent.

After what I thought was a pretty successful interview, the recruitment agent, an archetypal university-educated man in his mid thirties, turned to me and said, 'Well, Mr Pleasance, there is no doubt in my mind that you could do this job very easily. However, I'm not going put you forward for it.'

Well, obviously I was quite disappointed, so I got up, ready to leave.

'But hear me out,' he continued. 'You clearly have an extensive background in the retail market – in fact, such an incredible background that it would be remiss of me as a recruitment agent not to try to harness that experience and put you in a position where everybody will benefit.'

I returned to my chair, curious.

'Did you perchance notice the lady who was just leaving as you arrived?'

'Yes,' I replied.

'She has just given me the brief for a position that I think would suit you perfectly. She works for a company that makes computers, and they are looking for somebody to sell their business computers into the retail market.'

My interest was piqued.

'Truth is, they are not sure whether they should get a computer specialist who knows nothing about the retail market or a retail specialist who knows nothing about computers. And my advice to them was very clear: "I strongly suggest you get yourself a retail specialist, because that person can quite easily learn about the products". And I'll be honest with you, Mr Pleasance: I think you would be absolutely ideal for that role. I've not even had the opportunity to write it up yet, let alone advertise it!

'Oh, and by the way – the company is Commodore.'

Getting an appointment for a job that has not even been advertised? Talk about being in the right place at the right time!

So, just a couple of days later, I found myself in Browns Hotel, central London, having an interview with Eileen Stroud – the lady I had opened the door for.

Eileen, a very self-confident businesswoman, was the business development manager at Commodore. She explained more about the job and the company.

'We are looking for someone with extensive knowledge of retail channels who can introduce our small range of PET business computers – plus the peripheral devices to go with them – into this as-yet-untapped market.'

I expressed my excitement for the role and assured her I was a perfect fit.

'Commodore, as you will discover, is a very dynamic company where things happen and change quite regularly and quite rapidly. I think this could be a great opportunity for you.'

Satisfied with my interview, she put me forward for the position and I ended up having a final meeting with the then-managing director, Howard Stanworth (who I later learned had previously been employed at Associated Dairies). The interview went very well and I was able to convince him that I could do the job.

And so, within a couple of weeks, in June 1983, I began my career with Commodore.

*

I can clearly remember my first day at the office, which in those days was based out of Ajax Avenue in Slough. I was greeted by a gentleman by the name of Mike Tait, who had just recently been recruited to head the business division where I had been assigned.

Mike was a fairly typical mid-thirties sales executive and, in spite of his recent promotion, was not as assertive as I was expecting. In fact, I recall that while I was sitting in his office just a few minutes after I had arrived, his secretary Anita (who was Spanish, so we immediately got on well together) came in to tell him she needed to go to the supermarket to stock up on tea and coffee, and as he was new, she asked what his brand preference was for tea. Imagine my surprise when he telephoned his wife and said: 'Hello darling, what tea do I like?'

To be honest, he wasn't in the least bit prepared to have me working there – he had nothing for me to do. It was really rather strange.

Not wanting to just sit around, I searched out John Baxter, who in those days was Commodore's marketing manager. John was quite a good-looking chap with a dynamic personality (and, I later learned, a host of A-list connections).

I introduced myself and asked, 'Can you give me something to do?'

'Absolutely,' he said. 'In fact, a retail specialist computer shop has just recently opened on the North Circular Road – why don't you go and visit them and find out what they're up to, then write up a report and come and tell me what you think?'

I went straight there. The shop was a newly converted warehouse that had been extensively fitted out specifically to display – in 'live' format – computers and all things business-related.

'Who are you?' I was asked as I walked in.

I told him my name and said I was with Commodore computers.

'Oh, you're with Commodore? Do come in, you're most welcome!' they announced, and handed me a glass of champagne. I remember thinking to myself, 'I'm going to like this job!'

It turned out it was their official opening day – they had sent all the computer manufactures an invitation but nobody at Commodore had bothered to respond! (No surprises there, in hindsight!)

And that was my very first day at Commodore.

*

So, not having been given any direction, I made the decision that the best thing I could do to start my job properly would be to evaluate the state of the retail market in the UK, because I had been living in Australia for several years and of course things had changed quite considerably.

To begin with, I went from store to store visiting all the major consumer electronics retailers of the time – places such as Dixons, Comet and Currys – and it quickly became obvious that there was one particularly suitable store chain: a company called Laskys, who had 54 stores across the country.

Inside a typical Dixons in 1983
(from the cover of 'Dixons Group plc
– Reports and accounts 1983–84')

Laskys was a popular electronics store at the time that sold a range of TVs and other 'brown goods', and specialised in quality hi-fi equipment (i.e. no 'white goods' such as refrigerators, washing machines or other domestic appliances).[1] They were already well advanced and set up to sell business products because in 26 of their shops they had a 'store within a store' concept called Micropoint, where they were already selling some low-end computers, peripherals and software, making them an ideal vehicle for me and my principle objective to get Commodore PETs ranged.

Having determined that they would be my best option to approach initially, I went to their head office and received written permission from their managing director to go and visit all of the Micropoint store managers to 'research the market' and 'discuss our product range with them'. (In fact, what I was intent on doing was preselling into them.) So, I travelled the whole country intent on going to all of the Micropoint stores.

I was probably in store 24 of the 26, having an interview with its Micropoint manager, when I received a call from Commodore via the store's telephone. It was Eileen Stroud.

(Of course, in those days we didn't have mobile phones – luckily for me I was in the store where I said I would be!)

'David,' she said. 'Remember I told you things happen very quickly at Commodore?'

I said yes.

'Well, today is your lucky day. Our Consumer Products Division is doing so incredibly well with the VIC-20 and the Commodore 64 that they need a national account manager – and they've decided that you are it!'[2]

I dropped everything and returned immediately to the head office in Slough, where I quickly took up my new position, selling the VIC-20 and the hot new Commodore 64, as well as the full range of accompanying peripherals and accessories.

---

1   Laskys would eventually be bought out by Comet for £8.9 million in 1989.

2   I subsequently discovered the position had been held by Tim Chaney but he had resigned, and as I was already on the payroll I fitted the brief to replace him.

I reported to Paul Welch, the national sales manager at the time, who I could sense did not really like me, though it took a while to find out why. I later discovered that when budgets were tight it was not uncommon for Commodore to recruit staff from within the company, provided the person's background was a reasonable match, and in fact external recruitment was often not permitted during these times. In this particular instance, I was not personally selected by Paul Welch for this important role, and this was reflected in his attitude towards me.

In retrospect, this is the perfect example of two things about Commodore. Firstly, just how dynamic it was at the company. But secondly, just how disorganised it could be. The fact of the matter was – and it was a real lesson to be learnt – that the reason they took me out of the position I was specifically recruited for in the Business Products Division, selling Commodore PETs and other business products into the retail market, was that they didn't have enough PETs or other business products to satisfy the demand through their existing original channels, let alone supply a new one!

So, the whole purpose of me being recruited in the first place was nonsensical. It was the first of many great examples that showed, right from the beginning that Commodore, as a company, never, ever had a business plan.

Having said that, I am sure glad they did recruit me!

-3-

COMMODORE CORBY

SEPTEMBER 1983 - OCTOBER 1985

I transferred from the Business Systems Division to the Consumer Division as national accounts manager sometime in September 1983. I was thrilled with my new position, which meant I was dealing with all the major UK retailers, such as the electronics chains Dixons, Currys, Comet and Laskys, plus prestige department stores like John Lewis Partnership, Debenhams and Harrods. I took great pride in getting Commodore products into many of the supermarkets such as Tesco, Asda, Co-op and British Home Stores, plus catalogue mail order retailers Littlewoods, Kays and Grattons. I even managed to get Boots (a chemist), WHSmith (a national newsagent chain) and Woolworths (a toy store) to stock the VIC-20 computer and the Commodore 64.

But one thing that eventually paid huge dividends to Commodore UK was the appointment of five wholesale distributors, who between them sold products into the hundreds of small independent retailers throughout the country, including Lightning Distribution (run by Loretta Cohen and Norman Mandell), Silica Distribution (run by Mike West and Tony Deane), ZCL (run by Patricia Tordoff and Don Carter), Spectrum (run by Mike Stern) and Thompson Cook (run by John Cook).

The significance of this distribution channel is that it was the small specialist dealers who were best equipped to take care of serious purchasers and could help them install sound or video cards and other peripheral devices, and generally spend more time dedicated to assisting the consumer. This resulted in a growing number of sales being made through the small independent retail dealers, who became very influential, particularly when it came to guiding parents in what they should buy their children.[1]

Another advantage of having wholesale distributors was that they handled all the individual retailers' accounts payable themselves, which of course took quite a significant resource to manage, and removed from Commodore any financial risk that dealing with small retailers may present.

During my first few weeks as national accounts manager, the managing director Howard Stanworth decided to spend the day with me to learn how I did my job and to see for himself if I needed help of any sort. He confirmed to me that we were getting ready to move into a purpose-built assembly factory warehouse and office complex in Corby, Northamptonshire. It was a huge building that had been designed to fill the entirety of a 10-acre site, and for which we had received some substantial funding from the Corby District Council, as we were intending to employ in excess of 500 local people.[2]

To my surprise, Howard informed me he wanted me and my family (at the time, my wife Sheila and our 18-month-old son Marcel) to move to Corby, and that the company would pay for my moving expenses, legal fees and estate agent costs to buy our own home, plus substantial 'out of pocket' expenses (furnishings, carpets, appliances, that sort of thing).

---

1   This became more significant with the release of the Amiga 500. See part 1, chapter 5, 'Maidenhead, Pt. 2 – The Distributor Incentive Program' to read about the Distributor Incentive Program, which I came up with to push sales of the Amiga 500 in response to the release of the Atari ST.

2   The Corby region had been home to a huge plant owned by British Steel, who had brought hundreds of steel workers down from Scotland to work there. The company subsequently closed the plant, leaving their families without employment. Once Commodore had moved into its new head office, it employed many young workers from these families. Sadly this led to major behavioural problems from the assembly-line workers, resulting in irresponsible working practices, disruption and even vandalism (including in the ladies' toilets!).

The Corby office

This was a wonderful surprise. As a sales person I was, in effect, 'field-based', meaning I spent by far the majority of my time working from home or calling on customers at their head office or in-branch, so I did not expect to be offered this opportunity.

In fact, we were very lucky in a number of ways. Just a couple of weeks earlier we had put a deposit down on a house within reasonable distance from our office in Slough.

The house we had chosen was owned by a lawyer who, naturally enough, was representing himself to save on legal fees. Luckily for us, he was incredibly slow at responding to the requests our solicitor was asking of him – so much so, in fact, that our solicitor had sent him a notice of unprofessional conduct, which is a very strict and serious charge from one lawyer to another.

Of course, this ultimately worked very much in our favour, as we were then able to withdraw from the transaction without penalty or cost to us, and were immediately free to begin searching for a home much closer to Corby.

*

In the first week of December, the managing director of Spectrum Distribution, Michael Stern, a jovial and ebullient character (we seemed to hit it off very well together), offered me his airline ticket and hotel room booking for a trip to Las Vegas for the annual winter Consumer Electronics Show (CES) in January the following year.

Apparently when he had booked the trip he had not realised the dates clashed with a planned family trip to Marbella in Spain, where he owned a property, and his wife would not let him off the hook!

I went to seek permission from Howard Stanworth, who thankfully approved it on the strict understanding that I would spend some time on the Commodore stand at the exhibition, and bring back any new product information I could obtain.

So in January, I found myself travelling with Dudley Langmead, who was Spectrum's head buyer, and Scott Coghill, who was the (very young) buyer for the Edinburgh-based Menzies Group newsagents.

It was on the Commodore stand at the CES show in Las Vegas that I met Commodore founder Jack Tramiel for the first and only time. He appeared to me a very gruff man, shouting at his staff who were manning the insanely busy stand, and he hardly had any time for me. I moved out of his sight and spent my time looking at our products and displays, and making notes of new things I did not previously know about.

On the second day in Las Vegas, while having breakfast, I had a very heated – borderline threatening – discussion with a whole host of industry guys who were trying to bait me over the impending launch of the Japanese MSX machines, claiming that 'Commodore will be taught a lesson by these top-named and highly regarded industry stalwarts'.

They were intimating that, as a company, Commodore was too arrogant, and that we did not listen to the software companies, whereas the MSX boys were professional in their industry approach, and knew much better how to market their products. (This was well before I had the time or opportunity to get close to the software developers, something I did later on and quite successfully.) Basically, they were all in agreement with each other that we were going to get our 'arses whipped'.

I took great delight in telling them all my predictions for what would happen with the MSX market, which of course none of them agreed on (remember, I had lots of experience in the consumer electronics industry and, to be frank, I 'knew my shit').

'Currently we know there will be at least 16 different manufacturers of MSX machines, including top brands such as Hitachi, Toshiba, Panasonic, Sharp, Pioneer, Sony and so on, plus a small number of budget labels too. The challenge they will all face is that they have collectively reached an agreement to sell their machines for the same retail price [at the time expected to be £149]. But I will tell you now: as a policy within retail, that cannot work.'

'Why not?' they asked.

'Because not all of the 16 manufacturers will get ranged. Dixons, the largest chain, will range maybe four top brands – say Sony, Toshiba, Pioneer and Hitachi – and then perhaps their own brand, Saisho. The other retailers will range two brands at most. That means that of the 16 brands it is certain at least one or two will not get selected.

'The brands that do not get selected will not just disappear of course, so those companies will have no option but to sell at a discount price in order to get their products ranged – probably as low as £99 – disrupting the whole ethos of the plan.'

Of course, this is exactly what happened. Even better, many of the MSX machines that launched weren't even compatible with each other – certain software would run on some machines but not others. Nobody could have guessed this part of course, but as far as I was concerned it was a wonderful bonus result!

*

On my third night in Las Vegas – and because I had somehow ended up becoming his guardian – I decided to take Scott out, seeking adventure. So we jumped in a cab and asked the driver to take us to a place called The Big Piano, a bar someone had suggested we should go to.

'Why are you going there?' the cabbie responded. 'That is so yesterday's flavour! Let me take you somewhere much better – a really "happening" spot'. So we agreed, and to this day I do not know the name of the place or where it was.

When we walked in, it certainly was busy and had a great vibe. So we made our way to the bar and ordered a couple of beers, and soon got talking to a good-looking couple sat there who we seemed to get on with really well. They loved the fact that we were visiting for the CES show and loved our accents – particularly Scott, who, being from Edinburgh, had a strong Scottish accent.

It turns out that they were a married couple – he was an airline pilot for one very well-known US airline and she was an airline hostess for another – and they were apparently, in their words, 'out on the prowl', which it turned out meant they were looking for people to invite back to their house and 'party' with. There is no doubt the wife was a real stunner, nor would the husband have had any trouble 'pulling' just about any woman he fancied.

We ended up back at their house with two other couples and a girl on her own, and they certainly knew how to party. Several 'lines' were laid out on their coffee table (I should point out here that I did not partake!), and with plenty of marijuana and booze flowing freely it soon turned into a scene from a Harold Robbins novel! (I did not see what happened to Scott, but I must admit I did end up in the Jacuzzi with the pilot's wife and had a very memorable night!)

*

On this first of many visits to Las Vegas for CES, I also took the opportunity to enjoy some great live music. In those days, casinos would put top-name performers on the bill without charging too much to see them as a way of getting customers into the casino to gamble more.

So I looked to see who was performing during my visit and discovered that George Benson was there – being a guitar player myself (albeit in a completely different genre) I was quite a fan of his, and I figured he would have a really good six- or seven-piece band with him. Much to my pleasant surprise, he was accompanied by an incredible 12-piece band, with brass and percussion to die for, plus a 30-piece orchestra! To say I was in heaven is a real understatement – it was totally awesome.

On a later visit I got to see The Moody Blues backed by a 60-piece orchestra, plus on one trip I got really lucky and saw The New York Rock and Soul Review, complete with Donald Fagen, Walter Becker of Steely Dan, Boz Scaggs, Michael McDonald of the Doobie Brothers, Pheobe Snow, Chuck Jackson and many others – absolutely sensational!

*

Shortly after we moved into the new facility in Corby, there had been several changes to senior personnel – mainly, and not surprisingly, as a result of people simply not wanting to move from their current homes near London, where many had children settled into schools. Managing director Howard Stanworth and marketing manager John Baxter both resigned, at which point my boss, Paul Welch, was given the added responsibility of marketing the company.

Paul was only a couple of years older than me and was a somewhat short man with a huge attitude problem. I found him quite difficult to read as a person and as a boss, and I was quite dismayed at his new appointment; even though I had only been with Commodore a few months, I already recognised he had some serious flaws that were becoming major hurdles in terms of trying to grow the business.

Within a few weeks, a new managing director, Nick Bessey (ex-IBM), was appointed. I really connected with Nick – he was exactly who we needed in the senior role at Commodore UK. He was very astute, an excellent conversationalist, persuasive and, most importantly, he asked plenty of questions and was a good listener. Annoyingly he was a rather handsome and charismatic chap too! Don't you just hate that?!

Shortly after he joined the company, Nick asked to spend a day in the field with me, which I was very happy to do. So we set out early the next morning for an appointment to meet with the marketing director of Co-op Group at their head office in Wilmslow, Cheshire, a good 2-hour-plus car journey from the office in Corby.

In the car on our way there, Nick turned to me and said, 'OK, so tell me what is going on in your world: what is good and what is bad?'

'Do you want me to tell you what I think you want to hear or shall I tell you the truth, warts and all?' I replied.

He made it abundantly clear that he only ever wanted the truth, and warned me what the consequences would be if he ever caught me lying (I told you he was my kind of person!). Specifically, he asked me to tell him about Paul Welch.

Oh dear. I was not looking forward to answering this question, but I had no option.

I told him that many of our customers did not like Paul, which made my job of selling in to them very difficult.

He looked at me very quizzically, stared into my eyes and said: 'Are you exaggerating that somewhat?'

I swore to him I was not – I didn't know why he wasn't liked, but it was a sad yet true reality that I had to work around every day.

We arrived at the Co-op head office, and as we signed in at reception, the marketing director came downstairs from the executive offices to sign us in, shook my hand, and before I even had a chance to introduce him to Nick, asked, 'You haven't got that bastard Welch with you have you?'

Nick looked at me as if to say, 'You've set this up, haven't you?' which I later swore to him I had not!

He introduced himself to Peter and asked, 'Would you mind telling me why you just said that about Paul Welch?'

Peter replied. 'That guy is a liar and cannot be trusted, and he will never set foot in this building ever again.'

Nick pressed further and asked why. 'What happened to make you feel this way?'

Peter explained. 'It had been agreed that you would take back some of your products in exchange for a credit note, but it has been several weeks since that agreement was reached and nothing has happened.'

Nick looked at me, concerned, as the marketing director continued.

'Paul was in here two weeks ago, and just as I was about to go into a board meeting I told him I needed to know when he would collect the product and, more importantly, when I could expect the credit note, as we needed to adjust the accounts so we could close our quarter's books off. He promised me faithfully I would have it within two business days, and based on his word I told my board I had finally sorted it out. To this day I still do not have the credit note, and his lies have made me look completely incompetent in front of the board. I repeat: Paul Welch will never set foot in this building ever again.'

Nick immediately got on the phone and ordered the credit note to be issued forthwith.

Our return journey was most interesting. I assured Nick I had not set up the confrontation at Co-op headquarters, and in fact how could I? Until 6pm the night before I had no idea Nick was going to spend the day with me, and my appointment with Co-op had been made 10 days earlier.

So after quizzing me about the relationship between many customers and Paul, Nick came to understand how this situation was adversely affecting my ability to reach or exceed my targets.

'Look,' he said. 'I am not currently allowed to bring in anybody new from outside the company, so is there anyone already on the payroll who could do Paul's job?'

Well, I knew I was not up for consideration as I had not been in my role – let alone at the company – for long enough to have established any credible history of success. So I said to Nick, 'I would strongly recommend Tom Hart.'

He looked at me in disbelief.

'You mean the guy in the accounts department?'

'Absolutely!' I replied. 'First of all, our customers all know him, like him and, more importantly, trust him. He speaks with them nearly every day and his word is his bond. Second, I have struck up a really great relationship with Tom and his wife, and my wife and I go there for dinner sometimes and vice versa. I happen to know that Tom would do absolutely anything to be given the opportunity to join the sales department.'

The next thing I know, Tom Hart is my new boss, and Paul Welch has been moved on to a 'special project', never to be seen again (though he does eventually, a year or so later, turn up at Atari, as my rival).

Sadly, within just a few weeks, Nick Bessey had resigned. Back then, as managing director of CBM UK Ltd, Nick had also been responsible for the Commodore Electronics Ltd (CEL) countries, which were those places in the world where we did not have a subsidiary office. At that time, this included Australia and New Zealand, and Nick took himself on a trip to both of those countries to generate additional business.

Nick fell in love with New Zealand. It transpired that the Commodore distributor there was also an IBM distributor, and when Nick met the owner, they immediately got on very well. Nick was offered a partnership in the IBM distributors business, which he immediately accepted, and resigned from Commodore forthwith.

*

The next year or so was a fairly bleak time at Commodore UK – partially because we had no managing director, but particularly because we would have visits by some 'senior executives' from Commodore USA, such as Marshall Smith, Thomas Rattigan

Top to bottom:
Nick Bessey, Chris Kaday
and Tom Hart

and Henri Rubin, who would all make a nuisance of themselves for a few weeks then disappear back to the US.

This went on for several months, and it was during this period that Tom Rattigan – who had been appointed by Irving Gould as president of Commodore International Ltd and been tasked with getting the company back into profit 'at all costs' – decided to close down Corby, even though the plant was functioning more or less OK. Sure, there was the odd bit of assembly-line worker unrest from time to time, but sales in the UK were quite buoyant.

Eventually, USA management decided to appoint then-marketing manager Chris Kaday as 'acting' general manager. This was a disaster for me, personally. In my opinion, Kaday was a classic schizophrenic – and I hated both of him!

This is an absolutely true story that will illustrate what I mean.

It was October 1985 and we had all of our Commodore 64 packs on order through all the major retailers for each month up until the end of December. Effectively every C64 we were expecting to build in-house had been sold – a wonderful position to be in, and one that had taken a huge amount of effort from myself and my team in the Consumer Division.

I woke up one morning to discover that one of the retailers, Laskys, had run national newspaper advertisements offering the Commodore 64 packs at the low price of £169, when the recommended retail price was £199.[3]

When I arrived in the office I was distraught – I knew the knock-on effect of this would be all other retailers cancelling their orders, because they would not be prepared to invest in volumes of a product they would make almost zero margin on.

Chris Kaday saw how upset I was and ushered me into his office, where I explained why I was so distraught. I told him that I believed the other retailers would have no choice but to cancel all their orders.

He consoled me and spoke very reassuringly, even putting his arms around me, and told me not to get so distraught, that it was only business and that I should not take it so personally – to the point where I started to believe him! So after about 30 minutes I returned to my office and carried on working.

About two to three hours later, he strolled into my office and said, 'So Pleasance, we are still on for making all our targets this quarter, aren't we?', just as though we had never had the earlier discussion!

I was totally astonished. This was two different people sharing the same body.

---

3   Apparently, Laskys did this because they were the subject of a hostile takeover bid and needed the cash to help fight it – ours was a very hot product that they knew would sell out very quickly.

Kaday was also, I believe, a 'Moonie',[4] a fact that adversely affected his management approach, which was very bad for morale in the management team. Certainly he had some novel ways of settling disputes or disagreements between staff.

I recall one day I had a disagreement with one of my staff over the way he had handled a particular customer's issue. I was getting quite heated in my discussion when Chris suddenly intervened and made us grab a chair each and place it on the floor facing each other with our knees virtually touching. He made us put our hands on each other's knees, look each other straight in the eye and say nice things without breaking each other's gaze.

Some time later, that staff member and I would laugh about the incident because we both felt so completely ridiculous!

However, the very worst incident with Chris Kaday was when we were given instructions to permanently shut down the whole Corby facility at a time when we had in the region of 560 employees. From memory, we were reducing down to a total of just 29 people (luckily my team of seven and I were retained) and ultimately moved to offices in Maidenhead, back near Slough where Commodore had been based when I joined them in 1983.

The way Chris handled this was totally appalling. The day before he was to make the official announcement, he asked me and six other senior managers to stay behind after work. He told us to go the offices of all the less senior managers, remove their personal belongings in boxes, then lock the door and hand him the keys.

So there was a complete row of locked offices, outside which were boxes of all these managers' personal items – family photographs, flower pots, desk ornaments and so on – and on each door he stuck a note telling that person to make their way down to the canteen.

The next morning, everyone arrived at work as normal with no idea of what was happening. Then, with everyone assembled in the canteen, Kaday announced that from that moment onwards, every-body had been made redundant with immediate effect – company

---

4   A member of the Unification Church.

car drivers were asked to hand over their car keys, final pay slips were handed out and buses were provided to get everybody home.

It was shameful, and I will never forget being witness to this dreadful exercise in complete humiliation.

The large assembly-line workforce were given their notice on a slightly more normal timescale, although many of those people chose to simply never return to work. Can't say I blamed them to be honest.

*

As an adjunct to this chapter in the story, I must admit to a slightly embarrassing indiscretion, which is funny now, looking back on it.

We decided to have a farewell party in the last couple of weeks prior to the closing down of Commodore's Corby office, which somehow turned into a fancy-dress party. At the time I was extremely busy travelling all over the UK making sales, as Commodore International was in financial trouble yet again. As a result, I had left it very late to order myself a fancy dress costume, so on the day of the party, the only choice I had available to me was a rather embarrassing Billy Bunter outfit (which actually, with my bulk, was quite a good fit!).

The evening arrived and was held in a venue about six miles from my home. Despite the sad circumstances it was surprisingly good fun, with everybody – perhaps because of the fancy dress – in a party mood. Copious amounts of alcohol were consumed, but having just got back from a sales call down in Sidcup I was already tired by the time I arrived, so while I did not go crazy I must say it did not take long before I was, let's say, 'a little worse for wear'!

At the end of the evening I found myself driving along with a Roman gladiator trying to have his way with a nun on the back seat of my car. Thankfully their destination was a nearby hotel where several of the team were staying.

Once I had dropped them off and was on my own, I decided to drive the remaining four miles home using the much quieter back roads. I got within three minutes of home and fell asleep at the wheel, crashing into the back of a parked car which in turn crashed into the car next to it. It was about 2.30am, and luckily it seemed nobody had heard or seen the accident happen! Even though the radiator on my car was spewing water I managed to crawl home, which by that point was only a couple of hundred yards away.

At first light, I walked up to where I had crashed and made myself known to the owners, who by that time had already called the police. I assured these unlucky people that they would be well covered by our insurance and immediately made myself scarce, having my wife drive me to work where my boss Tom Hart was waiting for me, ready to drive us to attend our appointments in London all day.

By the time my wife had returned home, the police were there waiting in the vain hope of interviewing – and undoubtedly breath-alysing – me. Needless to say they were not happy and made sure I was charged with driving without due care and attention, for which I was found guilty. To be honest, I thought that was a bit mean – I was only asleep!

I was also charged with failure to report an accident and leaving the scene of an accident, but the magistrates dismissed those two charges because of the circumstances and the fact that I went back at first light, clearly not running away.

Thankfully nobody ever found out I was dressed as Billy Bunter when this incident occurred!

PLUS/4 PARTY TIME

This is one of my favourite stories, for reasons that will become clear!

As many of you will be aware, the Plus/4 was another example of our 'industrious leaders' producing something that nobody (at least in Europe) had been consulted about. It was a lemon from day one, and with no compatibility with the Commodore 64 there was little in the way of software titles for it. It was common knowledge that the four business software titles that resided on the ROM – the feature from which the model got its 'Plus/4' name – were not of sufficient quality to be much use.

In September 1985, Commodore Business Machines (CBM UK Ltd) – and indeed Commodore across the globe – had huge volumes of Plus/4 inventory in both assembled and component form that we simply could not sell, as well as a large volume of dedicated peripherals

'An idea of how I looked in my Billy
Bunter costume (made by me!)'

including monitors, external floppy disk drives and printers, all in
fetching dark grey.

Nick Bessey approached me one day to ask what we needed to do
to increase the stagnant sales. Clearly the price was an issue, but I felt
it was also important to give my sales team (and myself of course)
an added incentive, because the whole team were turned off by the
product's lack of acceptance by retailers. He, being new, came up
with the idea of offering a bottle of champagne for every (I think) 50
Plus/4s sold.

I held a consumer sales team meeting to make the announcement
that we were reducing the price to clear our inventory and let them
know about the extra incentive, which was very well received. So off
we all went on a mission to sell every Plus/4 we had.

The Commodore Plus/4

I put a bundle together that included the cassette drive and several games, designed to sell for just £99 – a very competitive price at that time. It was still a hard sell, though some of the team had minor successes. Luckily for me I had contacts at all the major retail chains and struck quite a big deal with Laskys who, at that time, had 54 stores nationwide. Pleased with my work, we arranged to have the agreed-upon volume made into packs for them.

Less than two weeks later, a man representing a large high street retail chain called Greens[5] made an appointment to see me in my office at Corby. He was a proper cockney Londoner who proceeded to tell me he had £25 million to spend with me to buy *all* the Commodore 64s we had coming into the UK for Christmas – in other words, they wanted to corner the market. Of course, I had to refuse him because I already had orders from all the major retailers for stock for Christmas and did not need to do a 'cut price' deal at all.

He was getting very upset and using plenty of bad language – he could not believe that with all that money I would not sell him anything! As he sat there with his feet up on my desk, picking his nose (true I swear!), an idea struck me, and in a pause between his cursing, I asked: 'Have you heard of the Commodore Plus/4?'

---

5   Greens was owned by Sir Philip Green, who has recently been held to account by the UK government over his dumping of the retail group BHS (British Home Stores), which he 'sold' for £1 – leaving behind millions of pounds shortfall of their Pensions Fund.

I did a deal with him where he would buy *every* Plus/4 we had in stock, including those that were only in component form in our warehouse, so that we could assemble them and clear our inventory completely. This did mean I had to go back to Laskys to get myself out of the deal I had previously agreed with them, but thankfully I had an exceptional relationship with their buyer and they were very understanding (plus I made it up to them later).

So Greens took delivery of the first several thousand Plus/4 packs, which they put into their stores in around mid October. Sales of the £99 pack were sensational and flew out of the stores in vast numbers – so much so that I went back with my boss at the time, Tom Hart (who was national sales manager) and sold them all of our Plus/4 peripherals as well! They were absolutely delighted.

I asked them whether they would be interested if I could get more stock. Well of course they were, so I took an order from them that meant we had to bring in all of our worldwide inventory in both finished and component form, which we assembled in our factory in Corby, as well as all of the peripherals we had left in stock. Tom and I were so euphoric we felt like doing cartwheels in Greens' car park!

This meant we'd cleared everything during the few weeks leading up to Christmas, and I ended up with 12 dozen bottles of premium champagne! (Sadly, the incentive had been capped at 144 bottles in line with UK inventory of Plus/4s.)

The real punchline to this story, though, is that during all the negotiations I had with Greens and their representative, I was never once asked if the Plus/4 and Commodore 64 were compatible – they just assumed it was. Which is just as well because, of course, they weren't!

So many thousands of Plus/4 packs were sold and given as Christmas presents, and for the first couple of weeks it was great – until people went to buy more software only to discover that none of the hundreds of available C64 titles were compatible. Oh dear!

4

INTERLUDE 1

SPIRIT OF THE STONES

This is a funny story that happened around the time Commodore had to close its Corby factory in early 1986.

I had been given the responsibility of disposing of all of the company's unwanted inventory – in particular the large volume of unsold software that was sitting in the warehouse. One of the programs was a Commodore 64 game – I guess today you would call it an ARG (alternative reality game) – called *Spirit of the Stones*, which was based on a book written by John Howard Worsley.

The premise was that in a secret real-world location on the Isle of Wight, some gemstones had been hidden by the author of the game, and if you solved the game's clues you could visit the actual location and dig to recover these gems. At least, that was the idea in theory.[1]

When the game was first released in 1984 it retailed for £19.99 or thereabouts, but by the time it came to disposing of the unsold copies

---

[1]   It is worth noting that across the pond, Atari had attempted a similar gaming experiment in 1980 with their *Swordquest* series, wherein players stood a chance of winning real-life prizes – including a talisman, a chalice, a crown, a 'philosopher's stone' and, ultimately, a sword – valued at $150,000. Of the four titles planned for the series only two were released before Atari cancelled the contest due to financial troubles leading up to the video game crash of 1983.

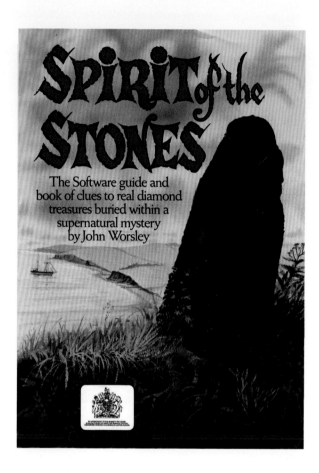

The Spirit of the Stones
software guide that came
included with the game

– almost three years after the game had first been released – all the diamonds had apparently been claimed, so the game had very little actual retail value. As a result, a well-known 'wheeler-dealer' friend of mine, Lou Fine,[2] offered a mere £2 per unit for them to clear the lot.

Around the time the game had been conceived, a deal had been struck with the Isle of Wight tourist board to promote it, who would then receive a £6 per unit royalty.

---

[2]   In the end, Lou bought hundreds of thousands of pounds worth of software and other clearance lines from Commodore when I emptied the Corby warehouse. Shortly after, I went over to Cork in Ireland to go salmon fishing with him. We were out there wading in the River Blackwater – both of us wearing all-in-one PVC suits – when he suddenly tripped on a rock and went over on his back, his wetsuit filling with water, giving him an appearance not unlike that of the Michelin Man. I almost wet myself from laughing so hard!

So I contacted them and said, 'Look, we're getting rid of all of these games and we've been offered £2 per unit – I'd like to give you £1 per unit for every one sold.' Problem solved, I thought.

Well, they refused outright: 'No way, not interested. Unless we get £6 per unit you are not allowed to sell them.'

'Well then, we will have to destroy them: we can't sell them for £2 and pay you £6, that's ridiculous!' I replied.

'We don't believe you,' they countered.

So, I called their bluff: accompanied by two lawyers to witness the act, we transported the software – of which there was several thousand pieces – to a remote location known only to me, the two lawyers and the driver of the JCB digger (who had signed a non-disclosure agreement), where we dug a very big hole, buried all the stock, filled it up and left.[3]

I wrote to the Isle of Wight tourist board to let them know the news: 'You've just lost any chance of getting any money at all – we have buried all the software,' and attached the affidavit signed by the two lawyers.

So, somewhere out there are several thousand games, buried in the ground. They're probably not worth much at all, but it just goes to show that from time to time the illogical actions of people in business lead to desperate counter reactions.

But hey, that's all part of the life's rich tapestry!

---

3   This recalls a well-documented moment in history when Atari buried thousands of unsold video game cartridges, consoles and computers in a New Mexico landfill site as a result of the US video game crash of 1983. In 2014, it was revealed that around 700,000 cartridges of various titles were buried there, including, famously, Atari's poorly-received *E.T.*, which many cite as the cause of the marketplace crash in the first place.

5

MAIDENHEAD, PT. 1

WE DON'T SELL COMPUTERS, WE SELL DREAMS

As we closed down the office complex at Corby, selling off the mountain of obsolete inventory left behind, it was decided to move back to Maidenhead in Berkshire, which was close to where Commodore Business Machines UK Ltd had previously been located. In part this was because the rent there was much lower, and this gave us access to quality staff who could not afford to live in the capital.

One Monday morning, without any warning, a man walked into our office, called every staff member into the central open area and announced himself to the room.

'I am your new managing director Steve Franklin. I want to see all of the Business Systems sales staff in my office in 10 minutes.'

Once they had assembled in his office, he proceeded to fire them one by one, to be immediately replaced by a team he had brought with him from his previous company, Granada.

That is, except for two people: Kieron Sumner, who was responsible for the newly released Amiga 1000; and Peter Talbot, who was responsible for the education sector, apparently because Granada had not been into education and had nobody who could do the job. Peter was doing an excellent job anyway, so it was good that he retained his position.

The Maidenhead office

The scary thing for me, as national accounts manager, was that for two weeks from the day he walked into the office, Steve spoke not one word to me. Silence.

Then one day he suddenly walked into my office and said, 'Pleasance, my office, now.'

I followed him to his office.

'I just wanted to let you know that if I knew anybody – anybody at all – who could do your job, you would not be here today.'

I was taken aback – this was obviously quite a shock to hear.

'Thanks for that vote of confidence,' I said.

'Look,' he continued. 'I have nothing against you personally – I don't know anything about you. But I have been brought into Commodore with the strict instruction to change everything – the whole ethos of the company. As you can see, I have brought in most of my own people on the business side, and if I could, I would have replaced you by now. But for now at least I am stuck with you, and as such, here are my rules.'

Steve Franklin

At this point he proceeded to tell me how everything we do has to reflect honesty, integrity and trust, and be totally above board in every respect.

Well this set of rules was how I always approached business as well as day-to-day life, so it was easy for me to agree whole-heartedly with the ethos he was outlining.

'I'll tell you what Steve,' I started. 'I'll make a deal with you.'

'You are in no position to make a fucking deal with me!' he suddenly interjected.

'Just hear me out,' I replied. 'I have a plan which, if it works as I believe it will, will either bring you more business than we have ever seen in this division or give you good reason to get rid of me.'

'What is this plan then?' he asked, disgruntled.

'Well, if you look at the Amiga 500' – I pointed to one sitting on a desk at the back of his office – 'it's very boring, just a piece of plastic with some keys on it. As such it is very difficult to sell, to the end user at least.

'Let me put a pack together that features the latest hot game, supported by two or three other trendy games, but – more importantly – also includes top productivity software to help justify to the parent why they should spend £399 in the belief that their children will get long-term educational benefit from this. The packaging will be so dynamic – complete with strong graphics and images related to the software, and hardly a mention of the computer itself – that the fact there is an Amiga 500 inside will be almost incidental.

'From this point on we do not sell computers – we sell dreams.'

The pitch worked, and Steve gave me permission to follow through with my idea.

So, I gathered my team – Dawn Levack, Kelly Sumner, John Smith, Jonathan Anderson, Bob Burridge, Pauline Wakefield and Ian Bourne

– and the brainstorming began. Everyone was asked to put forward suggestions for games they thought were destined to be very popular, especially ones they believed would be big hits.

OCEAN AND THE BATMAN PACK

Around that time, Ocean software had just announced that they had been to Hollywood and paid $1 million for the licence to produce the game for the new Batman film, so unsurprisingly *Batman: The Movie* became the most nominated game.

I made an appointment to see Jon Woods and David Ward, co-founders of Ocean, and a meeting was set up along with Gary Bracey, Colin Stokes and Paul Patterson, Ocean's software director, sales director and sales manager, respectively.

I opened the conversation.

'I am going to put a proposition to you that will need huge balls to go along with, and you'll either love it or you'll send for the men in white coats to come and take me away!'

This immediately broke the ice and got everybody laughing, so I explained my idea.

'Gentlemen, do you realise that you and I need exactly the same thing as each other?'

'What do you mean?' they asked.

'Well, we will both benefit immensely the more Amigas we get into consumers' homes – after all, the more hardware we get out there, the more copies of your games you are likely to sell.' Of course, they had to agree. I continued.

'To achieve this objective I want to completely change the way Commodore sells computers. From now on I want to feature a lead game on our packaging, in our advertising and in all our retail channels outlets. Alongside the lead game I want to include other, non-conflicting games, as well as top productivity software as a means of justifying to the parents – who after all are the ones paying – that they are investing in their children's future. The packaging will be designed to precisely reflect the artwork of whichever main game we choose, and even though we are selling an Amiga, the fact that there is a computer inside will be incidental. I have a very large advertising

The Batman Pack

budget, which means the promotion this whole project will receive will be, in a word, "immense". Clearly, I am interested in securing a deal with Ocean over your recently announced licence for the new Batman movie – can we seal a deal?'

David Ward was the first to reply.

'We only just paid $1 million just for the rights to the name, and we estimate it is going to cost us a further $1 million to develop the game. What do you propose?'

'Once the game is finished, I want it exclusively for my packs for two months, after which you can sell it as a standalone product. I want to pay you very little money for it, and commit to only 10,000 pieces.'

At this point, they all laughed and said in unison: 'Send for the men in the white coats!'

I'm not sure who at Ocean spoke next, but what was expressed was as follows.

'Well David, we are concerned mainly over two things. First, we think our dealers will be upset if we give you sole exclusivity for two months because they will feel they are losing business. Second, as we have said, we have already outlaid $2 million, and we have our own estimate for how many games we need to sell initially just to get our investment back and then the total we expect to sell to bring us an acceptable level of profit. We are concerned that our estimated volume of sales will be affected.'

I set to putting their minds at ease.

'I personally believe that while your dealers may well be upset for a couple of days, once they start selling our packs – which retail for £400, compared to your game which retails for £40 – I doubt they will be upset for very long. I know which I would prefer to sell if I was a dealer!

'And in relation to your estimated volume of sales, due to the significant amount of advertising we will be providing using the game's imagery, I suspect that will likely result in an improvement in numbers.'

Let me say for the record that Ocean Software are legends for having the balls to go along with what could easily have been seen as a crazy idea!

After some negotiation, they agreed to an amount of money we would pay for each of the 10,000 pieces to put into the bundle, and the first-ever pack was born. From that point on, we sold dreams.

The results of the experimental 'Batman Pack' spoke for themselves.

The dealers were upset, as expected, but for at most a couple of days, because very quickly they were making lots of £400 sales. And Ocean Software sold more than five times their highest estimated volume amount.

I ended up buying 186,000 pieces of the game as that is how many Batman Packs Commodore UK sold in the 12 weeks running up to Christmas.

I was delighted, and so was everybody involved in the whole project. The concept changed the home computer and then the games console market forever. It was history in the making.

MEHDI ALI'S BAG CARRIER

This is a good point to tell you about Petro Tyschtschenko, the man laughingly referred to by all the general managers as 'Mehdi Ali's bag carrier'.[1]

---

1 Mehdi Ali, Commodore's president at the time, is covered more in part 1, chapter 10, 'A comedy of errors – Our illustrious leader, Mehdi Ali'.

I was never afraid to take on a challenge
to promote business, as the cover to this
'Commodore Christmas Show Guide' shows!

Petro was solely responsible for inventory management – in other words, making sure that if a particular product was languishing in a subsidiary warehouse that was in short supply elsewhere, it would be moved to where it could best be utilised, and preferably sold.

Now, Petro would say – as he has on many occasions – that he was responsible for sales. A complete lie! It was inventory management, and he was lousy at it. Let me give you an example.

Suddenly, Commodore UK had orders for many thousands more Amiga 500s because of the success of the Batman Pack – we thought it would be a good seller, but we never could have imagined we would sell 186,000. It was easy to increase the production of our computers because we manufactured them ourselves. However, the availability of peripherals is usually a factor in how many computers you can sell, and I had considerably underestimated the number of 1084 monitors we would need, which were an OEM-sourced product.

Well, Mr Inventory Manager discovers we have a surplus of 1084 monitors in our Australian subsidiary, so what does he do? He flies hundreds of big, heavy monitors from Australia to the UK only to discover that due to a difference in polarity (not voltage), they weren't compatible with the UK models! In the end we had no option but to return them to Australia – imagine the expense!

PSYGNOSIS

The Batman Pack would be the first of many Amiga packs, and many of the finest software publishers were lining up asking for their games to be featured in one. As a result of its success, I was given free rein to produce the follow up, and it was decided we would release two packs a year in order to stay trendy.

After that incredible Christmas quarter, Steve Franklin and I were at the Winter CES trade show in Las Vegas in the first week of January having a meeting with Ian Hetherington and Jonathan Ellis, co-founders of Psygnosis, who were trying very hard to get us to feature their new game in our next pack. We hadn't even had time to think about the theme and featured game for the next one – nevertheless, they were keen to strike a deal and were already talking pricing with us.

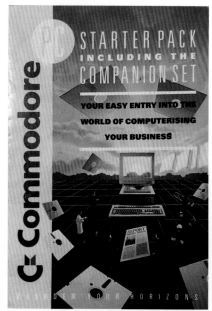

Clockwise from top left: The Cartoon Classics pack;
the Mindbenders pack; the Playful Intelligence
pack; the PC Starter Pack (featuring me on the
cover as the professor); the Night Moves pack; the
Light Fantastic pack; and the Hollywood pack.

At one point Steve had to go to the bathroom. While he was away, the guys leaned over to me and said: 'David, we are so committed to getting our game in your next pack that if we have to we will give it to you for free!'

Frankly, I was gobsmacked.

'Gentlemen, there is no way I would let you give us something for free that has cost you money, especially something we could conceivably take 250,000 pieces of – you would go bankrupt! And that's no good to me as I want you around for the long-term. We need each other!'

They looked relieved.

'But if you mention what you just said to me to Steve, I promise you I will never deal with you again – I know Steve and he will take you up on your offer without seeing the downside of what it would do for you financially. So, you have been warned!'

They made no mention of it to Steve, and we went on to produce the Cartoon Classics pack, which featured some great cartoon-based games along with Psygnosis' very popular *Lemmings*.[2]

PC COMPATIBLES

Given the success the Consumer Products Division enjoyed under my stewardship with the packs for the Commodore 64 and the Amiga range (which included the Amiga 500, 600 and 1200, as well as the Commodore 32), I wanted to prove that we could replicate the marketing model for our PC-compatible range. These included the PC10, PC20 and PC30, with the main difference between each being the processor (as well as some other features).

At that time PCs were very new and considered to be very complex, and most people did not know how to put them together or set them up for use. So although these were not 'consumer' products and did not fall under my purview, we decided to produce – with very little budget – a VHS tape featuring television celebrities Tim Brooke-Taylor (*The Goodies*) and Joanne Campbell in a light-hearted short film showing how to set the PC up and get started.

---

2   Psygnosis would go on to produce many successful games, and was ultimately sold to Sony Entertainment Europe for a lot of money.

When it came to the actual packaging, what I had envisaged was to feature photos of real people from every walk of life and all sorts of professions and trades – nurse, engineer, painter/decorator, architect and so on – to illustrate that a PC was suitable for everyone.

However, by this time we had run out of budget and could not afford to pay professional actors or models to pose for us – so we decided to use our own staff!

We hired costumes for everyone and had one of our advertising agency staff, who was a very good photographer, take the photos. It was such a laugh!

(For the record, I am the professor featured on the pack – the other characters were filled in by Julie Cottingham, Lindsay Smith, Bob Burridge, Kieron Sumner, Dennis Philips and Kelly Sumner.)

The results were really better than expected – in fact, one of our PC dealers, who was also an IBM dealer, rang us up to tell us IBM had just been in and bought one each of the packs to 'see what we were up to'.

Of course, the PC market was about to undergo rapid changes as Intel began releasing new processors at an alarming rate, each new one more powerful than the last and at increasingly affordable prices. In fact, Intel became known as the only company in the world that 'eats it own young'. This instability and volatility played havoc with all PC manufacturers, and Commodore certainly suffered during this period.

Commodore UK continued to produce many different and exciting pack offerings at a rate of about two per year. I defy anybody to accuse us of not doing any marketing![3]

----

3   We also applied the same pack marketing model to the ageing Commodore 64. The results were incredible, and this undoubtedly kept the C64 alive and popular in the UK for more than two years beyond its realistic life span. And we were the first company to package PCs with our PC10, PC20 and PC30 starter packs, in which we included VHS tapes featuring TV comedian Tim Brooke-Taylor, who took you step-by-step through putting all the components together and getting started in his own humorous fashion.

6

MAIDENHEAD, PT. 2

THE DISTRIBUTOR INCENTIVE PROGRAM

When I was moved into the Consumer Products Division in September 1983 – which was where the majority of the business was generated – I realised I had found myself a niche career position where I could put my extensive retail background to good use and really make a huge difference.

I have always been creative, and in my role as national accounts manager I felt I could really set about putting my personal stamp on every part of the job description in this fast-paced industry.

I have always prided myself on my ability to win customer confidence by being open, honest and straight to the point. I would get close to my customers by giving them marketing and promotional ideas that they could tailor to their specific retail outlet and earn favour with their bosses.

One area I noticed a big opportunity to grow sales in was with our national distributors, who would sell to all the independent retailers with whom we chose not to hold individual accounts because we were not set up for this kind of financial provision (i.e. holding hundreds of small accounts).

The independent dealers were, for the most part, incredibly well informed and knew their products exceptionally well, and as such were excellent at upgrading users to newer models with the latest release peripherals (many of which were made by third-party companies).

I really appreciated and understood the valuable service the independent dealers could provide to our more serious users, and I was determined to win them over and encourage them to provide outstanding service for Commodore and our customers on an ongoing basis. They were always 'on my radar' and I would devise a way to contact these important assets to the business in such a manner that we would work with them for the long-term.

So what did I do? My marketing budget was 5 per cent of the company turnover, which at that time was £100 million (something my team and I had worked very hard to achieve), so I went to my distributors one by one and made this proposal to them.

I offered them 4 per cent of their purchases from Commodore as a marketing budget and proposed that if they used half of that on the promotion then I would match it with an additional 2 per cent just for that promotion.

At that time we would allocate every single Commodore product a certain 'points' value, where the higher the monetary value the higher the points allocated. The dealer would accrue points for every Commodore product they bought or sold, and once they had accumulated sufficient points, Commodore and the distributor would take them on a fantastic holiday.

Each distributor would offer a different exotic destination to entice the independent dealer to buy from them (which not only generated loyalty to Commodore products, but also to the distributor that offered a destination with the most appeal).

The very first promotion we ran was with Lightning Distribution, and because our major product push was the newly released Amiga 500 – 'amiga' of course being a Spanish word – we chose to offer a fabulous two-destination luxury holiday to Mexico City and Acapulco.

I used a company called Creative Destinations who were located not far from our offices in Maidenhead, and the managing director Michael and I travelled together on an inspection visit, where we chose the hotels, the restaurants and any side tours we wanted to include (it was hell, but somebody had to do it!).

The Acapulco Princess Hotel, today

For this first promotion, we took 36 'holiday goers' – dealers with their wives or partners – and laid on the most incredible level of hospitality and entertainment imaginable.

We stayed in the best hotel in Mexico City, which was a day trip away from the Mexican pyramids. There was sensational three Michelin-star dining accompanied by a classical quintet, as well a visits to a typical locals' Mexican eatery, where we were entertained by genuine mariachis.

We then flew to Acapulco where we stayed at the Acapulco Princess, one of the top-five hotels in the world at the time. We took a cruise on a magnificent yacht in Acapulco Bay and had dinner up in a restaurant that had been recently converted from a castle, with an awesome view of the city.

On our last day, I had made personal arrangements to go big-game fishing, one of my biggest passions, and four of the dealers decided to join me. We caught some fantastic big yellowfin tuna and took some of it back to the hotel, where we asked the staff to cook it for our 'Finale Fiesta', which we had arranged to take place outside in

The Ballet Folklórico de México
ensemble, as they appear today

the lush gardens that night. We had a large stage built on which the world-famous ballet ensemble Ballet Folklórico de México performed exclusively for us. It was absolutely breathtaking.

A massive selection of food was laid out for us all, including the yellowfin tuna from our deep-sea fishing trip. This was a real treat, especially for those of us who caught them, and of course everybody knew how fresh it was.

The night ended with a spectacular fireworks display, culminating in a huge explosion that spelt out the names COMMODORE and LIGHTNING with our respective logos as the major highlight. Phenomenal.

The net result of this incredible first dealer incentive trip was that all those dealers, from the moment they arrived home, began to tell the world just how special the trip Commodore had provided was, and poked fun at those dealers who had not sold enough of our products to qualify.

This is exactly what I had hoped for, and it triggered a massive surge of activity from the other distributors who were now incentivised to do even better. (Although this was what we wanted, it did pose a huge challenge for us to keep finding better, more alluring venues to take the dealers to!)

The best outcome though – one we had deliberately targeted – was that we signed up Silica Distribution Limited (SDL) as one of our distributors. Although they were also Atari's sole distributor, there is no doubt in my mind that the promotion they did for their dealers – to Singapore and the Great Barrier Reef – contributed immensely to the Amiga 500 outselling the Atari ST. Any unsuspecting customer who went into an independent dealer's shop with the intention of buying an Atari ST was very convincingly talked out of it and persuaded to buy the Amiga 500 instead. The dealer incentives certainly did work, and subsequent trips would include The Bahamas, Bermuda, Thailand, Mauritius and an African safari.

Another really good idea we had for this promotion was to select an 'Employee of the Quarter' at Commodore – this could be anyone from any department, nominated by their peers – to go on one of these trips. So it was a very powerful staff incentive programme too, which everybody appreciated and embraced.

THE ANNUAL COMPANY CONFERENCE

One of the features Steve Franklin introduced into his management regime was an annual company conference during the first week of July. It was an opportunity to praise the people who had gone above and beyond during the previous fiscal year (which always ended on the 30th of June), as nominated by other people within the company. (It was also obviously an opportunity to kick some arse if necessary, though in fairness this was quite rare.)

Staff members who were nominated for their outstanding commitment to the company won the right to go on one of the distributor incentive trips.

These company conferences would take place in different venues and locations each year, such as Gleneagles' golf course (where a few of us had an afternoon session on Jackie Stewart's shooting range – amazingly, I won) and Cliveden House, a beautiful stately home where we had a wonderful wine-tasting experience.

Commodore staff at the
Cliveden House annual
conference in 1990

But the one company conference that stands out in particular was held at the Grand Hotel Brighton (the same place that just a few years earlier had been bombed by the IRA during the Conservative Party's annual conference in an attempt to kill Margaret Thatcher).

Once everybody had arrived, Steve ordered them all champagne. And not just any champagne mind you: Dom Pérignon. Bottle after bottle after bottle was bought until the hotel had run out. Steve was furious about this and he certainly let them know (he was well known for his use of colourful language).

He was getting quite drunk by this point, as indeed were most of us. I felt it prudent to get him away from the hotel for a while before we were all thrown out, so I suggested he, myself and a couple of the other senior managers go to the nearby casino. I knew Steve absolutely loved roulette from the several visits we'd made to Las Vegas for the annual Winter Consumer Electronics Shows. Luckily, I had driven down to Brighton three days earlier to register the four of us at the Casino for that evening.[1]

Now, I hardly ever gamble, but when I do, I usually set myself a modest amount of money to play with and try to make it last as long as possible. But once it has gone, for me that is it. I am quite strong-willed so it has never proven difficult to walk away.

Steve, on the other hand, was a very irrational gambler. He would cover several numbers or blocks of red or black at random, sometimes almost covering the whole table in one go.

Well, talk about luck. I have never previously, or since, seen anybody win so much. Everything he bet on won, time after time after time. It was truly incredible, one of those freakish winning streaks you hear about very occasionally.

Finally the time came when I needed to get him out of there – we still had the whole company staff back at the Grand Hotel. So, I grabbed one of his arms and dragged him across the casino floor towards the exit, his hands full of betting chips. As we went past

---

1   UK gambling law around that time required that you pre-register to play in a casino as a way of preventing people who were drunk from gambling on the spur of the moment and potentially losing lots of money.

the various roulette wheels he just kept reaching over and dropping chips more or less wherever they landed without looking to see what numbers or colours he was betting on – and he just kept winning! He certainly made a great deal of money during those one-and-a-half hours.

It was a very memorable night, and by the time we got back to the hotel he was in a wonderful mood and for the rest of the evening was very good company. He even forgave the hotel for running out of champagne!

*

Steve and I became good friends – much more than just business colleagues, as what I was generating in sales had made him a hero, at least in terms of the quarterly numbers CBM UK kept delivering.

He had promised me that if I kept delivering him outstanding sales figures he would promote me to sales and marketing director, which I had been striving for ever since I first joined the company, and had hoped to achieve by the time I was 40 (a fact he knew).

Around Christmas time in 1988, as the day of my 40th birthday approached, Steve arranged to come to my house in the tiny hamlet of Clopton, where I had moved with my wife during Commodore's Corby years. He and his wife picked us up in a chauffeur-driven limousine and took us to a wonderful, highly rated Chinese restaurant about 40 minutes from our house.

It was during the meal that Steve told me he was going to formally announce my title change on the 2nd of January (our first day back at work after the Christmas break) but that he wanted to tell me now, on my 40th birthday, so that I knew I had achieved my ambition. I believe that is a good indication of the relationship we had built together.

But as time passed – and being the 'hunter'-type salesman that I am – I started to get restless. It was clear that Steve was very well regarded and not going anywhere – he was enjoying being top dog in the Commodore hierarchy too much.

Then one day I heard that the position of general manager at Commodore Electronics Limited (CEL) in Basle, Switzerland was up for grabs. The role involved selling to the 36 countries Commodore did not have operating subsidiaries in, which was very appealing to me – it was another opportunity for me to prove myself and grow the business.

I applied for the position and, to my delight, got the role. In January 1990 I was on a plane with my family heading to Switzerland, finally fulfilling my dream of getting an international position – the goal I had originally left Australia in 1983 to pursue.

STEVE'S UNDOING

Some time after my promotion, I was summoned to Mehdi Ali's office in New York. I had no idea what the meeting was about, but of course arrived as quickly as I could arrange the flight. His attitude was quite aggressive, and the intense quizzing that ensued really shocked me.

(I have been advised not to reveal certain company names here, although none of the other facts have been altered in any way.)

'What do you know about Company ABC?' he asked.

I had to think for a moment because the name was familiar but I could not immediately recall who they were. Then I remembered – I had seen their name on a recent memo from Steve announcing their appointment as our exclusive authorised service agent for all UK warranty repairs on Commodore products.

'Absolutely nothing,' I said.

'So you don't know any of the people involved with that company in any way whatsoever?'

I replied honestly that I had no idea who they were, and that I did not even know where they were based or anything like that.

'Ok then – how about Company XYZ? What do you know about them?'

'Yes, I know them. The company is headed by a man who worked for Chelsea Football Club, where Commodore UK have a shirt sponsorship deal.[2] They arrange the hospitality events we take our best customers to, such as the finals at Wimbledon, the Prix de L'Arc de

---

2   Colin Proudfoot talks about Commodore's deal with Chelsea in more detail in part 1, chapter 16, 'Interlude 5 – Chelsea FC shirt sponsorship'.

Triomphe, Derby Day and so on. We use these opportunities to write additional business and do special deals and so on. All our clients know this and we even joke that they don't forget to bring their order books with them!'

Mehdi continued. 'What relationship do you have with this John Shaw?'

'Dawn Levack [my marketing manager at the time] and I liaise with him on the names of my customers and the numbers coming along, purely in his capacity as the person who arranges these events, and that is it.'

My curiosity piqued. 'Why are you asking me all these questions?'

'Allegations have been made that there is a personal financial relationship between senior management at Commodore UK and both of these companies,' he replied, 'and I wanted to talk to you face-to-face to find out if you're in any way involved.'

I was shocked – this was all news to me.

'Having spoken with you I think it's clear you know nothing about this. But you should be aware that Steven Franklin is no longer an employee of Commodore.'

It's amazing how things can change in just a couple of weeks. Steve had gone from hero to zero practically overnight! In some ways I felt stupid, being so close to Steve but not having the faintest idea of what had allegedly been happening right before my eyes. On the other hand I was relieved that I genuinely was not aware, because I would probably have had to look for another job if I had.

Mehdi Ali then told me he wanted me to take over as managing director in the UK. 'I know you were responsible for building all the UK business anyway, so I would be happy to put you officially in control.'

Well, what did I do? I turned him down. It was his turn to be shocked, and I could see it in his face.

'No? Did I just hear you say no? Why on earth would you not want this? I have always known it was you who built the business into what it is today – in my mind there is no question you deserve this opportunity.'

I told Mehdi that I am 'a hunter, not a farmer', and having just moved with my wife and two sons to Switzerland and – got both into an excellent international school there – I was quite happy, and excited at the prospect of building up our export business and proving my worth in my role with CEL.

I told him I was very flattered and that I sincerely appreciated the offer, but that for right then, it was not the best option.

'OK, well if you don't want it, what would you think if I appointed Kelly Sumner to the role?'

Kelly was the national accounts manager in the UK and had been with Commodore for many years (starting, I recall, in the Service department). He had worked his way up and was my second in command while I was there. He was a long-term employee who had built up experience in several departments over the years, and I explained to Mehdi that while I thought he was a good choice, he had a big ego, and as such would almost certainly not ask for help if he ever got into trouble.[3]

And so I returned to my new role as general manager of CEL in Switzerland and Kelly Sumner was duly appointed to managing director of Commodore UK.

I was quite upset to find out from my former team that soon after Kelly took over from Steve Franklin he apparently started bad-mouthing me, though I have no idea why. You can never tell what some people will do with the opportunities that come their way.

---

3   When I later returned to the UK in 1993 to take up my position of joint managing director with Colin Proudfoot, I discovered that my prediction about Kelly was correct. During the last quarter of his tenure in charge, we discovered he had made a deal on several thousand Amiga 1200s on a 'sale or return' basis, something we had never done before or since – presumably because he was short of his sales target. This was bad timing from our point of view – our parent company was in a dire financial position and we needed a lot of cash flow at that time. Having to accept returns and issue a refund was exactly what we did not need.

7

COMMODORE ELECTRONICS LIMITED

BASLE, SWITZERLAND

In February 1990, I was promoted to general manager of Commodore Electronics Limited (CEL). CEL was based out of Aesch, a village in the canton of Basle, where companies paid no tax – just one of the ways they benefited from being based in Switzerland (many of the world's pharmaceutical companies are also based there because there is a high level of protection from lawsuits).

This worked out well for me and my family – by then I had two sons, Marcel and Emile, who I managed to get into a very good international school, where they mixed with children from many different countries.

I was responsible for all 36 of the initial export countries where Commodore did not have an operating subsidiary, including Turkey, Finland, Cyprus, Greece, Iran, Malta, Bahrain, South Africa, Morocco, Algeria, Kuwait, Lebanon, Israel and Egypt. It was a fantastic opportunity for me, personally – the challenge of having to grow business in these countries was exactly what I relished doing.

The business of selling on an export basis is a completely different model to that of selling into countries where we had our own office and staff who could warrant, advertise, market and promote, all of which had to be accounted for financially and calculated within the framework of cost pricing vis-à-vis the retail price. So, we would buy our product from the corporation, calculate the cost to provide the 12 months' warranty and to pay for marketing and the sales force, and then calculate the VAT charged by the UK government.

So, as a fictional example, say the Amiga 500 cost Commodore UK $200 to buy in from Commodore International – taking the UK subsidiary as an example, our recommended retail price was £400 (well, £399.99 because it sounds cheaper!), which meant both Commodore UK and the retailer or distributor/dealer had a margin for profit.

At CEL, I sold at my lowest possible price because my customer – the appointed distributor[1] – would have to provide the warranty and market the products himself, as well as pay for his own staff and so on. In most of those export countries there was no recommended retail price – instead, it was more a case of 'get as much as you can for it'.

What I was able to bring to my role, which previous incumbents had not, was the marketing ideas that had worked so well in the UK. Ideas such as bundling our products (primarily the Commodore 64 and the Amiga) in the same packs as the UK, but with the packaging printed in the local language. This also helped in terms of identifying a legitimate product, as opposed to products sold illegally by Commodore subsidiaries into countries under my jurisdiction, simply to enable them to meet sales targets.

The most prolific of these was without doubt Commodore Germany, followed closely by Commodore Netherlands. Both often boosted their domestic sales figures by drop-shipping[2] several 40-foot containers of C64s and Amigas (especially into Turkey, as they shared a border).

On one occasion, we were alerted about a large shipment of Amiga 500s hitting Turkey via a black-market route. So I took a team from CEL to my authorised distributor and we manually went through his entire warehouse stock of Amiga 500s, recording

---

1   In each country I appointed an exclusive distributor, and no country was sufficiently large to warrant more than one.

2   Drop-shipping is where goods are delivered directly to the retailer or customer by the manufacturer.

every single serial number. This way we could help him identify any product that found its way back to him under a 'warranty' claim and reject any that were not registered as having come from him in the first place.

Exercises like this meant we maintained fantastic relationships with our customer; however, they came at significant expense, and had Commodore been stricter in its control of illegal export activities, this cost would not have been incurred by Commodore and it would have been more profitable.

TURKEY

Turkey became one of my favourite business destinations while at CEL, and in no small part thanks to my clients at Teleteknik. I became particularly good friends with Osman Babaoğlu and Fatih Ariman, director and purchasing manager for the company respectively, particularly because they were both big fans of live music – mainly jazz – and we went to many wonderful clubs together.

Through them we pulled off a major coup in Istanbul at a high-profile computer exhibition organised by IBM. Teleteknik were involved from the beginning and arranged for Commodore to sponsor some live music.

Just prior to me taking over at CEL I had signed a sponsorship deal in the UK with a young group of jazz musicians who I convinced to change their band name to Jazz Amiga. They performed halfway through the exhibition, and with the announcement of each song they were going to perform they kept promoting the Amiga computer – much to the dismay of IBM!

On another occasion, in Ankara, I managed to get some of Commodore's PC-compatibles into the education system through a process called 'downward auction', whereby manufacturers reduce (rather than increase) the price of their product (in this case, PCs) until the last manufacturer stops. Mehdi Ali was constantly on the phone giving me a hard time, but in the end I had a batch of 500 units accepted.

One time I managed to persuade Mehdi to pay a visit to my customers in Istanbul. He never stopped complaining from the moment he arrived until the moment he left about the pollution in the air. He was a terrible company ambassador.[3]

INDIA

When I first took over as general manager at CEL I was surprised to find that we had no business of any kind with India. When I asked Mehdi Ali about this, he – being from Pakistan – said: 'We do not want to do business with them – they cannot be trusted!'

'How can we ignore a nation on such a huge growth path?' I contested. 'There must be some big opportunities to establish business there.'

'Well how do you propose we find somebody to commence business with?' he asked.

'How about I put an advert in the *Times of India* calling for existing consumer electronics distributors who are interested in adding home computers to their portfolio?' I asked.

'That won't work!' he exclaimed.

Well, of course it did work.

I placed a quarter-page advert in the newspaper, and again three weeks later, requesting written submissions from interested parties, particularly those already distributing consumer electronics (Pioneer, Sharp, National, Sony, etc.) because I knew they would already have an existing customer base, which meant we could get up and running very quickly.

I received quite a large number of replies and subsequently went to Bombay (now Mumbai), where I stayed in the Searock Sheraton Hotel and invited along applicants I felt had what I needed.

One of these applicants was the authorised distributor for National (a now defunct sub-brand of Panasonic), who later took me out to dinner – surprisingly – at a Chinese restaurant, where I had the best

---

3   After my relationship in Finland had finally come to an end (which I allude to later in this chapter), I found new solace in Istanbul with a lady named Deniz Akgul, who I met at a jazz club and with whom I shared lots of fun moments. Istanbul is my favourite city in the world with the most amazing food, and I love the way people of all nationalities and religions seem to get on so well together.

Chinese meal I have ever had in my life (and I have been to China several times!). Truly magnificent food, with king prawns larger than lobsters – sensational in every respect. Delicious!

I also invited a fledgling start-up to present their application, mainly because they were young and very enthusiastic about the Amiga. They gave by far the best presentation of all the contenders and certainly knew their stuff when it came to the products, so I happily appointed them. They hadn't even named their company yet!

And so I added another country to CEL, and business was quite good for a fledgling market. But the biggest problem we faced was the very high import duty put on finished goods landing in India.

I made a proposition to my customer there that they consider setting up an assembly line, which would reduce the import duties significantly (as opposed to manufacturing, which would have been much more intricate and considerably more costly to establish). This would bring down the retail cost and widen our market by making the product more affordable to a lower socio-economic group – a very worthwhile exercise if we could do it.

We set about drafting a business plan, found some suitable premises, did a whole costing exercise and, based on the much lower price that local assembly would allow us to sell at, produced a very workable, compelling and viable proposition to present to banks.

We made an appointment with the State Bank of India – the largest and most prestigious bank in India at that time – presented our proposal and requested suitable funding. (This was for my clients, not for Commodore – I was there only to add credibility and to show Commodore's support for the application for funding.)

The presentation was superbly put together, if I say so myself, and showed a very profitable result, even though we decided to show sales forecasts well below what we were already achieving by paying high import duties, so we could be certain we would achieve what we had presented to the bank.

The two gentlemen from the bank had a quick and quiet word with each other, at which point the more senior of the two said, 'That is all well and good Mr Pleasance, but what is in it for us?'

'Well you can see from our figures – which we have only forecast on a modest basis – that the bank is going to do very well out of this,' I replied.

He looked me straight in the eyes.

'I'm not asking about the bank – I mean us,' he said, pointing to his colleague and himself. 'What is in it for us?'

He was asking for a backhander! At that point I asked my clients to say their farewells and we walked out of the bank, empty-handed. I never enter business under those sorts of corrupt and potentially punitive conditions.

It's a shame really, because I know that had we been able to strike a deal with the bank, the outcome of being supported by a loan enabling the establishment of an assembly plant would have resulted in much lower import duties, leading to lower consumer pricing. This would have benefited everybody, particularly people in the lower socio-economic group who would be able to afford a computer for their children. Considering how India has developed as a nation – especially now, with a huge pool of well-trained IT professionals – we could have been in a much stronger position, with excellent brand recognition.

FINLAND

Finland was a very good market for me at CEL. It was more western-ised than most of the countries in my remit, with a strong and stable economy, nice people and a huge following of particularly Amiga fans.

For my first ever visit, I asked the contact I had been given there, Marjut Mymme Kaislakari, to set up a conference meeting in Helsinki with a whole bunch of Amiga fans. I went along with two of my tech support people to do a presentation and answer all their questions, with the objective of revitalising the whole scene.

I also asked her to invite some media and press people to video the event, and report in the national newspaper and dedicated Amiga magazine.

Approximately 80 attendees turned up, and it proved to be a very successful way to introduce myself and to get the whole Amiga community on side and believing in our commitment to giving them a much higher level of support than they had experienced from Commodore before.

While at the initial conference I succumbed to that age-old temptation and fell head over heels for Marjut's younger sister, Minna Kaislakari. Thus began a love affair that lasted well over a year and would change my life forever.

Marjut Mymme and Minna Kaislakari

*

At that time, our distributor in Finland was a guy called Grels Westman, who was based in Vaasa. I had deliberately not invited him as I wanted to find out what all the Amiga fans thought of him and his service to them. The feedback I received was not good, and it made me even more wary beyond my gut feeling, which had turned out to be right.

Sure enough, he ended up cheating us by deliberately using incomplete documentation, resulting in him taking delivery of a shipment of Amigas and not paying us for them. I immediately cancelled his distributor agreement with CEL and set about appointing a new and significantly better company called Toptronics, who were based in Turku, the former capital of Finland.

Toptronics had a large dealer network as they were distributors of software, games and accessories. But as they had never previously sold any hardware, they needed a product marketing or sales manager to handle the Amiga range. I proposed Minna work with them and she was ultimately hired. This was an excellent solution both from a business and personal perspective, as every time I held distributor meetings anywhere in the world, Minna would be there representing my distributor from Finland. It worked brilliantly for our relationship and we had lots of fun together while working.

While CEL never recovered the money stolen by Grels Westman, I did eventually get my own back.

Immediately after Commodore put themselves into liquidation, I went for a meeting with Franklyn R Wilson – Commodore International's elected liquidator – in The Bahamas.

As I entered the office, I spotted Grels Westman sitting there in reception. Imagine his shock as I walked in – his face sure was a picture! I assume he was interested in bidding, either on his own or in some sort of consortium. Well, it turned out my meeting was before his, so when I went in to see the liquidator, I alerted him to the fact that Grels Westman had stolen a shipment of Amigas from CEL, and so not only was he in no way to be trusted, but he actually owed us, as creditors, money. There is no doubt I put a stop to any devious plans he may have been proposing to the liquidator. Revenge sure is sweet!

-8-

INTERLUDE 2

COMMODORE NETHERLANDS

This story is a prime example of what happens when a subsidiary is allowed to get away with, at best, poor administrative practices, and at worst, illegal practices.

Commodore's Netherlands subsidiary was run by the late Bernard van Tienen.[1] He was famous for his regular end-of-quarter bragging to all of us general managers that if he was short of reaching his sales target (for which he – and all general managers – were paid a bonus), he would 'create some false invoices, load product onto trucks and send it on a long journey, only to be returned back into stock a few days into the new quarter'.

He would do this every quarter without exception, and was quite proud of the fact. This highlights the major failings of all of Commodore's corporate presidents: they never performed random unannounced auditing on any of the subsidiaries, which allowed this kind of practice to flourish. It's no surprise that Commodore was never seemingly aware of their true financial position at any given time.

During my time as general manager of Commodore Electronics Ltd

---

1   Bernard went on to became director of Escom. See part 1, chapter 15, 'Management Buyout'.

in Basle, Switzerland, I witnessed many instances where Commodore Netherlands illegally exported products into the countries I was responsible for. It was incredibly disruptive and counterproductive to long-term business when trying to support the appointed distributor in any country.

One day, the premises Commodore Netherlands had been renting for several years came up for sale. Bernard suggested to Mehdi Ali that it was a good proposition to buy it as the repayments would be less than the rent and would give Commodore equity. Mehdi Ali outright refused, exclaiming: 'Commodore is not in the real estate business!'

So Bernard bought the building himself and became his own land-lord – what a bizarre situation that turned into!

During the final days of Commodore UK, when we were left no choice but to declare bankruptcy, Colin Proudfoot and I had cause to deal with the liquidator of Commodore Netherlands. It was he who brought to our attention some rather unusual expense claims that had been processed by Bernard for 'services rendered' at an extremely well-known establishment in Amsterdam call 'Yab Yum', which was considered to be a 'very high-class' brothel. The whole bizarre incident became considerably more intriguing when it was revealed that the expenses claimed were to the tune of $480,000!

Bernard van Tienen was subsequently the subject of subpoenas issued by the Dutch liquidator in the amount of 300 million guilders.

The irony is that Bernard – who had allegedly set up bogus Commodore accounts and spent huge sums of Commodore money in a notorious brothel – was in fact protected from those legal proceedings by an insurance policy established and paid for by Mehdi Ali, Irving Gould and the rest of the Commodore Board at an estimated cost of $5 million, money that lawfully belonged to Commodore creditors. So the insurance policy designed to protect Mehdi and Irving's backsides ended up helping someone suspected of inappropriate conduct to escape a massive legal bill![2]

---

2   Wim Meulder goes into more detail about the false invoicing conducted by Bernard van Tienen, as well as the fake bank accounts he set up to allow this practice to go unnoticed, in part 2, chapter 10, 'Wim Meulders – Death by management, customers and users'.

The following is an article printed in the Dutch newspaper *de Volkskrant* in 1997 reporting on the incident, printed with permission (the English translation follows on page 93).

Curator pakt ex-directeur Commodore aan

Lucas van Grinsven, 2 September 1997

Bernard van Tienen, de voormalige directeur van vier failliete computerbedrijven, krijgt een schadeclaim van driehonderd miljoen gulden aan de broek.

Daarom wordt hij aansprakelijk gesteld voor het hele tekort dat aan het licht kwam bij het faillissement van de Nederlandse dochters van Commodore in 1994, zegt curator A. van Hees. 'De dagvaardingen liggen al klaar. Het duurt geen maand meer voor ze worden verstuurd,' zegt de advocaat.

Behalve Van Tienen worden ook Commodore-directeuren aangeklaagd in de Verenigde Staten en de Bahama's. Van Tienen was directeur van de Nederlandse tak van de Amerikaanse computerproducent Commodore.

'Ze hebben een puinhoop gemaakt van de administratie. Sommige vennootschappen hebben in het geheel geen boekhouding,' zegt Van Hees. Om die reden kan hij onmogelijk traceren welk gedeelte van de miljoenenschade is veroorzaakt door wanbestuur, en welk door marktomstandigheden. 'Daarom vorderen we gewoon het volledige tekort.'

Eén van de misstappen van Van Tienen is dat hij omzet boekte die nog niet was gerealiseerd. Hoewel de curator dit zogenoemde voorfactureren niet kan bewijzen, twijfelt hij niet aan het bestaan ervan. 'Dat gebeurde bij Commodore op grote schaal,' zegt hij.

Ex-medewerkers, die niet met name willen worden genoemd, bevestigen dat Commodore Nederland jarenlang op die wijze heeft gewerkt. Bij het faillissement stond voor circa 15 miljoen gulden aan verkochte pc's in de boeken, die in feite niet waren geleverd. Ook dochterbedrijven van Commodore in Duitsland en Groot-Brittannië maakten zich schuldig aan deze praktijken, zeggen zij met de curator.

De prachtige omzetgroei en winstgroei die Commodore liet zien, was geflatteerd door voorfacturering en droeg bij tot het faillissement toen de marktgroei begon tegen te zitten in 1993. 'Dat kun je niet volhouden. Op zeker moment komt het uit,' zegt een medewerker die bij de afwikkeling van het faillissement is betrokken.

Om de fiscus om de tuin te leiden, maakte Commodore gebruik van een tweede magazijn bij de Amsterdamse Coentunnel, waar de zogenaamd geleverde goederen werden opgeslagen. Ook detailhandelsketen Dixons zou zijn magazijnen ter beschikking hebben gesteld, reden voor het vertrek van directeur Jacobs. Dixons was niet meer bereikbaar voor commentaar.

Vorige week kwam Bernard van Tienen al in het nieuws met het faillissement van het nieuwe Commodore, dat na slechts een jaar alweer over de kop is gegaan. Uit de boedel van het oude (Amerikaanse) Commodore dat in 1994 failliet ging, kocht Van Tienen de merknaam Commodore voor gebruik in Nederland.

Naast een assembelagelijn voor pc's in Nieuw-Vennep (een schroevendraaierfabriek) had het nieuwe Commodore ook 35 winkels. Hiervan zijn er 17, na het vorige week uitgesproken faillissement, verkocht aan concurrent Dynabyte.

Van Tienen heeft ook nog twee andere bedrijven geleid. Net voordat het oude Commodore failliet ging, verliet hij dit bedrijf in 1993 samen met enkele collega's die hij nog kende uit hun tijd bij Olivetti om computerwinkelketen The Champs te beginnen, met hulp van Olivetti. The Champs was geen lang leven beschoren. De torenhoge ambities konden niet worden waargemaakt. Het Duitse Escom, eveneens geleid door een ex-Commodore-directeur maar dan die van Duitsland, nam The Champs over. Escom werd gesteund door Siemens.

Escom op zijn beurt ging vorig jaar over de kop. Van Tienen was er als de kippen bij om de Nederlandse restanten voor een prikkie op te kopen, met hulp van de Rabobank dit keer. De curator van Escom, H. Bouma, laat weten dat hij Van Tienen niet aansprakelijk zal stellen voor het faillissement.

Here is the English translation

Trustee goes after former Commodore director

Lucas van Grinsven, 2 September 1997

Bernard van Tienen, the former director of four bankrupt computer companies, has received a fine of 300 million guilders.

He is being held liable for the entire deficit that came to light in the bankruptcy of the Dutch subsidiaries of Commodore in 1994, says bankruptcy trustee A. van Hees. "The subpoenas are ready and will be sent within a month," says the lawyer.

Besides van Tienen, Commodore directors in the United States and The Bahamas are also being sued. Van Tienen was director of the Dutch branch of the American computer manufacturer Commodore.

"Their administration is a mess – some of the companies have no accounting at all," says Van Hees. As a result, he cannot possibly trace how much of the millions in damages were caused by maladministration and how much were caused by market conditions. "That is why we are simply claiming the full deficit."

One of Van Tienen's missteps is that he wrote sales in the books that had not yet been realised. Although the bankruptcy trustee cannot prove this so-called pre-invoicing, he does not doubt its existence. "That happened at Commodore on a large scale," he says.

Ex-employees, who do not want to be named, confirm that Commodore Netherlands has worked in this way for many years. At the time of the bankruptcy, approximately 15 million guilders of sold PCs were in the books that had in fact not been delivered. Commodore subsidiaries in Germany and Great Britain were also guilty of these practices, the bankruptcy trustee has been informed.

The excellent sales and profit growth that Commodore showed were bolstered by pre-invoicing and contributed to the bankruptcy when market growth started to stall in 1993. "You cannot keep that up – it will come out at some point," says one employee involved in the settlement of the bankruptcy.

In order to mislead the tax authorities, Commodore used a second warehouse at the Amsterdam Coen Tunnel, where the so-called delivered goods were stored. The retail chain Dixons would also have made its warehouses available, which at the time was reason for the departure of director Jacobs. Dixons did not want to comment.

Last week, Bernard van Tienen was again in the news because of the bankruptcy of the new Commodore after just a year. Van Tienen bought the brand name for use in the Netherlands from the estate of the old (American) Commodore, which went bankrupt in 1994.

In addition to an assembly line for PCs in a former screwdriver factory in Nieuw-Vennep, the new Commodore also had 35 retail stores, 17 of which were sold off to competitor Dynabyte after last week's bankruptcy.

Van Tienen has previously led two other companies. Just before the old Commodore went bankrupt, he left Commodore in 1993 with some colleagues he knew from their time at Olivetti to start the computer shopping chain The Champs, with the help of Olivetti. The Champs did not last long either – its unachievable ambitions could not be realised. German company Escom, also led by an ex-Commodore Germany director and backed by Siemens, took over The Champs.

Escom, in turn, filed for bankruptcy last year. Van Tienen was very keen to buy the Dutch remnants for next to nothing, this time with the help of Rabobank. The trustee of Escom, H. Bouma, has announced that he will not hold Van Tienen liable for that bankruptcy.

I should take a moment to explain about the reference in this article to Commodore UK also doing 'false invoicing'.

The fact of the matter is that Kelly Sumner – who went on to become Commodore UK managing director – did boost his final quarter-end sales by processing a single sale-or-return deal with ZCL, one of our distributors, in order to get his bonus prior to resigning from Commodore.

Colin Proudfoot and I discovered this when after we took over as joint managing directors at a critical time when our parent company desperately needed cash flow, and ZCL insisted we take back a high level of stock 'sold' under these terms.

We at Commodore UK had never before recorded sales 'with the right to return' and it was very upsetting to discover this underhand practice within a previously 'squeaky clean' subsidiary.

- 9 -

COMMODORE INC.

WEST CHESTER, PENNSYLVANIA, USA

On the 4th of January 1992, I was attending a general managers' meeting hosted by Mehdi Ali in the offices of Commodore Germany in Frankfurt, in my position as general manager of Commodore Electronics Ltd.

We had a pretty normal meeting in which we discussed targets, budgets and expenses, and then as we were finishing up, Mehdi called me back to talk further.

'Right, Pleasance,' he said. 'You have been on at me for a very long time about this and today I'm going to grant you your wish: I'm sending you to America to take over the Consumer Products Division as vice president. Jim Dionne [then-president of Commodore Inc., the US sales company] will think you are reporting to him but really you will be reporting directly to me – just don't tell him that!'

I was shocked but absolutely overjoyed at the news. He was right – I had been asking for almost three years to be let loose in the US. For some reason it was an area where our retail business was particularly terrible. I felt certain I could make the changes necessary to get our consumer business back on track.

I was even more shocked when Mehdi said he wanted me on the 7pm flight out of Heathrow that night – it was already 1pm and I was

Concorde

in Frankfurt! He then wanted me to fly on to Las Vegas to meet up with Jim Dionne at the annual Consumer Electronics Show, where Commodore had a stand as he wanted me to take over the division at that show. He sent me upstairs to the administration office immediately to make sure I was booked on the flight to New York.

To my complete surprise and delight, it turned out my arranged flight out of Heathrow was on none other than Concorde! Of course, it never occurred to him to do otherwise because he would fly Concorde all the time – it was just one occasion when Mehdi Ali made a huge mistake that worked out well for me!

To be honest, I found the Concorde somewhat underwhelming. It was a very narrow aircraft with only two seats on each side of a narrow aisle – a window and an aisle seat that were roughly the same width – and it had about as much legroom as a business-class seat on a 747.

But the most disappointing thing, I felt, was that as you were flying at over 50,000 feet there was no real sense of the speed at which the aircraft was travelling – the only way you could tell how fast it was going was by reading a digital speedometer at the very front of the plane by the entrance to the cockpit.

That said, stepping off the plane in New York less than four hours after leaving Heathrow showed just how fast that beautiful aircraft could really travel – I do feel incredibly fortunate, especially as that plane is no longer in service. Thank you Mehdi!

*

Once I was finally in Las Vegas, I met up with Jim Dionne.

I had met Jim a couple of times before, although I did not know him very well. We decided to go out for dinner at a Mexican restaurant where we had a nice meal accompanied by a few Dos Equis beers. After we finished our meal we exited the restaurant and tried to hail a cab to no avail, so ended up walking the long way home.

At the time I was still suffering from a torn cruciate ligament – the injury had occurred during a game of football just a few months earlier while attending an industry conference as a keynote speaker in Marbella, Costa Del Sol.[1] Suffice to say, walking all that distance on my first night in Vegas was quite the ordeal (not that I let Jim Dionne know that!).

At this stage I should tell you about the poor state of consumer product sales at Commodore US up to that time – it is a great example of how not to conduct business.

Around the time the VIC-20 was released in the US in June 1980, Commodore had quite a good distribution network throughout the country with all retailers – from small independents right up to the national chains – and they were all keen to stock the hot product at that time. Then when the Commodore 64 was released in August 1992, things changed dramatically as it became the 'must-have' home computer for families in the America.

In the run up to Christmas, Kmart decided they wanted to use the C64 as their major 'loss-leader' product – selling it at more or less cost

---

1   Foolishly, myself and a few other reprobates had decided to play the game while hungover. The pitch was tarmacked, and being incredibly overweight at the time and somewhat clumsy, I ended up twisting my knee and tearing a ligament. This resulted in a three-night stay in hospital back in Basle.

price – in order to win all the sales from the other retailers, at which point they would upsell the consumer further accessories such as the Datassette drive, joysticks and, of course, games, all at full margin.

They ended up advertising and selling the C64 for just $99 – a mere $1 over the price they paid for them! This resulted in all the other retailers – including the small independents and all the other national chains – cancelling their orders and refusing to stock the product, which they would have had to sell at a loss to try to keep up with Kmart's aggressive pricing strategy.

Under normal circumstances, any manufacturer who understood their business would somehow 'manage' this unacceptable situation – they might, for example, suddenly have an unexpected huge shortage of product so they could not supply Kmart with their orders. However, the brains of Commodore's Consumer Division management decided, in their infinite wisdom, that as they were selling every C64 they could get, it was not necessary to bring order back to the market, and so just let it happen.

As a result, Commodore Inc. lost its entire retail network – with the exception of Kmart – more or less overnight.

It is interesting to note that once other games consoles came on the market at lower retail prices, Kmart dropped the C64 like a hot potato, showing absolutely zero loyalty to Commodore.

DOCTOR D

My first day in West Chester is etched in my mind forever.

On my way to my office in the far corner of the first floor, a voice from the office next door shouted: 'It's the Doctor! It's Doctor D!'

As mentioned before, the first band I was in, at the age of 20, was called 'The DR. D Revue', so named after the first initials of the three group members, David, Robbie and David – 'DR D'.

Somewhat spooked, I stopped in my tracks and entered the next-door office to find the vice president of Business Systems at the company.

'What did you just call me?' I asked.

'Doctor D!' he replied.

Naturally I had to ask him why.

'That is what you are known as by everybody here – when there is a problem in the company, you get sent in to fix it. That is why we call you "The Doctor". Doctor D!'

What a spooky coincidence!

After my first cup of coffee in my new office (I cannot function without a big caffeine fix every morning!), I decided to say hello to the engineering team – after all, without them the company would not be in business. We had a mere seven Amiga engineers but I was very shocked to find that we had 40 PC engineers!

This was such nonsense – by that time in January 1992, the idea of Commodore making its own PC compatibles was truly outrageous. There were many companies in East Asia who made PCs considerably cheaper than we could, and it would have been much easier to have had them cosmetically designed for us with the famous CBM badge on the front, then ordered as sales were made on a 'just-in-time' basis. This way you would never get caught with obsolete stock as new models were being released at a very fast pace.

Apparently, the reason why we had this many PC engineers was because Mehdi Ali, who had a very poor reputation for recruitment skills, had just hired a new head of engineering – a gentleman by the name of Bill Sydnes, who prior to Commodore had been a project manager at IBM where he had been responsible for the ill-fated IBM PCjr (the 'PC Junior'), which was described in the December 1984 issue of *Time* magazine as 'one of the biggest flops in the history of computing' and is certainly one of IBM's biggest failures.

It was commonly believed by the staff at West Chester that Bill Sydnes had given out jobs to 40 of his mates. It certainly did not make any commercial sense given Commodore's weak financial position, and because its real strength was clearly in its unique Amiga range of products, which at that time had no competition.

My first team meeting with the US Consumer Products Division Sales and Marketing Team was a real eye-opener.

It transpired that the reason there had been no sales for several months to any of our major retailers was because they all owed money and none of them were paying their bills. This seemed incredible to me, and even more strange was the fact that none of my staff knew why this was so. I told each of my sales guys to make appointments for their customers to meet with me so I could get to the bottom of this unusual problem.

The first customer I got to visit was Sears. We went to the 14th floor of Sears Tower in Chicago and were met by a team of 10 senior managers and directors, all sitting round a large boardroom table and looking expectantly at me.

I introduced myself and explained that I had been with Commodore for around nine years, in both the UK and international market, and that my new role as vice president of Consumer Products meant it was my responsibility to ensure we had a profitable and healthy trading relationship with Sears. I went on to explain that I was a person of great honour and integrity, and that I hoped to enjoy a similar level of business dealings from them, which they acknowledged and agreed.

I proceeded to ask if they wouldn't mind explaining why they were not paying their outstanding invoices, which were several months overdue.

'Well Mr Pleasance,' they replied. 'We are simply waiting for Commodore Inc. to come and take back all our stock and issue us with a credit note. After that we will owe you nothing.'

I was a bit taken aback by this.

'Well that's strange,' I said. 'In my nine years at the company I have never known us to be a "lending library"'.

At this point, their accountant slid a piece of paper across the table. I picked it up.

It was a letter confirming the transaction for a volume of Commodore products on a 'sale-or-return' basis, signed by president Jim Dionne. To say I was gobsmacked would be an understatement – we simply never did this.

To my horror, the product that was the subject of this sale-or-return deal was the CDTV, a product that had been a complete disaster – it was so far ahead of its time that it was almost impossible to sell by tech-savvy outlets, let alone Sears, whose shop staff could barely ring up a sale on the cash register and place it in a bag.

I was in no way prepared for this, and having only just assured them

The CDTV

I was an honourable guy and that Commodore was an honourable company, I felt somewhat humiliated.

I had to think quickly. So to buy some time, I explained to them that it was not their fault this product had not sold in their stores and brought them up to date with how well certain other products were doing for Commodore in Europe – especially the Amiga 500, which was selling in vast numbers.

This gave me an idea.

'Gentlemen, I told you I am a man of my word, and Commodore will of course take back the volume of CDTVs as per the letter. However, I have a duty to you, as a major US retailer, to ensure you have the same opportunity as all the successful retailers in Europe – if I produce an exclusive Amiga 500 pack just for Sears, would you consider giving me an order to exactly the same value as the stock of CDTVs I am giving you credit for? In effect, you will be swapping non-saleable inventory for a very desirable product, and will be back on trend again.'

Luckily they went for it, so while I did not start my career in America with positive sales in the first quarter, I did not have negative sales either.

*

Frustratingly, the situation at Sears was exactly the same in all the major chains throughout the US – Jim Dionne had put CDTVs into all of them on a sale-or-return basis. Unsurprisingly, every chain had the same problem: no sales and no credit note issued, so none of them were paying their bills.

What a crazy situation: the president of the sales company made these deals – and collected his 'bonus' for meeting or exceeding his target – without telling the sales representatives what he had done, so they obviously did not understand why their customers were not paying their bills! Luckily I managed to resolve and reverse each problem with the same approach I used for Sears.

(Sadly I did get shafted by one chain: Tandy Name Brand.[2] The general manager there stitched me up when he agreed to place an order for Amiga 500s to match the value of the CDTVs I took back and gave them credit for – then duly cancelled his order. He would have ended up regretting it, as all the other stores who ranged the A500 did very well with them.)

This was yet another example of the repercussions of Commodore having no independent auditing systems in place, meaning anybody in a high enough position who felt inclined to do so could easily cheat and get away with it. It also explains why the US retail channel was in such a mess. After a very long time and no small amount of work, I was able to get us back in stock in the stores that mattered, and we continued to trade with them from that point until Commodore's eventual bankruptcy.

The interesting part of this story came at the quarter end, when all the staff in charge of sales had to report to Mehdi Ali what had

---

2   Tandy Name Brand was a chain of stores set up by RadioShack – who traditionally only sell their own brand merchandise – to sell other well-known brands.

transpired during the past 12 weeks in terms of sales figures and expenses, as put against the targets set at the end of the previous quarter.

It just so happened that at that time I had booked a two-week holiday over the last week of the quarter, and spent one week with my two sons (who I had flown out from the UK) at my house near the office and one week on my boat, which was moored on a marina at Rehoboth Beach, Delaware, about an hour-and-a-half's drive south from West Chester.

I absolutely loved making this trip most weekends – it was a wonderful area with a traditional boardwalk that had plenty of amazing restaurants, one of my favourites being a crab shack that was all-you-can-eat for $10 and where jugs of beer cost $5. I would sleep on the boat and then first thing in the morning go fishing for a few hours. Bliss!

I was on my boat when the quarter-end review took place in Mehdi Ali's office. Jim Dionne was there with my figures for the quarter, which of course showed a neutral figure as all the CDTV returns had to come off the positive sales figures. Mehdi went ballistic. He immediately got me on the phone and started shouting and swearing about the negative figures.

I told him to ask Jim for the envelope I had sent along with him on my behalf. The letter explained to Mehdi exactly what I had been faced with, that Jim had made all these 'non-sales' many months earlier (for which he had claimed his commission and bonus) and included copies of all the letters from Dionne offering sale-or-return deals. All this time, Mehdi was unaware of Jim's sale or return transactions – until now.

I wish I had been in that room after Mehdi hung up on me. No doubt there were fireworks aplenty!

But at least I got Commodore USA trading again, and after a long period they mostly did very well indeed. I introduced tailored bundles to each chain that included some of the great games that were popular in the US alongside the stalwarts *Wordsworth* and *Personal Paint*.

THE WINE CELLAR

While I often cast my own disapproval of many of Mehdi Ali's poor decisions, there was one occasion during this period of my life where he really surprised me in the nicest possible way.

One afternoon I was having quite an intense meeting with him in his New York office when completely out of the blue he asked me if I would join him and his family for dinner that evening and stay at the house.

I was shocked as I had never seen this side of him before – I'm sure I must have stammered my thanks.

That night we travelled in his chauffeur-driven Mercedes back to his beautiful house where I met his wife and two of his children. We all went on to a steak house and had the most superb meal and very enjoyable conversation.

Afterwards, when we were back at his house, Mehdi showed me down to his impressive purpose-built cellar – all temperature and humidity controlled – where he had a truly magnificent collection of vintage ports and fine wines. He chose a bottle of port and we went back upstairs and drank the lot.

Well as anybody who knows me can confirm, I am a very persuasive salesman. So after we had been through bottle number one, I got him to fetch a second – and we finished that one off as well!

So that one time I did get to see a softer side to this man – and in spite of the almost contemptuous way he could treat me at times, I knew then that he must have had a certain respect for me, as I am not aware of any other person in the company to whom he extended that privilege.

MOVING ON

After almost a full year as vice president of the Consumer Division, I told Mehdi that at least for now my job in the US was done, and that he should send me somewhere else.

'What the fuck are you talking about?' he said.

'Well, all the retailers are now trading well and I have no intention of selling them any more Amiga 500s for now,' I explained.

'Why not?'

A 1948 Triumph Roadster

'Because you and I both know we have the Amiga 1200 getting ready for release over the next few months, and if by the time it is launched I have sold further A500s into them, they will undoubtedly be asking me to take stock back or they will not be able to buy the new model in – it will be a repeat of the situation with the CDTVs. If they need additional A500s they can certainly order them, but if I have not sold into them they will have no chance whatsoever to ask for returns.'

Mehdi had no choice but to accept my reasoning (it was one of the rare times he did). So he asked me to operate out of the UK but to also readdress the CEL market – the market I used to run before moving to the US. Since I had left there it had been split up to be handled between the UK and the Netherlands, and business had dropped considerably. It was decided that I would return to the US once I had launched the Amiga 1200 in the UK.

As things turned out, I was kept very busy in the UK while overseeing CEL business and did not end up going back to America, instead taking over as managing director of Commodore UK jointly with Colin Proudfoot.

*

Once I knew I was going to be based in the USA at Commodore Inc.'s West Chester office for the foreseeable future, I decided to ship my gorgeous 1948 Triumph Roadster over.

I had bought her as a complete 'in pieces' restoration project not long after I was appointed sales and marketing director at Commodore UK. Although I had started the restoration myself, it became clear I was not really qualified to do it, nor did I realistically have the time needed for such a huge project. So I did some research and found a professional restorer Doug Elliot living in the Fens, not too far from Corby. Doug took it on and did a great job.

After much expense and many weeks, the car finally arrived at the docks in New Jersey. The very nice lady in charge of importation rang me and told me it was not a simple matter to get the car released, and there would be lots of documentation to complete. She kindly volunteered to do everything necessary and promised to keep me informed of her progress.

After six or seven months, she finally rang me and excitedly declared, 'It's all cleared and ready for you to collect!'

Well, by that point I had just been advised I was returning to the UK! So I told her and asked if she could please put the car on the next ship back.

So I never got to drive it even once in the USA. A very sad and expensive mistake!

10

A COMEDY OF ERRORS

OUR ILLUSTRIOUS LEADER, MEHDI ALI

It's difficult to know where to start here. The events portrayed through the following recollections have probably the most significance in the whole story of the unfortunate demise of a once great and dynamic company.

Irving Gould – chairman and major shareholder of Commodore International – fell out big time with Jack Tramiel, who in 1984 was refused permission to bring his sons onto the board, resulting in Jack leaving Commodore. There is much conjecture about whether Jack was fired or quit – and as both have sadly since passed away, I doubt we'll ever know for sure.[1]

Irving appointed Marshall F Smith – an executive from the steel industry with no knowledge of the computer market – to CEO, and he immediately put in place a series of cost-cutting exercises. Smith was replaced by Thomas Rattigan, previously CEO of PepsiCo, Inc., and

---

[1]   In the recent documentary 'The Commodore Story', Leonard Tramiel (Jack's son) states that the falling out was due to annoyance at Irving's personal use of the company plane – the 'Pet Jet' – to help with his permanent 'tax exile' (which I discuss in part 1, chapter 11, 'Interlude 4 – Irving Gould'). However, Irving himself told me the falling out was over Jack's insistence on his three sons joining the board.

Mehdi Ali

he was even more aggressive in his cost-cutting, closing the newer pur-pose-built assembly plant in Corby in favour of the ancient Braunschweig facility in Germany (stupidity personified).

Despite bringing the company out of a $237 million three-quarter loss into a $22 million profit in the space of one quarter (a rather short-term view of the real financial status of any company), Rattigan was fired by major shareholder Irving Gould, who tem-porarily took over as CEO. Rattigan subsequently sued Commodore for $9 million of lost income.

Mehdi Ali was a managing director of the restructuring division at Dillon, Read & Co., who were brought in by Irving Gould to assist in a refinancing/restructuring programme, something that was desperately needed at that time. One of the most significant negoti-ations made by Mehdi Ali for Commodore was a $50 million loan by Provident of America.

Irving Gould seemingly became friends with Mehdi Ali and ulti-mately appointed him to the position of president, despite Mehdi having no knowledge whatsoever of the computer business (nor, as it turned out, much interest in even attempting to understand it).

I remember in the early days of the Corby office being approached by a guy who had been developing 3D glasses for use with computer games at a time when the concept of 3D games was very hot. He needed a small amount of funding to complete the prototype – from memory, around £20,000 – and produce around 100 finished sets from which to take orders. I negotiated so that if we provided the money it would become a Commodore-branded product and we would earn a 20 per cent royalty on every pair sold, as well as add it to our portfolio of products to sell into our existing retail channels, thus earning commission on the sales. As deals go, it was a real no-brainer.

Clearly I needed to get Mehdi Ali's approval for this, and I assumed it would be very easy as it was such a potentially profitable investment. So I phoned Mehdi and arranged a time for me and the guy to fly to New York for a meeting to discuss the whole venture.

By complete coincidence, within a few days of having made the appointment with Mehdi, another inventor came to see me with an incredible invention for which he also needed further funding to complete – this time I seem to recall it was around £40,000–£50,000. He had invented a special formula coating which, when applied to glass – screens or lenses of any sort – magnified the image to an unbelievable degree. It was phenomenal. Again, I negotiated a cracking deal for Commodore, subject, of course, to our investment.

So, I got my brain working overtime here, and I'm thinking: 'If I can combine these two products we'll have 3D glasses that gave you a giant screen image while playing the latest video game – and all under the Commodore brand name. What a dynamite proposition!'

On that basis, I added Mr Coating Man to the appointment with Mehdi in New York, and I was excited at the prospect of bringing such a strong proposition to the attention of the Commodore top dogs.

Imagine my disdain when the very day before the appointment Mehdi rang me up to cancel the whole thing.

'Pleasance,' he said, 'it is too important to me that you be there in the UK to keep getting sales in – don't come to New York tomorrow.' I was gutted.

I never found out what happened with the 3D glasses, but I do know that Mr Coating Man, not long after our meeting, sold his invention to Canon for a whopping £6 million!

One of Mehdi's biggest failings was his inability to select good outside people for critical positions within the company. Though he often used Heidrick & Struggles, a highly regarded international executive recruitment consultancy, his final selections were often simply appalling choices. Bill Sydnes's hiring – which I covered in the previous chapter – is a prime example of this.

At around the same time Mehdi hired Bill, he also hired a new head of manufacturing (name withheld) who insisted we set up assembly in the Philippines. This was crazy – we had absolutely no customers in Asia, and shipping by sea from the Philippines to Europe, our major market, took around five weeks, which was expensive and risky as prices could potentially change while the products were in transit.

It later transpired that the only reason he had convinced Mehdi to do this was because he had worked in the Philippines with his previous company and wanted to continue to visit the mistress he acquired over there! Awful reasoning for a huge investment into an already nonsensical business decision.

INTERNATIONAL MARKETING

One of the things that used to really upset me at Commodore was the amount of money the company wasted on each subsidiary being allowed to produce their own 'marketing campaigns' – a term I use loosely given the many pathetic efforts some countries came up with!

I was particularly annoyed that our strategy for marketing and selling our consumer products in the UK was not adopted by at least the other European subsidiaries, as we had proven exponential growth in our volume sales quarter on quarter. After all, it is commonly accepted that western children (our target market) are pretty much the same in marketing terms wherever they may live, and so what we produced was as likely to appeal to children in Italy and France as it was in Germany and Spain.

As it was, up until then, each subsidiary did their own thing, with no consistent marketing message. So I approached Mehdi Ali.

'I've just been on holiday with my children to the Costa del Sol, and when we arrived at Heathrow Airport there was a huge poster advertising a Sony product. When we landed in Malaga, lo and behold, there was exactly the same advert, but in Spanish. This is global marketing, and it is spreading the same message wherever you go in the world, strengthening brand awareness.'

'So? What do you want me to do?' he replied.

'Well, instead of awarding each subsidiary 5 per cent of their respective turnover for them to spend on whatever they chose, allocate a "Central Marketing Fund" to be used to produce one TV commercial with one message, but produced in the subsidiary's native language. And let's get all our literature printed the same way in multiple

European languages, using one design company and one printer, who then ships the relevant brochures to each country to use.[2]

'Not only will we – for the first time ever – be spreading a uniform marketing message around the world, which will be phenomenal in itself, but we will also save the company a fortune. And if we have all of our subsidiaries sell the same Amiga packs that we design and put together in the UK, it will give us even greater price negotiating power because we will be talking about massive increases in volumes of software that we will be able to commit to – thereby reducing our cost and adding margin directly to our bottom line.'

My idea fell on deaf ears. There is a saying that goes: 'There are none so blind as those who will not see.' Mehdi Ali was the epitome of that expression.

*

I have an adjunct to this story that is another example of Mehdi's poor choices in recruitment.

One day, Mehdi called me on the phone.

'Pleasance,' he began, 'you will be pleased to know that, based on your suggestion, I have just recruited a marketing director to set up Commodore Marketing International. He will be operating out of the UK and has recruited a consumer specialist and a business systems specialist. I want you to give them all the help and assistance you can.'

I told him I would be happy to.

The first thing that this new guy (I believe his name was Peter) did was rent a central London office space at an enormous expense, even though we had spare office space in Maidenhead. He then ordered himself a bespoke suite of office furniture at a cost of £135,000 (a desk, side table and glass-fronted tall cupboard, which I subsequently sold during the liquidation of CBM UK Ltd for the grand sum of £400).

I never actually met Peter, and I have no idea what he actually did to contribute to our global marketing efforts.

---

2   We had no internet in those days and thus no email, but it still would have worked out cheaper to post artwork to each subsidiary company and have the brochures printed locally.

Meanwhile, his 'consumer specialist' – I cannot even remember his first name – did ring me up once.

'I understand you are the man with all the consumer knowledge within Commodore – can I come and talk with you please?' he asked.

'At long last', I thought to myself, 'someone with a bit of interest in what's going on!' I jumped at the chance and an appointment was made.

He came to my office at the agreed time, sat down in front of my desk, asked me a handful of basic questions and then, seemingly having run out of further topics to discuss, excused himself and left, all within precisely 14 minutes – not one second more! – never to be seen again. What a waste of time.

After that, nothing happened – no marketing activity of any kind was ever undertaken by those two – nor the 'business systems specialist' – and quite quickly (though not fast enough in my eyes) the 'New International Marketing Division' was shut down.

THE AMIGA 600 DEBACLE

At CBM UK Ltd, with some very clever marketing, we had managed to keep sales of the Commodore 64 buoyant for two years beyond its realistic sell-by date. But in February or March 1991, after analysing the results from the UK Christmas sales, it became obvious that the C64 as a saleable product was dying – in fact, for all intents and purposes, it was dead.

I went to New York for a meeting with Mehdi Ali during which I explained to him that we now desperately needed a very low-cost entry point Amiga to replace the C64. The idea was to attract that same demographic target audience, ideally with a similar retail price point of £200, although I believed we might get away with an entry-level price of a maximum of £249.

I explained that the way to achieve that price point was to design and manufacture a very basic, low-spec Amiga, but with the potential to be upgraded, as consumers funds allowed, with the addition of external hard drives, extra RAM and so on. In this way, we would attract and convert the previous C64 buyers, whose demographic profile showed they were less affluent than buyers of our Amiga range.

It was agreed per my suggestion to call the new model the Amiga 300, which, I explained in great detail, would easily identify to the Amiga community and the public in general that this was a 'lesser' model in the range compared with the existing Amiga 500. Remember, at that time the Amiga 500 was selling in very big volumes and was a profitable line for Commodore. My idea was to add the Amiga 300 to the range as a replacement for the now defunct C64 (which had not been selling anywhere in volume for years outside the UK), so this move would considerably boost our worldwide sales volumes and revenues.

In September that year, all the general managers met in Frankfurt to agree the final basic specifications of the A300, and we left the meeting confident that corporate management were probably – and for the first time ever – doing what we, and the market, had actually asked for.

Imagine our surprise when in May 1992 we took delivery of a large quantity of computers with the model number A600 and not A300!

It transpired that after our Frankfurt meeting the German subsidiary – who had clearly missed the whole point of the need and demand for the A300 – had underhandedly told Mehdi Ali that they could not and would not sell any Amiga that did not have a hard drive included, thereby sabotaging the whole well-thought-out plan to entice C64 buyers into an affordable upgrade path. Mehdi Ali simply rolled over and conceded, but never had the balls to talk to me or any other GM about the change of plan.[3]

This A600 would become a catastrophic disaster for the following reasons:

- Though it was smaller and had fewer features than the A500, it cost *more* to manufacture.
- Being called the A600 gave consumers the impression it was a higher specification machine than the A500, resulting in sales of the A500 slowing down significantly, virtually destroying that existing (and profitable) market.

---

3 On a related note, Commodore had instructed the production of an upgrade of the Amiga 500 called the Amiga 500 Plus at around the same time – and I am not aware of a single general manager or managing director from any subsidiary who asked for this or even knew about it. (Though in fairness, the A500+ did at least cost less to manufacture than the A500.)

- We had prematurely killed off the A500 by introducing the A600 instead of the planned A300 – and on which we made considerably less money.
- Consumers who bought the A600 believing it to be a superior model to A500 were very upset, believing they had been misled (which of course they had).
- The press, with whom we had an excellent relationship, absolutely lambasted our misguided rationale, and justifiably so.

AMIGA 500 PLUS

Although it was officially introduced in the spring of 1992, at around the same time, Commodore had already sold out of the remaining stocks of Amiga 500s before the run up to the profitable Christmas sales period. So in order to meet the demand for A500s before Christmas, Commodore used stocks of the new 8A revision mother-boards destined for the A500 Plus. Many users were unaware that they were purchasing anything other than a standard Amiga 500 because they were in the original A500 case and packaged entirely as a standard A500. Confusion reigned.

The saddest thing is that the first several thousand A600 machines produced had 'A300' printed on the motherboard.

As well as once again highlighting Mehdi Ali's complete incom-petence, this is another perfect example of Commodore corporate management never having a 'plan' of any kind, which resulted in them shooting themselves in the foot.

CD32

As Commodore's engineers designed the basic specifications of the CD32[4] – which appeared to be, for the first time ever, the subject of a well-planned and considered product launch – we managed, under strict non-disclosure agreements, to seed CD32 development machines into most of the major games software development houses. They had begun writing games especially designed to utilise

---

4 Beth Richard talks in excellent detail about the design process of the CD32 in part 2, chapter 6, 'Design many, ship few'.

the full capabilities and features this 32-bit CD-based machine had to offer so that at the planned launch – scheduled to be in late spring/ early summer of 1994 – there would be a plethora of fantastic games launched at the same time.

As a result of this, I was asked by Ian Hetherington (co-founder, with Jonathan Ellis, of Psygnosis) to arrange a meeting with Mehdi Ali at their studios in Liverpool. Mehdi was not very happy with the idea, but I ignored his moaning and drove him there.

Ian explained to Mehdi that with a few seemingly quite modest design changes, the CD32 could have an incredible boost in performance at very marginal additional cost. He also pointed out the benefits it would give developers like Psygnosis and other major players in the industry, who would find it easier to produce even better-quality products and enhance the reputation of the CD32 and the games publishers – a genuine 'win-win'. Ian had not requested any financial reward for this – it seemed he simply wanted to offer considerably improved games performance and to be credited for his contribution.

Well, it went exactly as expected. Mehdi was rude and ignorant, and clearly had no idea what Ian was talking about. But instead of just admitting that, he more or less turned on Ian, as though he 'must be crazy telling us how to design our computers!' I ushered Mehdi out of the building feeling very ashamed, and it was quite a while before I plucked up the courage to talk to Ian again. Luckily for me, Ian had realised what kind of a person Mehdi Ali was and held no bad feelings towards me.

The real sting to this story is that Psygnosis subsequently sold their company to Sony Computer Entertainment Europe, with Ian Hetherington being made head of Sony PlayStation Europe – and I often wonder to myself: 'If Mehdi Ali had not been such an obnoxious prick, would Commodore have had that technology?'

TAIWAN
One day, Mehdi phoned and asked if I could get perhaps two or three significant individuals from within the UK computer games industry to travel with me to meet him in Taiwan. He had apparently set up a meeting with someone and 'wanted me to explain what a good

business we had in the UK and how we did what we did.' (To avoid embarrassment to the highly respected individuals who travelled with me, I will withhold names.)

After a very long flight and a few beers, we all went to sleep as we had an early meeting the following day, which turned out to be at the head office for computer company Acer.

This was one of the strangest business encounters I have ever witnessed. Mehdi was incredibly uncomfortable as he sat there sweating and was almost incoherent in his rambling conversation. It was frankly very embarrassing.

He asked me to explain our 'consumer bundle' strategy, so I showed the Acer guys some packaging examples and then handed over to my colleagues, who each took turns to explain how good their relationship was with Commodore and how successful the collaboration had proven to be, and in particular how the increased sales of Commodore hardware had led to much increased sales of software. Another win-win situation.

We had no idea what we were actually doing there or what the objective actually was – until later, when Mehdi finally let it slip to me that the whole purpose of us all being there was that he was hoping to sell Commodore to Acer!

My god, if only he had told me that before we left the UK – imagine what a presentation I could have given to Acer? Sophisticated, accurate, with all the relevant sales and overhead figures – one hell of a compelling display. Instead it was, by my own admission, like a damp rag, as I was of course totally unprepared.

What might have been? To this day I cannot understand his rationale for not telling me the real purpose of our meeting and allowing me to really put on a show.

I've noticed recently on Mr Ali's Bloomberg profile that he credited himself as having accomplished 'a major operational turnaround' at Commodore. He certainly did – as president of the company they lost so much money they had to declare bankruptcy!

11

INTERLUDE 3

IRVING GOULD

I was very fortunate to have met Irving on many occasions, usually on the Commodore stand at the CeBIT trade show in Hanover,[1] but also in the Manhattan offices he shared with Mehdi Ali, and I would always try to say hello with each visit. While I often found him frustratingly stubborn, I admired much about him.

My favourite memory is when he answered a very forward question of mine (which I really had no right to ask in the first place).

'Irving, obviously you are a wealthy man – would it be impertinent of me to ask how you came to make your fortune?'

His answer completely floored me: 'I took the best piss of my life!'

Naturally I had to probe further. He continued.

'I was having lunch one day with a couple of friends at the Four Seasons in Manhattan and suddenly I needed to go to the bathroom. So I arrived at the urinal and was just starting to relieve myself when a young man came in, cursing loudly to himself, "Those fucking idiots! I can't believe they just said no! They are fucking insane!"

---

1   This was a very large two storey stand with a VIP hospitality area upstairs. It was so big it ended up being much cheaper to keep it permanently erected and just pay for its rental all year round, rather than pull it down and rebuild it each time!

Irving Gould

'Seeing how animated the man was, I asked "I take it you are upset with somebody?"

'The young man replied. "You bet I am! It's my stupid bosses – I just gave them a fantastic opportunity to make an absolute fortune and they just turned it down! Fucking idiots!"

'I prodded further. "Would you mind telling me what this opportunity is?"

'"Gladly," said the man. "You know how currently goods of all sorts, shapes and sizes are moved from country to country by sea, and it's a real nightmare trying to load a cargo ship with these goods because you're always left with gaps, and the stuff often moves around and gets mixed up and becomes very difficult to deal with? And then it takes ages to load and even longer to unload? Well, I know these guys who have come up with a way of dealing with the problem by using 20 and 40-foot containers that can be loaded individually, moved around by trucks at each end and then loaded onto specially designed container ships. And my company have just turned down the exclusive rights to use them in the whole USA!"

'Spotting an opportunity, I said to the young man, "Fear not, you've just found the person who will take this on – and for bringing this to me, you can be a part of it!"'

He had indeed taken the best piss of his life.

*

Because Irving was a Canadian national, and owing to his wealth, he constantly had to play a game with the tax authorities. As I understand, from what he told me, he was not allowed to stay in the US or Canada for more than three days at a time, so every couple of days he would have to move between them, taking regular breaks in The Bahamas, where he kept his beautiful deep-sea fishing boat.

Knowing I am also a keen big-game fisherman, he did invite me to go fishing with him, but sadly for one reason or another it never happened.

Regarding his work at Commodore, he was nowhere near as astute as you would expect. Believe me, I tried so many times to advise him of the many mistakes Mehdi was making and to warn him of the consequences of so many misguided decisions. But he would repeatedly reply with, 'I put the man in charge and I am leaving him to run the business.' I honestly raised this topic on many occasions, but I got the same response each time.

A large part of Commodore's demise can be apportioned to Irving, who chose to abdicate his responsibility and deliberately ignored the warnings of many people – certainly I was not the only one trying to advise him of impending doom.

There is a very old but true saying: 'You can lead a horse to water, but you can't make it drink.'

-12-

THE LAUNCH OF
THE CD32

In my opinion, what Commodore had planned for the launch of the revolutionary Amiga CD32 was the most professional and well thought out roadmap of any of the company's previous product releases, certainly within my 12-plus years working there.

At CBM UK we had, over many years, established excellent relationships with nearly all of the major games developers. We did this in part, of course, with the game and productivity software bundles, as well as by showing ongoing support against the rampant hacking and copying practices that prevailed over the years – we were the first hardware company to join and subscribe to the Federation Against Software Theft (FAST), for example.

As such, we had gained the trust of these major developers, and so, when the time came, we sent them all early CD32 development kits, for which they signed non-disclosure agreements. Soon they were secretly developing brand new titles to take advantage of the additional power and features the CD32 boasted so that on the day of the launch there would be – for the first time ever – a plethora of titles that really showed off the products capabilities.

The timing we'd afforded the development of these dedicated games was perfect, and the CD32 hardware was on schedule to meet

The Amiga CD32

the launch date of late spring/early summer 1994.

Meanwhile our UK-based Consumer Products business was in a very healthy position – we had taken massive orders for the Amiga 1200, scheduled for specific volume deliveries from September through to Christmas from all the major retailers. It was a profitable product with a healthy margin for Commodore at both corporate head office and in the UK.

Imagine my dismay at being instructed by Mehdi Ali that the UK – and worldwide – release of the CD32 was being brought forward to September, in the misguided belief that Commodore would reap the rewards of sales of both products, bringing in much needed cash flow and additional revenues over the Christmas period.

Believe me, I argued and argued with him that this was entirely the wrong strategy for two main reasons.

Firstly, once the launch of the CD32 was announced, consumers would opt for this new product and cancel their plans to buy the Amiga 1200, which was of course a healthy, profit-making product.

Secondly, none of the software that was being developed especially for the CD32 platform would be ready in time, so we would have to get developers to simply port existing Amiga 1200 games, and so there would be nothing special to display on our 'new baby', even though it was well designed and perfectly capable of doing so.

David's slogan for the
CD32 launch invite

Sadly I was not listened to. Instead, I was forced to secretly arrange a launch that was merely a few weeks before the product would be coming off the production line in the Philippines.[1]

Luckily for me, I had the best marketing department and team, led by Dawn Levack, and we set about devising a powerful way to launch the product. Dawn came up with the brilliant idea of using the Science Museum in London to host the event, so we booked it for the 16th of July 1993 and built our whole campaign around it.

As this was the world's first 32-bit, CD-based games console, I came up with the slogan '16 will never be the same again', to convey how it would smash all 16-bit offerings. (It's also the reason why we picked the 16th for the launch date.)

Through our PR company, we booked TV presenter Chris Evans to co-host the launch with me. We were always way ahead when it came to using celebrities for endorsements and things like product launches, often selecting those who were themselves rising stars, and Chris Evans certainly fit that profile perfectly.

Now, sometimes in life you get lucky – very lucky – and we certainly did then. Approximately three weeks before our scheduled launch

---

1   There was a somewhat insalubrious reason behind Commodore's decision to manufacture in the Philippines, which you can read about in part 1, chapter 10, 'A comedy of errors – Our illustrious leader, Mehdi Ali'.

David with Chris
Evans at the launch

there was an interview in a computer magazine with Tom Kalinske, president of Sega of America at the time. During his interview, he was asked about '32-bit, CD-based consoles', to which he replied words to the effect of: 'No way, it cannot be done. If anybody can do it, we at Sega would have done it – but we haven't.'[2]

This was music to our ears. At the launch in the Science Museum, we had a professional voice-over announcer read aloud the quote from Tom Kalinske, at which point we opened curtains to reveal the CD32 in all its glory, gloating from our announcement that it would be available to buy in shops in the UK in September, ready for Christmas.

The launch was a sensation and incredibly well received, and we got a long, standing ovation from the retailers, journalists and software developers who had filled the venue to capacity.

*

2   I have searched high and low for this article to find the actual quote to no avail – but I know it was said.

About two or three weeks later I received a phone call.

'Hi David,' said the man on the other end. 'You probably don't remember me but I certainly remember you – we've done business together before and I was impressed by the way you deal with people.'

I thanked the man and asked what the call was about.

'We have several hundred poster sites across the UK and I have a fantastic deal for you. We have three 96-sheet poster sites [the largest size] in prime locations in London, and the client who reserved them for the run-up to Christmas in advance has now had to cancel having paid 50 per cent of the fee. So I can offer you these three sites for the 50 per cent balance owed.

'Oh, and by the way – one of them happens to be right in front of Sega's head office.'

Well this was far too good an opportunity to pass up – we booked all three immediately, then set about determining what 'message' to put on them.

I'm not sure who actually came up with the idea – I think it was our advertising agency – but it was pointed out that Sega's whole pro-motional tag line at the time was the famous spin on their company name: 'To be this good takes AGES. To be this good takes SEGA.'

So our punch line – based on Tom Kalinske's own admission in that magazine interview – was:

TO BE THIS GOOD WILL TAKE SEGA AGES.

The campaign drew massive publicity all around the globe, and left me and my team feeling very smug indeed!

The poster went up just a few days prior to our annual industry dinner (known as 'InDin'), held at The Grosvenor Hotel, where exec-utives and staff from major companies in the industry came together to hand out awards and so on, all with the aim of raising money for charity. Commodore had three tables there and of course Sega were in attendance too.

At one point, Nick Alexander, the then-CEO of Sega Europe, walked up to me and said, 'A bit close to home, Mr Pleasance. A bit close to home.' To which I simply replied, 'Where needs must, Mr Alexander.

The CD32 billboard
advert in position
outside Sega head office

Where needs must', and smiled. No words were spoken on that topic
ever again after that!

*

On the downside, as I predicted, the launch of the CD32 had a
negative effect on the sales of the Amiga 1200. Consumers who had
planned to buy the A1200 were confused into thinking the CD32 must
be considerably better, when in reality it was just different. It was not
a computer in its basic form – it needed a keyboard and other peripheral add-ons to offer the same functionality as the Amiga 1200, plus
the only games available were ports of existing Amiga 1200 titles that
were not specifically written to take advantage of the CD32 superior
architecture. The whole outcome was, in a word, disappointing.

Commodore UK certainly suffered in revenue terms, and all because
yet again our 'esteemed leader' had completely screwed the company,
wrongly believing the CD32 would make for additional sales. And the
result was sadly replicated throughout Europe.

A perfect example of 'panic decision-making', which Commodore
had rightly earned a reputation for, and was most certainly another
major contributing factor to the company's demise.

THE SCI AMIGA 1200 MANUFACTURING SAGA

In 1992, a Scottish company called SCI started to build Amiga 1200s for Commodore International. The manufacturing contract was issued out of Commodore Hong Kong, who bought the machines from SCI and sold them to Commodore Electronics Limited (CEL) in Switzerland, who would then sell them on to the various Commodore entities around the world. But by the end of the year, Commodore International was running out of cash and ended up short-paying SCI by $20 million.

Early in 1993, Commodore notified the Securities and Exchange Commission that its financial future was at risk and therefore that Commodore UK could be deemed to be trading while insolvent (without a parent company Commodore UK could not survive, and if there is a material risk of failure then you are deemed to be insolvent). The directors of a company in this condition become personally liable to the creditors for any act that puts the assets of the company at risk.

With the inventory of Amiga 1200s dwindling, Mehdi Ali proposed a deal with SCI to build 400,000 units of the computer for Commodore UK, who in turn would pay them directly for the cost of the units plus $50 per machine to cover the old debt. Payment would be made as the inventory sold through.

We among UK management had not been involved in the nego-tiations and had no knowledge of their goings on, and the situation turned out to be a double-edged sword.

One day in March, a copy of the contract between SCI and Commodore International arrived in our office. We were stunned and sent it on to our liquidation counsel for advice. A few days later we got a reply.

'Don't worry about it,' they said.

'Why not?' we asked. 'Does it not bind Commodore UK to these actions?'

They told us it didn't. 'Commodore UK is not a party to the contract – legally, we don't have to follow it. Commodore UK's legal purchase of the Amigas from Commodore Switzerland creates an intercompany liability. How you pay that liability is up to you and Mehdi Ali – just make sure you do not pay more than that debt.'

During the third quarter of 1993, new machines started arriving from Scotland, invoices started arriving from Switzerland and we started remitting cash to SCI.

As Christmas approached, Mehdi called and told us to send some money to the US. We replied that the money was promised to SCI.

'Let me worry about that,' he said. 'Just send me the money.'

As we knew we were not a party to the SCI contract, we sent Mehdi the money and credited the balance on our intercompany account.

Early the following year, we sent more money to SCI – and also more money to Commodore US. By February, we had completely paid off the intercompany debt for the machines we had purchased. Out of courtesy, we called SCI to say we would not be sending them any more money. The proverbial hit the fan.

We were personally threatened by SCI that our professional repu-tations would be ruined, that we would never work in tech again and that we would be held personally accountable.

One Sunday morning, Colin Proudfoot, our legal director at the time, received a phone call from Mehdi and Gene Sapp, the president of SCI, and Mehdi told Colin he had to pay SCI more money.

Colin said that he couldn't because there was no debt to pay the money against.

The Amiga 1200

'Send it anyway!' was Mehdi's reply.

Colin again refused, telling them that paying money without debt in the circumstances Commodore was in was illegal.

'Make it legal!' Mehdi barked.

Colin, aware of the personal liability he was under if he conceded, offered to resign. This would have left Commodore UK without a legal director and would probably have required that someone in the US step in and take on the position (and potential liability).

Colin offered that if anyone could come up with a UK counsel's opinion that deemed such a payment legal then he would happily make it. They hung up unhappily.

On the 19th of April 1994, Commodore International went into liquidation, but Commodore UK continued to trade. SCI started to harass Commodore UK's customers, demanding that they pay any moneys owed to Commodore UK directly to SCI. Naturally, they all refused.

In June, SCI issued writs against Commodore International, Commodore UK and Colin Proudfoot. The jurisdiction for the case against Commodore UK and Colin was England and the trial was set for August in the Royal Courts of Justice on the Strand.

When Colin walked into the trial anteroom on the first morning of the trial he was greeted by SCI's barrister, who thumbed his lapels, looked down his nose and introduced himself ... sort of.

'Ah, you must be Mr Proudfoot. I'm working on the basis that you are a liar and a cheat.'

'Pleased to meet you too,' Colin replied.

SCI's opening argument basically surmised that Commodore owed them money and that UK assets had been illegally withheld. Our defence was that Commodore UK – and therefore Colin – was not a party to the contract.

The plaintiff went first to lay out their case and called Gene Sapp as their first witness.

Two hours of direct testimony laid out the argument that Commodore was crooked, that Mehdi Ali was a fraudster, that a deal was a deal and that Commodore should pay.

Our barrister got up to cross examine and held up the contract.

'Do you recognise this document, Mr Sapp?'

'Yes, it's the contract we negotiated with Commodore, the thieving–'

'Did you read it before you signed it?'

Sapp stammered. 'Well, no. I rely on my general counsel to read that sort of stuff.'

'No further questions, your honour.'

Next up was SCI's general counsel. Again, what followed was two hours of testimony on how crooked Commodore was and how Mehdi had deliberately played SCI. He got the same cross-examination.

Yes, he recognised the contract. No, he hadn't read it before asking Mr Sapp to sign it; he relied on the finance guy – he was concentrating on the annual general meeting and hadn't paid much attention to the deal.

On Wednesday morning, the finance guy took the stand. The same two hours of complaints followed – Commodore is outrageous, etc, etc.

Yet again our silk gets up to cross-examine.

'Do you recognise this document?' he asked.

The finance guy asked to look directly at the document, studied it for a few minutes and looked up at the counsel.

'No,' he said, 'it's not the contract I negotiated with Commodore. It doesn't include Commodore UK – somebody took that out.'

'But do you agree that this is the document that your president signed?' our silk asked.

'Yes,' he said.

'Well, what happened?'

'I went on two weeks' vacation and somebody must have changed it while I was away,' came the reply.

'No further questions, your honour.'

When Thursday morning came it was the defence's turn. Ed Goff, Commodore's general counsel, took the stand, taking questions on direct.

Yes, he recognised the contract and yes, Commodore UK was not a party to the contract – that was how Commodore had wanted it and that was how the final contract read. Commodore UK had no part in the negotiation of the contract and in fact had not been informed of its existence until after it had been signed.

During the lunch break, SCI's barrister approached our team. 'What does it take to get my client out of this travesty?' he asked.

Because we felt that all along Commodore UK was a bystander in the deal, we decided that SCI had been naïve in their negotiations – and as SCI was a potential future provider of Amigas should we achieve a buyout of the business, we agreed to settle with SCI simply covering our legal costs.

-14-

INTERLUDE 4

THE PC WEEK LAWSUIT

BY COLIN PROUDFOOT

PC Week used to have a back-page gossip column where the 'Mole' would dish dirt on the goings-on in the computer industry. In one particular issue they said there was a 'smell' coming from Commodore.

The moment I saw it, I called my brother, a city lawyer. He said libel is a specialist field but he knew a libel lawyer, and that if I sent him the article he would get their opinion. So I did.

A couple of hours later he called back – his libel lawyer friend had apparently said this was what he called a 'Friday special'. It turned out a 'Friday special' was a story written just before the publication deadline that legal folks don't get a chance to vet.

I asked him if he thought we had a case and he said 'yes' – turns out my brother's friend was counsel for the publisher that owns *PC Week*! He advised my brother to seek counsel from a libel specialist and said the best firm in London for libel was Schilling & Lom. So he arranged an appointment for me to go to see Keith Schilling.

When I met Keith, who was maybe in his early forties at the time, the first thing he said to me was: 'I've been practising law for 15 years and have never lost a case, and that's because I only take cases I know I'm going to win. Show me what you've got.'

I showed him the article and talked about Commodore, SCI, the

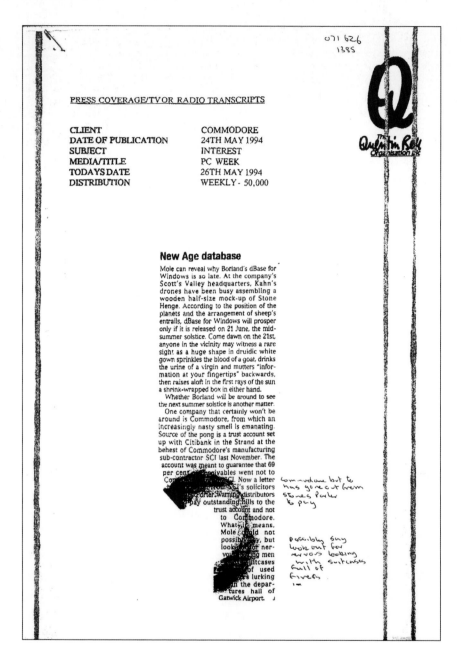

071 626
1385

PRESS COVERAGE/TV OR RADIO TRANSCRIPTS

CLIENT	COMMODORE
DATE OF PUBLICATION	24TH MAY 1994
SUBJECT	INTEREST
MEDIA/TITLE	PC WEEK
TODAYS DATE	26TH MAY 1994
DISTRIBUTION	WEEKLY - 50,000

New Age database

Mole can reveal why Borland's dBase for Windows is so late. At the company's Scott's Valley headquarters, Kahn's drones have been busy assembling a wooden half-size mock-up of Stone Henge. According to the position of the planets and the arrangement of sheep's entrails, dBase for Windows will prosper only if it is released on 21 June, the midsummer solstice. Come dawn on the 21st, anyone in the vicinity may witness a rare sight as a huge shape in druidic white gown sprinkles the blood of a goat, drinks the urine of a virgin and mutters "information at your fingertips" backwards, then raises aloft in the first rays of the sun a shrink-wrapped box in either hand.

Whether Borland will be around to see the next summer solstice is another matter.

One company that certainly won't be around is Commodore, from which an increasingly nasty smell is emanating. Source of the pong is a trust account set up with Citibank in the Strand at the behest of Commodore's manufacturing sub-contractor SCI last November. The account was meant to guarantee that 69 per cent ▓▓▓▓▓▓ceivables went not to Co▓▓▓▓▓▓▓▓▓▓. Now a letter ▓▓▓▓▓▓▓▓▓ SCI's solicitors ▓▓▓▓ Warning distributors ▓▓y outstanding bills to the trust account and not to Commodore. What it means, Mole could not possibly say, but look ▓ of nervous ▓▓g men ▓▓▓ litcases ▓ of used ▓▓s lurking ▓ the departures hall of Gatwick Airport.

[handwritten note:] Commodore but te has gone out from Stones Parker to pay

[handwritten note:] possibly say look out for nervous looking with suitcases full of fivers in

A photocopy of the legal
document, featuring a copy
of the offending article

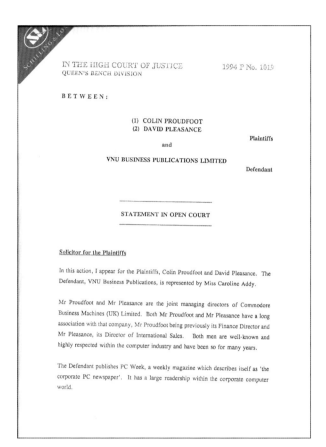

IN THE HIGH COURT OF JUSTICE   1994 P No. 1019
QUEEN'S BENCH DIVISION

BETWEEN:

(1) COLIN PROUDFOOT
(2) DAVID PLEASANCE
                                                    Plaintiffs
                    and

VNU BUSINESS PUBLICATIONS LIMITED
                                                    Defendant

STATEMENT IN OPEN COURT

Solicitor for the Plaintiffs

In this action, I appear for the Plaintiffs, Colin Proudfoot and David Pleasance. The
Defendant, VNU Business Publications, is represented by Miss Caroline Addy.

Mr Proudfoot and Mr Pleasance are the joint managing directors of Commodore
Business Machines (UK) Limited. Both Mr Proudfoot and Mr Pleasance have a long
association with that company, Mr Proudfoot being previously its Finance Director and
Mr Pleasance, its Director of International Sales. Both men are well-known and
highly respected within the computer industry and have been so for many years.

The Defendant publishes PC Week, a weekly magazine which describes itself as 'the
corporate PC newspaper'. It has a large readership within the corporate computer
world.

A photocopy of the
solicitor's statement for the
plaintiffs (Colin Proudfoot
and David Pleasance)

accusations and the reality of what we did. He asked if we could back
it up and I told him he could contact Wilde Sapte, the law firm we had
used to make sure we were operating with integrity.

A few days later he called back and said he would take the case.
There was never any doubt about the guilt of *PC Week*, it was just a
question of how much they would pay in damages.

PC Week went on to argue that the article didn't mention either
David or myself by name and therefore that we were not harmed. So
our PR agents compiled a selection of 500 articles published in the
previous six months that named us and Commodore, proving that as
Commodore management we had been harmed by association with
previous writing.

PC week capitulated, published a front-page apology, and in open
court testified that their malicious assertions were unfounded.

15

MANAGEMENT BUYOUT

JULY 1994

Not long after our parent company Commodore International declared bankruptcy, Colin Proudfoot and I decided to find out if there was a viable business to be resurrected from the assets that were soon to be auctioned off to the highest bidder at a time and place yet to be determined by the liquidator, Franklyn R Wilson.

I travelled to The Bahamas to meet with Mr Wilson, both to formally express our interest by gathering the relevant documentation and to protect the interests of Commodore Business Machines UK Limited. Through conversations with various interested parties, I was able to ascertain that a figure in the region of approximately $15 million would probably win the bidding – it was not in any way scientific, but it proved useful in calculating our strategy.

On my return, we began what became many weeks of burning the midnight oil while formulating what we hoped would be a viable business model to adopt and deploy, ensuring all the financials were in place to interest potential investors.

I must pay particular homage to Jennifer Laing, managing director of Laing Henry, our advertising agency at the time – she not only gave us an office to use, she also gave us access to all her staff for the duration of this business-planning process. They supported us in every way imaginable, designing graphs, making illustrations, conducting research, you name it. They were all, under Jennifer's guidance, magnificent.

The first thing we decided to do was to completely ditch all products prior to the Amiga range – actually a very easy decision to reach. We also came up with some plans for how to generate revenue from the other brand names (which I will get to later).

But our main business was to continue producing, for as long as we could, the current Amiga range.

My plan was to bring in the very low-cost, basic-as-it-can-be Amiga 300 to replace the Commodore 64, but with a predetermined upgrade path.[1] The idea was that this would appeal to the sorts of buyers who could only afford machines like the Commodore 64 or similarly low-cost machines and give them a way to at least get onto the Amiga platform, after which they could upgrade with selected add-ons or peripherals as and when they could afford to.

A large part of this initial plan centred around our tower case concept. This had already had designed for us by German company Mikronik and was to give any Amiga owner a way to upgrade their Amiga easily and affordably. The tower case was to be the vehicle by which we would introduce this concept to our already large user base, and it would work like this:

Say you had an Amiga 500 but you wanted to upgrade. You would take your Amiga 500 to one of our independent dealers – usually one-shop businesses which, as I have said in previous chapters, were the absolute backbone of our Amiga business in the UK – and they would sell you one of our specially designed tower cases. They would then offer, say, a newer-model motherboard according to your choice and budget – a 1000 or a 2000 or a 3000 and so on. These motherboards would work with any of the peripherals you already owned (floppy drives, etc.) and could be fitted into the tower case, which was designed to accommodate their different shapes and sizes.

[1]   This plan was originally screwed up by Mehdi Ali – see part 1, chapter 10, 'A comedy of errors – Our illustrious leader, Mehdi Ali'.

The 'Project Amiga'
business plan

The dealer would also give you an allowance for your old mother-board because he would be able to fit that into the tower case for somebody who wanted to upgrade from an Amiga 300.

Using this method, you could upgrade right up to a top-of-the-line Amiga 4000 if you wanted to. We would make the motherboards for all models available to purchase separately, and any new product within the Amiga range would be designed to fit into this tower case, thereby giving our platform as long a lifespan as possible (at least until we introduced new technology, which I admit we knew would not be possible to produce while maintaining backwards compatibility).

This concept was conceived by our team at Commodore UK and it was Kieron Sumner who came up with the brilliant name 'Amiga Infinity'.

So we produced a business plan containing manufacturing costings for the A300, A1200, A3000, A4000, a newly designed A5000, the CD32, the Infinity cases and a whole line of peripherals. We concentrated on reducing the costs of all of these models, and having manufacturers in China as partners would have enabled this without too much difficulty (although we would likely have sourced our peripherals as OEM products from specialists who deal in the high-volume manufacturing of those items).

Having worked out our model range and costed each of them, we then determined what realistic retail price points we could achieve through our existing distribution channels. These price points enabled us to determine with some degree of accuracy the volume of products we would be likely to sell, which in turn allowed us to determine the staffing we would require in sales, administration and technical support, and thus the size of the premises we would need and the minimum overheads required.

Processing all of this data came naturally to Colin and the set of figures he produced was, if anything, deliberately understated. It was a realistic business plan, and factored in the fact it that we would have to self-finance the whole operation for at least seven months because no component supplier would give us normal trading terms since Commodore had left all of them with numerous debts after the bankruptcy.

On this basis, we knew we needed to raise $50 million – but if all went to plan, within 18 months we would be a profitable business with minimal debts.

*

With our determination made, we set about trying to raise the funds.

We contacted the Management Buyout Division of Coopers & Lybrand, who had recently successfully raised venture capital for two even larger management buyouts than ours. Thankfully, upon reading our business plan, they accepted our brief and thus began the quest to raise $50 million – not much if you say it quickly, but a significant sum in 1994.

These next few lines are quick to type and even faster to read, but they disguise the vast amount of work that went into this next part of the story. There were countless meetings, a plethora of negotiations, innumerable contract rewrites, many, many late nights, and a persuasive dialogue that became so fine-tuned and sharp you could cut a cigarette paper with it.

Through Coopers & Lybrand, we eventually formed a consortium of investors and managed to raise the $50 million. This consortium was a combination of high-wealth individuals and a small venture capital company who between them put up $25 million, while the remaining $25 million came from a Chinese manufacturing company called New Star Electronics, who up until that point had allegedly been manufacturing pirated Sega and Nintendo consoles (apparently the Chinese government had told them they had to become a legitimate business!). From our point of view, this made them a perfect match, because it meant our investor was also our manufacturer, which would ensure our pricing was always competitive.

Now for the rest of the business plan.

I had always recognised that our brand names were – or at the very least could be – highly valuable commodities, and if used properly could provide a steady and very lucrative income. Take CBM (Commodore Business Machines), for example – at one time, as a billion-dollar company, it was at least as valuable and as highly regarded a brand name as IBM.

My plan was to license the CBM name to a chosen manufacturer of PCs and peripherals for a royalty in the region of 2 per cent of their wholesale sales price. Our only expense would be to set up our own Quality Control Division, which we would need for our own products anyway, to ensure any product sold with our badge on it met our high criteria, so as to protect the value of the brand.

In addition to the ongoing revenue from licensing the CBM name, we would also offer the use of our sales teams, who were already selling into the ideal retail channels, to sell the CBM-branded products (or indeed any brand they may also manufacture) on a commission basis. This would mean that we, as a company, earned revenue from the sale of PCs and peripherals without having to manufacture them or invest in any inventory – simply selling on the manufacturers behalf with none of the risk. We take and place the order, the manufacturer makes and ships it, and we get paid when the goods are delivered. So far, so good.

Similarly, my intention was to offer out the licence to use the Commodore brand name for basically anything with a plug on the end: toasters, kettles, hairdryers, other such small appliances – you name it. The principle was the same: a 2 per cent royalty, our overheads limited to quality control, and the same offer to let us sell your Commodore-branded products into our existing retail distribution channels on a commission basis. Again, no manufacturing costs, inventory management or warranty issues – we take the order, place it with the manufacturer, they manufacture and deliver it, and we get paid when goods are delivered. All in all, a win-win situation.

As for the Amiga brand name, we were intent on retaining that for our own developed products, except yes, we recognised a demand for Amiga-branded designer clothing, tracksuits, t-shirts, golf jackets, baseball caps and various novelty items, all of which could be licensed in the same way or sold by us on commission – the same method by which we sold the CBM and Commodore brands.

As for the CD32, I recognised an incredible opportunity: sell the technology to any and all manufacturers of hi-fi stacking systems on the premise that they include a front-loaded iteration of the console in place of a CD player. This would not only achieve substantial additional revenue, it would also help realise a long-held desire we had to get our computers into the living room. We would manufacture and sell keyboards, mice and any other peripherals needed for this to work.

The software developers would have loved and no doubt strongly supported this concept because of the considerable number of extra CD32s that would be out there. And remember, the Japanese had just made a disastrous attempt to enter the market with the MSX – here was an opportunity for them to get into it again without risk. We would have encouraged them to use any new technologies they had for add-on peripherals as developed (such as wireless keyboards and controllers, for example).

But this whole concept – as valuable as I'm sure you can see it would have been – was deliberately left out of our business plan. It was to be our safety net in case anything should go wrong with the business plan we had put forward, and from which, remember, we had already raised an incredible $50 million. We were in a very good place.

WHAT COULD POSSIBLY GO WRONG?

It was during our extensive due diligence process, while Colin examined the financials and I probed the engineering team about any future technology, product modifications and cost-reduction programmes, that we became aware that the representatives of New Star Electronics – a Mr Lee (the managing director) and his wife – were spending quite a lot of time in West Chester, where Commodore had been based for some years (though according to the engineers they were not looking at the technology).

It transpired that the paths of New Star Electronics and ESCOM had inevitably crossed, and ESCOM became aware – presumably because New Star Electronics were too stupid to keep their mouths shut – that they were intent on doing a deal with Colin and I.

And in the end, with a mere 36 hours to go until the commencement of the auction in New York, New Star Electronics advised us that they were withdrawing from our consortium, and therefore that their $25 million was no longer available to us.

Even though we still had the other $25 million and we were confident that the assets could be bought for around $12–15 million, we had to make the extremely difficult call to withdraw from the auction. We knew we needed the full $50 million to be able to trade for the next seven months, during which time we would have to purchase components on a cash-up-front basis until we had established some trust and a line of credit, sufficient to operate our business model.

As men of the highest integrity, Colin and I knew there was no way we could even consider using the $25 million we still had knowing full well we would run out of cash very quickly indeed, thereby triggering our own bankruptcy. So we contacted our remaining consortium members and advised them of our decision to withdraw.

Colin rang the staff at Commodore UK to give them all the tragic news – he says it was the most painful phone call he has ever had to make.

The Commodore UK staff had been magnificent, giving their total support throughout a very busy and traumatic period. We will never forget this team of people for their sheer dedication and determination – and though we did not come back with the spoils, there was nothing that they could have done differently to change the awful outcome.

I've always had my suspicions that New Star Electronics had been 'got at'. Our plan made excellent business sense and they had said they were content with all our ideas – they had, after all, committed to invest $25 million, and would not have done so if they had any doubts.

We attended the auction anyway – even though we could not make a bid, we had to protect the position of Commodore Business Machines UK Ltd as the company's directors. While we were there, we found out that New Star Electronics were already fraternising with ESCOM, which lent credence to my suspicions about them having been approached.

What we didn't know at the time was that Petro Tyschtschenko – who I already had an extremely low opinion of[2] – had somehow wormed his way into the ESCOM camp.

Eventually, we found out that ESCOM had stolen New Star Electronics from us. ESCOM said that if New Star Electronics pulled out of the consortium so that we could not bid, ESCOM would let them manufacture and distribute in China for just a few million dollars. Of course, ESCOM ultimately reneged on that deal, leaving New Star Electronics out in the cold, and they came away with nothing.

I spent the following years knowing we had been cheated out of what should have been the perfect solution for the long-term future of the Amiga and Commodore brands. I was naturally very bitter about it all, and even though I was unsure of the fine details, I was

2   See part 1, chapter 5, 'Maidenhead, Pt. 1 – "We don't sell computers, we sell dreams"', for an example of why!

fairly certain – though I could not prove – that Petro Tyschtschenko was involved ...

*

In 2015, I was invited as a guest keynote speaker to the Amiga30 celebration in Amsterdam, which I was proud to say yes to. Petro was also invited to speak but insisted on charging a fee (summing up his entire ethos and loyalty to the Amiga community: take, take, take), and had set up a display area outside the marquee from where he was selling various bits and pieces (Amiga-branded playing cards, keyrings, etc.).

As soon as I arrived – and in spite of my sour feelings towards him – I went out of my way to find him and say hello. We managed to keep things surprisingly pleasant for few minutes, after which I headed into the main conference area.

Later, Petro became quite obnoxious towards the organisers of the event, Marvin Droogsma, Marcel Franquinet, Paul Hamer, Folkert de Gans, Robert-Jan van Meersch and Rene van der Steen. He was disgruntled about not being allowed to speak for the whole hour he had insisted upon – he was given 40 minutes because there was simply not enough time to fit the several other VIP speakers in.

At the end of the conference many of us went on a dinner cruise on a canal boat, arranged by the lovely people who organised the event. Petro gave up his place and stormed off like a spoilt child for not getting his own way – he was not missed.

A few months later, I was invited to speak at another Amiga30 event in Neuss, Germany, and this time I had managed to get Colin Proudfoot to come along and give a talk – although Colin had been living in the US for several years, he happened to be in the UK from San Francisco for a family wedding in London so he was 'in the area', so to speak.

Just after the event had ended, while I was in my room getting changed for the evening dinner, it transpired that Colin had approached Petro and, straight to his face, asked: 'Did you persuade New Star Electronics to abandon our consortium and join forces with ESCOM?'

Petro admitted that he had. Effectively, Petro told New Star Electronics that ESCOM would sell them the CD32 licence for $5.1 million. ESCOM put that money towards their bid for the Commodore assets.

Finally, we had the confession we had always believed to be true: Petro Tyschtschenko had cheated us out of our management buyout. Had I been present when the admission was made, I would have floored Petro there and then.

So, to all of you who have hailed Petro as some sort of saviour, you now know the truth to make up your own minds – and about time too!

Imagine how different things might have turned out if we had been able to bring our plans to fruition? I am not saying everything Colin and I had planned would have worked out perfectly – and I'm sure we would have made some mistakes along the way – but there is no way we could have screwed things up the way Escom and Petro did. In my opinion, a set of professional saboteurs could not have done a better job of destroying whatever potential there still remained at the time of the auction.

16

INTERLUDE 5

CHELSEA FC SHIRT SPONSORSHIP

BY COLIN PROUDFOOT

In 1987, Commodore became Chelsea Football Club's first long-term shirt sponsor. When David and I assumed control of Commodore UK, one of the first decisions we made was to change the logo from the Commodore symbol to the Amiga symbol. We did this for two reasons. First, the Commodore-branded PCs (including the Commodore 64) had reached their end of life and were a much smaller part of our business, and with the Amiga 1200 and imminent CD32, we felt that a focus on the Amiga brand would give us better leverage. The second reason was that, with fewer letters, the Amiga logo would be much more visible on TV, as well as in the stands.

To our surprise, Chelsea was very supportive: changing the logo meant they didn't have to redesign their shirts – they could use the same as the previous season – but supporters would all have to buy the new shirts to be current. Chelsea made more money from their shirt provider Umbro than they ever did from the Commodore sponsorship.

In 1992, the Premiership League was established and TV rights and coverage expanded. Our deal with Chelsea was mainly about getting our logo seen by the largest potential audience – it is much cheaper than any other form of advertising in terms of brand awareness.

Football clubs know this and structure sponsorship deals accordingly so that bonuses are payable based on league position and cup results (both league cups and the FA Cup, as well as European appearances).

These bonuses can add up to big money – if Chelsea won the FA Cup, it would cost us half a million pounds. Getting to the FA Cup Final would cost £350,000 and so on down the table, and in the various rounds of the cup competitions.

Clearly, potential exposure to large liabilities such as this posed a problem for the business. Yes, good results meant we would get more TV coverage, bigger crowds and more brand recognition – but how do we budget for the potential expense?

The Amiga-sponsored home and away Chelsea shirts

The answer? Lloyds of London.

At Lloyds, you could insure pretty much anything – including against Chelsea doing well. At that time in 1993 there were a couple of brokers who would specialise in insurance coverage for sponsors of football teams. So we sent them the structure of our Chelsea contract and asked for a quote to cover the liabilities should Chelsea do well in the 1993/1994 season.

I have no idea what actuarial tables the brokers used to calculate the premiums or how scientific their approach was, but we nevertheless obtained quotes for the 1993/1994 season.

Part of the basis of all insurance quotes is claims history. In the 1992/1993 season, Chelsea ended up mid-table in the Premiership (so no bonus) and were knocked out in the third round of the FA

Commodore Germany also sponsored Bayern Munich (left) while Commodore France sponsored Paris Saint-Germain (right)

cup (so no bonus), but they reached the quarter final of the League Cup, receiving a bonus and leading to a modest claim on our policy.

As a result, the policy quote for 1993/1994 was significantly higher than the previous year. Perhaps the appointment of Glen Hoddle as player-manager had made the loss adjusters optimistic? Well, optimistic for Chelsea but pessimistic for our policy.

Faced with an – in our minds unacceptable – increase in costs from Lloyds, we turned to an alternative market, and there were two options: William Hill and Ladbrokes. We could place a bet on Chelsea winning the premiership, for example – I think they were 12–1 against, so if we bet just under £42,000, we could cover our exposure on that. Calculating the odds on each occurrence we had exposure to in our contract, we determined that Ladbrokes was by far the cheapest option.

Now, some readers will know that you can't just walk into Ladbrokes and lay down upwards of a £100,000 on one football club – they just won't take bets that size and they will likely change the odds against you. Fortunately for us this was 1994, and technology was not as advanced as it is today. So we hired a specialist company to spread the bet.

On a given day, at the given time, 40 'consultants' would walk into branches of Ladbrokes in 40 different cities across the country and place bets on Chelsea. They were flawless, and all got the published odds and covered our financial exposure.

The next morning, headlines in the back pages of the paper read:

ODDS OF CHELSEA WINNING THE PREMIERSHIP
HAVE BEEN SLASHED FROM 12-1 TO 4-1

Only our consultants and us knew the real reason why ...

-17-

AFTER COMMODORE

Rather traumatised by the debacle that ended the management buy-out bid at Commodore, I decided to adopt a less regimented lifestyle and returned to my roots in music.

I set up the music-recording business Tangent Music Design and built a studio in Hayes, Middlesex, and started the company off by producing my concept album 'Everybody's Girlfriend' (a play on 'amiga', the Spanish word for 'female friend'). Released in 1995, the album was a 'Celebration in music of 10 years of the Amiga' and featured 14 different genres of music to cater to a target audience of Amiga lovers who typically covered many different age groups. I perform solo flamenco guitar on the track 'Para mi Amiga', which is dedicated to the 'Father of the Amiga', the late Jay Miner. The recording has no multitracking, perhaps an indication of the level of playing I am capable of! I also composed the ballad 'Prisoner of Passion' – the solo lead guitar in the middle of this song is played by Marcel, my eldest son, who was only 15 years old at the time of recording.

*

Cover and CD art for
'Everybody's Girlfriend'

In 1997, I took a holiday to Dominican Republic to go big-game fishing and had the best catch of my life – meeting Francia and her then six-year-old daughter Lucidely.

Francia was still legally married to Lucidely's father, though they had been separated for a long time, and in order for Francia to get a visa to come to the UK for us to marry, we had to implement divorce proceedings.

Around that time, I was renting an apartment in Santo Domingo, the Dominican Republic capital, through two lawyers Celia Feliz and Joselyn Matos, with whom I became very close friends. So naturally I requested that they instigate the divorce for us – which, because of the corrupt nature of the authorities in that country, became a long and painful 14-month process predicated with bribery.

Eventually, Celia and Joselyn got Francia her divorce and the British Consul in Santo Domingo granted her a visa to enter the UK for the purpose of marriage. So in June 1999, we travelled to the UK and married on the 6th of November 1999 – a very significant day for me.

Three weeks after the wedding, Francia and I emigrated to Australia, though we decided to initially leave Lucidely with family in Santo Domingo because we did not want to disturb her schooling while we decided on a place to ultimately settle.

David with Francia, not long after they first met in the Dominican Republic

We entered Australia under a business visa, which are issued in two phases: in phase one you are permitted into the country for the purpose of either establishing a new business or buying an existing one – but to enter phase two you need to have run that business for approximately three years, employed a certain number of Australians and reached agreed turnover figures, at which point permanent residency status is granted, allowing for citizenship and Australian passports. (Oddly enough, there are no requirements to be profitable!)

So, both of us being fluent Spanish speakers, we decided to buy a large, 160-seater Mexican restaurant called Karakas that overlooked the marina in the beautiful town of Mooloolaba on Queensland's Sunshine Coast and was situated next door to the popular tourist attraction Underwater World. I introduced live music to Karakas seven nights a week, with my son, Marcel, working and even performing there.

Although I had spent many years living in Australia in the past and believed I knew my way around the myriad rules, regulations and procedures – and even with English as my first language – I found the process of finding out the criteria necessary to obtain permanent residency extremely difficult. While there was plenty of information available, it was disorganised and very difficult to find, and it occurred to me that the process must be even harder for the many business migrants arriving in Australia from non-English speaking countries.

So I decided to set up a new business helping incoming business migrants meet the country's strict requirements and achieve permanent residency, which I called PRIME Network (Permanent Residency

David with Lucidely in 2003

and Integration Made Easier). The business depended upon migration agents sending us leads that put us in touch with migrants as soon as they arrived.

After just a few months, we realised we would do much better if we did migration too, so we employed a licensed migration agent and set up a sister organisation called The MAIN Company (Migration to Australia International Network), which we established and ran concurrently for the last three of the five years during which I also ran Karakas.

Finally, in 2005, having successfully run the business for the required length of time, Francia, Lucidely and I received our permanent residency status, as well as our Australian citizenship and passports.

However, unsurprisingly, Francia became very homesick and longed for her family, who were thousands of miles away – she particularly missed her parents, who were very old and quite frail. So I decided to open an office of The MAIN Company in Miami, with the intention of helping professionals and skilled workers from Latin America migrate to Australia. The idea was particularly apposite for the time – the US was closing its borders, and Australia was desperate to get its hands on qualified professionals and trades people. Clients of

The MAIN Company would automatically be registered as clients of PRIME Network, thereby feeding one business revenue into another.

Prior to moving to Miami, Francia, Lucidely and I spent a few months back in Santo Domingo in the Dominican Republic and opened up another PRIME Network office. I set up all the systems and established cooperation with an English language institution in order to help prepare potential migrant candidates for the English test they would need to pass to qualify for skilled or business migration.

Unfortunately, in 2007, I fell prey to a con-artist migration agent from the US. I had met the man three years in a row at the giant Migration Expo at Sandown Park in the UK, where PRIME Network had been invited to share the Queensland Government stand. Each year we would have dinner together and would often talk about collaborating, and when I decided I wanted to set up shop in Miami he seemed like the natural fit. So I hired him, paid him $6,000 and sent him all the company paperwork and everything else he asked for in support of our application for a business visa.

He was very slow in returning my correspondence, but at the time I put that down to him just being busy. Eventually, after chasing him quite aggressively, he sent an email just before Christmas saying he had lodged our application and expected we would have the visa by the 14th of February (I remember because it is, of course, Valentine's Day).

Based on that information, over Christmas we bought a house in Miami with a substantial mortgage. To our shock, we found out in January that he was in jail and had never actually lodged our application. Sadly, by the time I discovered this, it was too late as all the business documents from Australia in support of this visa application were now out of date. As I understand it, he had scammed many people to the tune of over $2 million.

I was particularly upset because I had assumed knowing him for three years was some sort of endorsement as to his integrity. Thankfully I have not made many other mistakes in my life in my ability to judge people!

My wife was determined to stay in the US even if it meant doing so illegally, but of course there was no way I could conduct a legal

Caricature of David courtesy
of Design Directions

migration business helping people get into Australia if I was operating in the US illegally. Sadly, Francia and I parted soon after, divorcing in 2008.

*

I decided to move back to Peterborough in the UK and returned once more to my musical roots, establishing the agency Musos4U, where I was agent and promoter for mostly acoustic performers.

Naturally I made my first act my son Marcel, a solo singer-songwriter, but the roster soon expanded to a point where, at its peak, we were representing in excess of 90 acts, and supplying artists to 40 venues in the surrounding areas. I even supplied artists for the Acoustic Stage at the three-day long Willow Festival in 2013 – at the time the largest not-for-profit music festival in the UK.

That year I also started a free, monthly live music event at the prestigious Key Theatre in Peterborough, which I called 'The Glasshouse Acoustic Sessions'. It quickly became a popular Sunday afternoon destination, and the event is as popular as ever to this day.

In January 2014, I teamed up with my friend Gordon Leed and devised and produced the 20-track CD 'Hearts in Harmony'. The album featured 20 local acts performing 19 original songs and one cover song, for and on behalf of Peterborough-based children's charity Little Miracles, who specialise in helping children with special needs and life-threatening conditions.[1] (The 'cover' song was a superb solo rendition of 'Somewhere Over the Rainbow', which we specifically chose to match the Little Miracles' logo of a rainbow). One of the donated songs was 'Concrete' by my two sons' band, The Deltaphonics.

The performing artists all donated their songs free of charge, and when the CD was launched in March that year, 17 of the 20 acts gave live performances over two stages and three floors of a packed venue – it was, without doubt, a massive success.[2]

---

1   www.littlemiraclescharity.org.uk.
2   Hearts in Harmony CD Launch www.idea1.org.uk/event/hearts-in-harmony-cd-launch.

Above: The Willow
Festival 2013 programme

Left: A flyer for the
'Hearts in Harmony' CD
launch and live concert

More recently, Marcel and Emile have formed a new band, Satya Dub Orchestra, and are currently recording their first full album of original dub reggae material.

*

The year 2015 marked the 30th anniversary of the launch of the first ever Amiga computer, the A1000, a date that was celebrated with special events all around the world. I was delighted and surprised to be invited as a keynote speaker at the Amiga30 celebration that June in Amsterdam.[3]

3   I also helped organise the UK event in Peterborough and was a guest keynote speaker at Amiga30 in Neuss, Germany.

David with Francia and
Lucidely in 2015

It was here, as I walked off the stage having given my speech, that I was approached by the Norwegian co-founders of the Friend Unifying Platform, Hogne Titlestad and Arne Peder Blix, who spent some time explaining to me what they were developing. Even though I am a self-confessed 'dumb-ass' when it comes to technology, somehow I very quickly understood, and I was thrilled when they asked me to join their new company as director of international sales and marketing, to which I said yes. The software is based on the best features of the Amiga OS, but updated for the 21st century by utilising the cloud, the internet and the World Wide Web. The decision to join the company was an easy one, and one that I am incredibly proud to have made.

Friend Software Corporation (FSC) have been incredible supporters of this project, bringing the true story of Commodore out into the open. Colin Proudfoot (ex-co-managing director of Commodore UK), Paul Lassa (ex-designer of the Commodore 65 and Amiga 3000), François Lionet (author of AMOS), Dan Wood (host of *The Retro Hour* podcast) and USA-based Adam Spring (host of the Remotely Interested Podcast) are now all part of the great Friend Software Corporation team.

In August 2017, FSC decided to enter into the realm of block-chain, de-centralised computing and cryptocurrency. We wrote a comprehensive white paper and launched a presale in early 2018, followed by a full initial contribution offering in June.

I am extremely proud to be associated with FSC and I feel that, as with Commodore, this is a company which I have no doubt will change history for ever. I can't believe I could be so lucky two times in my life.

As a side benefit, I was able to present Friend Unifying Platform to many of the leading engineering figures from Commodore and Amiga who still

Emile (top) and Marcel (bottom)

live in the Philadelphia area, including Dave Haynie, Dr Ed Hepler, Peter Cherna, Jeff Porter, Christian Ludwig and Jeff Frank. I also got to meet YouTube's The Guru Meditation (aka Amiga Bill and Anthony Becker), who filmed the whole event, as well as Zach Weddington (creator of the *Viva Amiga* documentary) and Adam Spring (host of the *Remotely Interested Podcast*). The event was incredible and reintroduced me to so many Amiga legends.

As if that was not enough, I was able to use the opportunity to reconnect with my ex-wife Francia and my stepdaughter Lucidely, who live in nearby New Jersey. Since then I have been spending quality time with both of them and our relationship is wonderful – I am hopeful of a reconciliation soon. If this happens I will most likely relocate to Miami, a city and lifestyle I love, with the two ladies in my life I totally adore.

*

So here we are in 2018, and I am so incredibly grateful for my life and career. Working during the early years of what is now one of the leading global industries, and being fortunate enough to make a difference in how things have developed, has been and still is a total honour.

In spite of the many poor business decisions made by the board members of Commodore – and especially the president – it was an incredible buzz, and I know I speak on behalf of my team at Commodore Business Machines UK Ltd when I say just how exhilarating every day was.

One can only guess as to what would have happened if we had not been cheated out of our management buyout, though I truly believe we would have delivered a much more satisfactory outcome for the many owners and ardent fans of the Amiga.

My life has been amazing and continues to be as fulfilling, rewarding and full of joy as I could ever wish for – I feel truly blessed. A huge thank you to everyone.

PART 2
COMMODORE MEMORIES

-1-

ONE MORE UNTOLD AMIGA STORY

RJ MICAL

GEPPETTO'S IDIOT APPRENTICE

Back in 1986 – wow, 32 years ago – a group of Amiga people went to see a Peter Gabriel concert.

Picture it, if you will. We're in a big, smoky, dimly lit concert hall, which is only half-filled because we got there early to enjoy the pre-show ambience and to get some t-shirts. And there is beer – yes, Dale[1] was there so we got beer. Everyone was thrilled – it was a Peter Gabriel show and that meant we were in for an awesome experience. A pleasant half-roar of excitement already filled the air, and the occasional whiff of burning weed wafted under our noses.

To our delight, we had pretty good seats. We were fancy, rich high-rollers now, what with all the success of the Amiga, so these days we splurged on fancy concert seats!

OK, just kidding – we weren't really high-rollers, and no one ever got rich off of the Amiga, and Dale was the only one who was, you know, fancy. But we *were* high on the success of our baby, that's for

---

[1] Dale Luck, Amiga's Software Wizard Extraordinaire, ran the entire graphics OS effort *and* was a near-daily contributor to the hardware design effort (Dale single-handedly added line-draw to the Amiga's hardware blitter).

sure, and getting good concert seats was part of the ongoing celebration. We had plenty of reason to feel joyous! The Amiga had made it into the market and it was selling reasonably well.

Not too far from our seats was the main stage. We could see everything pretty clearly but we were geeks at heart, and serious geeks always bring binoculars to a concert, even if the seats are good. So we started checking out the pre-performance Peter Gabriel stage using the binoculars.

It was quite interesting! We studied everything in great detail and told each other excitedly what we were seeing: the lights, the amplifiers, the rows of instruments, the road crew setting up the stage just so ... There were cylinders with 'DANGER' markings containing, what, fireworks for the performance? Oh, and what do we have here? An Amiga computer! There, amid the equipment onstage at a Peter Gabriel concert, was an Amiga.

An Amiga! Imagine our astonishment!

What was it doing there?! It was part of a stack of gear facing the keyboard performer's stand, and only its rear end was facing out at us – but we could tell from its shape and from the monitor that it was definitely an Amiga. Were they going to use an Amiga as part of the Peter Gabriel concert?!

We were agape with amazement. Then we wondered: *What* were they going to use it for? We had to know. We had to find out. We had to go see what was on that display!

The concert stage was set up inside a sports arena with seating that went all the way around, so we decided we could probably walk behind the stage to see what was on the Amiga's monitor. Off we went, the intrepid explorers! But when we got back there, the monitor was blocked on one side, and directly behind the stage they had closed off the passages and hung a heavy black drape that obscured all view. So it turned out we had to walk all the way behind the stage, past the security barricades and into the darkness to try to see the display from the other side. All the aisleways were sealed off, so we inched our way through the shadows between the rows of ghost-filled seats.

Picture us, tiptoeing our way through the darkness, slightly naughty and nervous, like characters in some adventure story – which of course we were! Breaking the rules a little bit. That was us!

Creeping through the darkness like that, I was reminded of one of the mock commercials we made after Commodore bought us and proceeded to introduce the Amiga to the world via one of the worst marketing campaigns ever conceived.

They were truly awful! In response we joked that even we dumb Amiga people could create better commercials than Commodore's. We made a bunch of Amiga ads – a dozen or so – some of them a take on popular commercials of the time but others just goofy jokes that we invented. It was harmless fun.

The one I'm thinking of was a night-time commercial with one of us acting as a salesman trying to convince people to buy the Amiga while behind him the rest of us were moving everything out of the building – oscilloscopes, keyboards, chairs – as if we had all given up and were trying to sneak away under cover of darkness. It was funny at the time, but later it became ironic.

I have VHS tapes of those commercials. They're hilarious! Has anyone ever grabbed a copy of these homemade Amiga commercials? Does anyone even remember what a VHS tape is? I'm sure there must be digitized copies of those commercials by now. I ought to get mine digitized someday, as I have early-generation copies of the originals. But someone (Dale?) must have the originals. We should try to get our hands on those.

But have you ever seen those original Amiga commercials from Commodore? Dare I call them some of the worst commercials ever made? Yes, I dare. I've never seen worse – I've seen as bad, but never worse.

If only Commodore had had at least one good marketing or advertising person in charge – just one. It seems they did not. That was the heartbreaking dichotomy of Commodore – the engineering half versus the business half. Some of the Commodore engineers are among the best I've known in my career (I'm looking at you, Hedley!),[2]

---

2   Hedley Davis was Commodore engineer deluxe, equally comfortable with hardware and software, and contributed to projects across the board (representative of those many fine Commodore engineers and production people).

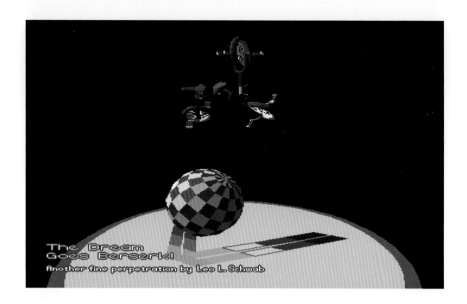

A still from 'The Dream
Goes Berserk' animation

but the challenges of the Amiga – of growing into the future – were too much for the business half of the company.

One of us – the inimitable Leo Schwab – was convinced that his own adverts would be better than the Commodore ones, and many agreed, including me. (I hope Leo's commercial concepts are available somewhere in the Amiga museum – if they're not, they ought to be!)

Leo created a lot of the truly spectacular early work on the Amiga. You might remember one particular animation gem, 'The Dream Goes Berserk', based loosely on a popular Pixar animation of juggling that had already been parroted, and which was further parodied by Leo. That demo alone sold more Amiga computers than all of Commodore's early advertising efforts.[3]

Leo was not a Commodore fan. In fact, excluding the company's engineering department, whom we adored, no one in California was really a fan of the rest of Commodore. Over the years, my Amiga

---

3   The demo – and Pixar's lawyers – also taught Leo some important facts about trademark protection. He ended up giving it the subtitle, 'My First Lesson in Intellectual Property Law'. Heh, it's a funny story – you should ask him sometime.

colleagues have said a *lot* of negative things about Commodore – which was understandable, because there was so much negative material to work with.

And there might have been a little snobbishness on our part mixed in there too, I think. From the beginning there was at least a scent of 'Commodore is a typewriter company, not a modern computer company. How can a company like that ever rally enough smarts and resources to do what the Amiga computer needs them to do?' (Witness the infamous sentiment buried in the ROMs by Amiga engineers: 'We made the Amiga; they fucked it up.')[4] The feeling that Commodore was responsible for the death of the Amiga was pervasive. And to a large extent it was true, in the end.

But 'the end' came later. The Amiga was fatally limited long before that, in my opinion, because of mistakes and unfortunate choices made right from the beginning.

I always felt my fellow Amigans, who were Commodore haters, went too far in knocking the company that had helped us survive. It was as if to say: 'Thanks for keeping me alive yesterday, but what have you done for me today?' It was understandable that they felt so much bitterness toward Commodore, sure – we had all watched in abject horror as the slow-motion train wreck of Commodore crushed the amazing Amiga opportunity.

But sometimes they seemed to forget how weak and poor we had become before Commodore. When Commodore bought us, we were at the very the end of our rope. Pennies were being pinched, the Amiga execs went unpaid, our vendors went unpaid – Darlaine, our account manager, started wearing a fire chief hat around the office because she had to 'put out so many fires' every day. Jay Miner even took out a second mortgage on his home to make one of the payrolls. I sat through those executive meetings where we discussed the possibility of The End.

---

4   This infamous Easter Egg was hidden away in Workbench 1.2 and shipped with a significant number of units. The message can be seen by holding down both Alt keys, both Shift keys, inserting and ejecting a disk from DF0, clicking the left mouse button on the 'Screen to Back' gadget window, and re-inserting a disk into DF0.

And then suddenly the Commodore floodgates opened and in poured a torrent of cash, equipment, and access to a whole bunch of brilliant and seasoned engineers and production people. We could breathe again! The Amiga would see the light of day after all!

Commodore meant survival, and it meant life not under the lash of Atari. These were two very good things.

(Speaking of Atari, I found out recently that Jack Tramiel was a fellow Pole. So at least he had one good thing going for him.)

I always looked on Commodore as the saviour of the Amiga, and it's always been true that I have less of a negative aftertaste from the overall Commodore intercourse than my fellow Commodore and Amiga colleagues. I celebrated what the company did for us (though of course I lived through their fatal weaknesses too).

And besides, while we worried whether Commodore would do right by us, it turned out that the biggest obstacle we would face was ourselves. I'm talking about the early releases of the operating system and the feeble filesystem, which were so lousy that it literally impeded the launch success of the machine.

In the years since, I've noticed that it's easy for the original Amiga engineers to forget about the poor quality of those early operating system releases. Not me. I hang my head in shame when I think about the Amiga OS 1.0 – especially my part in it – because of the impression the OS gave to the computer-buying public right from the beginning.

The 1.0 release of the Amiga OS was abysmal, and it was entirely our fault. It was so buggy and crash-prone that right from the beginning the Amiga started to develop that 'stink factor' that became part of its early reputation, and which crippled its lifetime sales accordingly. People thought that the Amiga was not a 'serious computer' like a PC.

I remember listening to a salesperson talk with a customer about the Amiga versus the Macintosh. 'Oh, that new Amiga has colour, audio and video editing, and the *best* games! It's like they took the Commodore 64 and tried to turn it into a real computer! But if what you want is a real computer, you should get a Mac.'

I stood there, stunned and humiliated, like Geppetto's idiot apprentice.

COFFIN LID CLOSED

And then the Amiga died.

The West Chester engineers held a 'Deathbed Vigil' to mourn the end of their beloved Commodore. But before that came the 'Amiga Wake'.

Secret confession: I did not like the Amiga Wake.

Do you know about the Wake? It marked the end of Amiga, when Commodore fired most of the remaining Amiga people in 1987, just two-and-a-half years after Commodore gave us the money to stay alive. By then, Commodore was hurting terribly for cash and the disagreements between the bipolar, bicoastal departments of the company finally led to the dismissal of most of the West Coast crew. There was a lot of bitterness and an abiding sense of heartbroken abandonment. Management didn't show much compassion, but for the people with boots on the ground on both coasts it was devastating.

The survivors came from all over to join the newly dead at one last big celebration: the Amiga Wake.

I had fun being with all my friends again, but the 'wake' part of it – the coffin and the talk of death and the sadness about our failure – was all too heartbreaking for me, and pointless too. I left early.

I was sad that my friends had lost their jobs and I was sad that the Amiga era had reached its end, but I felt we were focusing too much on the demise of the dream. Now we were free to dream of bigger, better things! And there was some seriously bitter sentiment expressed at that wake, which depressed me even more than the firing of the Amiga crew.

As I slunk away from that moribund, black-draped affair, quietly slipping out without saying goodbye, I vowed to myself that I wasn't going to let that be me. I would shake it all off and go on to do ever more interesting things with my life. Which I have done – at least, from time to time.

The wake suffered especially unfortunate timing as it was held just a few weeks before the birth of my first child, and I did not want any psychic or chronological connection to bridge that all-important birth with the sense of death and despair that the Amiga team was suffering.

In the end, Commodore took the entire beating for causing the death of the Amiga – but in truth, Commodore was only part of the problem.

As I've said, I believe the seeds of the Amiga's destiny were sown in those early days. Yes, the original Amiga marketeers were over-whelmed by the marketing mastery at Apple, so we couldn't reach the high-end consumer. Yes, the original Amiga was expensive compared with the Commodore 64, so we couldn't quite reach the masses. And yes, the original OS had many components that were bug-ridden piles of poop, giving the Amiga a stink that lingered long after the problems were fixed.

But the number one reason the Amiga computer didn't become a champion is because of the filesystem. There were a lot of other reasons, sure, but this was 'the big one'.

The poor performance of the filesystem was the Amiga's Achilles heel. Even more than the fuzzy display or any other shortcoming, it was the weak filesystem that kept the Amiga from being regarded as a serious computer.

Now, don't get me wrong – I love the TRIPOS[5] people who created the filesystem we shipped on the Amiga, and I am overjoyed that we had any filesystem at all, thanks to them. These people came to our rescue after those jerks in the desert, who were creating a filesystem according to our spec, tried to extort money out of Commodore and got fired instead, leaving us without a filesystem mere minutes before the launch.[6]

Fortunately, the TRIPOS knights came galloping to save us. Plus, they gave the Amiga undertaking more of an international flavour, which was much needed (though of course we did have engineers like Spence Shanson and Barry Walsh to bring a bangers and mash sensibility to the effort).

---

5   TRIPOS, which stands for TRIvial Portable Operating System, is still in use today. Its development started in 1976 at Cambridge University and was headed by Dr Martin Richards. The first version appeared in January 1978 on a PDP-11 and it was later chosen by Commodore Amiga in March 1985 to form part of AmigaDOS.

6   The identity of these people is lost to antiquity, and that's probably a good thing, eh? There are a lot of Amiga fans who would like to have a word with them …

Alas, the TRIPOS filesystem was designed for a different purpose and a different hardware architecture. TRIPOS wanted to be the OS that controlled the hardware – but we couldn't have that. So we had to use a hammer to force TRIPOS into the Amiga, on top of the Exec kernel, and we had to do it in a big hurry so we could make the launch.

And it worked! But the interface was slow and clunky, and there was no way we could ever 'fix' the inherent differences of that system. If we ever wanted better, our only option would be to bite the bullet and create a whole new filesystem for the Amiga, one that coupled tightly with the Exec and our device drivers. It would have been costly in so many ways, but it would have been worth it.

The sad thing is that we had a chance – a brief, magical moment of opportunity – to fix the filesystem problem, to create a whole new filesystem for the Amiga, and that magic power was at my fingertips for a brief time. But I couldn't make it happen.

Throughout 1986, I had the attention of Commodore upper management, and especially Dr Henri Rubin, the one person at the time who could make things happen at the executive level. While working a contract for him in Germany, I convinced him that the Amiga's greatest hope for success was to create a new filesystem, one that worked according to our original excellent spec but also maintained compatibility with the current install base. I pitched and won approval for a plan to create a file compatibility mode for existing software while all future software would have the advantage of this sparkly new filesystem designed specifically for the Amiga. Yes, we would have to live with the legacy of supporting the original code – possibly forever – and that would suck real bad. But all newly developed Amiga software would run on this new-and-improved filesystem, and our performance problems would have been solved.

This would have changed the world! We could have made it happen! Alas, there was one obstacle I couldn't overcome: there was only one engineer I knew – Carl[7] – who could have pulled off this miracle, but I couldn't persuade him to do it. He wouldn't work for

---

7   Carl Sassenrath was the Amiga software engineer who created the multitasking kernel known as Exec.

Commodore again – at least, not at that time. Commodore shrugged, and the opportunity passed.

For me, THAT was when the coffin lid closed on the Amiga. Years later the engineers cured all of the original Amiga sins and Carl went on to do other projects for Commodore, but it was too late: Apple had already won. Such a heartbreak. Imagine how different the world might be today if the Amiga had prevailed! Oh my god, just imagine that world ...

So, if you must blame someone for the failure of the Amiga, blame me for my terrible software and for my failure to get us a custom high-performance filesystem. I tried, but fell short.

But again, this was no fault of the TRIPOS people. They were our heroes, and I hope to see Tim[8] again someday soon so I can buy him yet another beer of gratitude. They saved our bacon and their AmigaDOS became an integral part of the Amiga story. Cheers to them all.

PLAYING GAMES

But meanwhile, what about that Mac? It just wasn't fair.

From the beginning, the Apple Mac had a perceived quality that the Amiga lacked. This was unfair because the Amiga was the superior machine in many respects. Sure, the early release of the OS was buggy, but the early Mac OS was buggy too, and we eventually fixed our OS (well, except for the filesystem, alas). We had colour, amazing audio, awe-inspiring games and video, and multitasking. And we had the best paint program ever made for a computer! Yay *Deluxe Paint*![9]

Yet, to our collective chagrin, the Mac won. But it won based on perception more than facts.

The Mac did have a few very real advantages over the Amiga. It had a crisp display, for example, with non-fuzzy pixels. A lot of people in the early days felt the Apple was a better machine because the

---

8   Dr Tim King, one of the original TRIPOS developers, got TRIPOS running on the 68000 processor line and was chiefly responsible for getting TRIPOS to work with the Amiga OS.

9   Did you know that Electronic Arts released the source code for *Deluxe Paint* to the Computer History Museum in California in 2015?

display looked more professional. The Amiga was designed to work with the fuzzy NTSC standard – so you could plug into *any* television and get satisfying results (ask Stan[10] sometime for a funny story about that!). We tried to create a computer for the common person, not just those who had a fancy computer monitor.

But nobody wanted fuzzy numbers in their spreadsheets. So the Amiga got all the games while the Mac got all the professional software. The Amiga was by far the best at graphics and video production! But the Mac was better at satisfying business needs, and business spending proved to be the biggest spending.

'Speaking of Electronic Arts, have you ever noticed that the Amiga was particularly good at playing games?' he asks the audience with a sly grin.

If you are hip to the history, you probably already know that the Amiga was the best game system of its era. This was because the Amiga was designed with games in mind. Sure, we had plenty of features that allowed the Amiga to be more than a game system, such as support for mouse and keyboard, external storage, hardware expansion, and a powerful architecture with the most sophisticated OS ever released on a personal computer underlying it all. We created the *first* multitasking OS ever released on a personal computer. But from the beginning, we wanted a system that would play games better than any other in the market, and we succeeded.

I've been asked what my favourite Amiga game is so often that I have turned the process into a bit of an analysis game itself.

When I'm asked I say the first one that pops into my head, and over the years the most repeated answers have included: *Populous, Crystal Hammer, Cannon Fodder, Marble Madness* and *Road Rash*. But my absolute favourite Amiga game will always be *F/A-18 Interceptor*.

I also played a *lot* of *Microsoft Flight Simulator* to pass the time during compiles while working on the Sidecar project (on aptly named project as the Sidecar was developed and built in Germany).

---

10   Stan Shepard was director of QA for Amiga, and as such had to 'herd cats' every day of his life. Plus he got exotic jobs such as buying the cheapest, most miserable televisions he could find to make sure the Amiga would work on them.

A Sidecar attached to an Amiga

Sidecar was an entire PC that you could plug into the side of your Amiga, adding complete PC compatibility ... because Sidecar was a complete PC! It had its own CPU, memory and storage, and it connected to the Amiga bus, so you could transfer data easily and rapidly between the two computers. The entire PC desktop view was displayed in a window on the Amiga, which you could control and arrange just like any other Amiga window. I got a big laugh out of that – with one click you could push it to the back, or close the PC completely whenever you had had enough of it!

But the biggest laugh came from the way I used *Microsoft Flight Simulator* during Sidecar development. I would run this superb PC flight sim in an Amiga window, trying to learn how to land, while testing the new version of the PC software on the Sidecar. If the software crashed, my plane would crash too! But if the software worked, phew, I was OK to fly (and work) another day!

I thought of the Sidecar as yet another coprocessor for the Amiga, and I loved the thought that we could contain the entire PC in an Amiga window. I also had my own secret code name for the Sidecar project: 'Zaphod', after Zaphod Beeblebrox, the two-headed character from classic literature where the two heads were constantly bickering with one another. *That* for me was a perfect description of the Sidecar project, both in terms of the technology and the engineers working on the project.

For the *real* biggest laugh of my Commodore Germany experience, ask me sometime for the story about 'screwing the lid' at the Braunschweig office.

Actually, for an even *bigger* biggest laugh, ask me sometime about the coffee and the fluorescent lights where we worked in Germany. We were such naïve foreigners! We may have been smart in a few ways, but boy we sure were dumb too, as Dieter Preiss can tell you – or Torsten or Frank or Wolf. Or Herr Doktor Rudolf Goedecke. My, I wonder where those fine engineers are now ...

The Amiga was a great game machine – mostly because of the blitter, but generally because of the whole architecture, and don't forget the CPU, and ... OK, there were a *lot* of reasons why the Amiga was great at games. But the device that gets the least credit is the Copper.

Here's something new for this chapter that you may not have heard before (with a tip of the hat to Ron Nicholson, one of the chip's original designers): the Copper – that amazing specialised graphics coprocessor unit – was one of the *original* RISC devices.

RISC – which stands for Reduced Instruction Set Computer, in case you don't know – was, once upon a time, the new revolution in chip and architecture design. In fact, we had invented one of the very first RISC devices, we just weren't smart enough to call it that.

I think the same can be said about the revolutionary 6502 chip series – I claim the 6502 was a precursor to modern RISC chips.

Someday, I want to program for a device with a 4Ghz 6502 driving a modern-day Copper. I wonder what sort of Copper would work with modern display devices? 'Scanline' and 'vertical blank' have fluid meanings these days.

LITTLE-KNOWN SECRETS

I once read that the option to transform the Amiga from a game console into a proper computer was cleverly hidden.

Maybe to 'the suits' it was hidden, but it was not so well hidden to an engineer, and at Amiga we didn't have any suits working for us. Everyone from Sales, Marketing or Engineering, to our bubbly receptionist Cheryl … we all knew we were secretly building the world's next computer.

Here is one of the little-known secrets about the Amiga: Mitchy the dog did *not* design the Amiga.

Jay Miner's dog, Mitchy, is credited as having designed the Amiga for Jay. But this was just a joke. Mitchy didn't actually design anything. Mitchy was just a dog – an excellent dog to be sure, but not much of a chip designer. Although I'm pretty sure Dave Haynie's kids do all his hardware design for him.

Here's another little-known secret from the Amiga development days: we played a lot of *Jack Attack* .

We had an Atari 800 set up in the office courtesy of Jay and there was this game called *Jack Attack* in which deadly blobs of doom tried to destroy everything we'd built. *Everyone* at Amiga played that game – almost non-stop during business hours. We didn't know we were seeing into the future.

Here's a correction for you: it took seven months to develop Intuition, the Amiga's user interface engine – not one week.

It is true that I locked myself in my office for most of those seven months, eating meals that kind people brought in for me, sleeping on the floor or staying in a local hotel instead of 'wasting' the time to drive home and back again. It took seven whole months of gruelling, 100-hour weeks (yes, an average of 14 hours per day) to get to the 1.0 release.

Recently, I read the claim that I had developed Intuition in one week. I nearly hurt myself laughing at the thought! At one point I *lost* a whole week's work because I hadn't backed up my data!

Here's a fun little-known secret about the industry: there was this Chinese restaurant in Silicon Valley that was a well-known hangout for engineering types where one could occasionally overhear high-tech discussions and gossip.

We used to go in there and talk intentionally loudly about the Amiga computer we were creating, making up details that weren't true – sometimes inflating and sometimes minimising – to be eaten up by the press and Atari, in order to spread disinformation and help the Amiga win. And often it worked! Oh, what naughty scamps we used to be. Good thing we've all grown up since then (he says with a wink).

Speaking of restaurants, here's a story you may not have heard.

Once upon a time in a fancy Silicon Valley restaurant, I bumped into Jack Tramiel (actually, he spotted me and came over to my table). This was to be the last time I ever saw Jack.

At this point the ST had already lost, but the Amiga wasn't doing too well either. He came over to gloat about the lack of Amiga success, scoffing that we picked wrong, that we should have chosen to go with him. He punctuated each point by poking his finger into the air between us. Then, in his arrogant way, right there in the middle of this restaurant, he lit up a big cigar, just in order to blow smoke at me I guess.

Now, you can't smoke a cigar in a restaurant in California – and he knew that, but he did it anyway. Immediately this waitress came hurrying over to tell him to put it out. Instead, he made that Unhappy Jack face at her, scowling unflinchingly until she was cowed into turning away.

Bullying people was one of Jack's specialities, but after she was gone – although before the manager could get there – he ground out the cigar and walked away. Being tactically savvy was also one of his specialities.

But he left me abruptly, without an end to our story. And now he's gone. And I'm left wondering: Would the Amiga computer have done better in the long run if Jack had acquired it?

LOST HEROES

The peerless David Pleasance asked me to write this chapter for his book. He asked me to try to dredge up more untold stories about the Amiga. After so many books, so many conferences, so many speeches, so many drunken late-night laughs in reminiscence, I did not think it would be possible to find one more untold Amiga story. I never realised how many stories there were still to come out of me. I'm sure

David never realised how long it would take me to write this chapter – I owe him a huge debt of gratitude for his patience. (And I owe great thanks to the magnificent Marcel Franquinet and the meticulous Simon Busby for helping make this happen.)

But, though I'm having great fun writing this, to tell the truth I literally wept while wishing that Dave Needle[11] was here to help me remember the stories, the people, the fun ...

Long live Dave Needle.

Here's a little story you haven't heard, about a Dave Needle prank.

Dave and I once went to Disneyland with our lovely long-suffering wives Margo and Caryn. At one point we went on the Small World ride, which got stuck and left us stranded and motionless for about five minutes.

We had to listen to that unchanging Small World song over and over again for five whole minutes. The scenery and the soundtrack had been charming up until the moment we stopped moving, but after five monotonous minutes of that robotic repetition 'we wanted to rip off our ears and gouge out our eyes'.

Of course, it became a great joke between us, and we spent the rest of the trip singing that song to each other. I called Dave's room at 6am to sing that song to him! Then, unknown to me, the day we left for home, Dave snuck into the gift shop and bought a greeting card that played the Small World song when you opened the card.

He waited a whole month to spring the prank on me. He extracted the small circuit board from the card, mounted a gravity switch and then found a way to hide this booby-trap inside the paper roll next to my toilet. Imagine my delight – sitting there, my pants around my ankles, pulling on the roll to get some paper – when suddenly, and quite unexpectedly, I was treated to a performance of our cherished Small World song. Courtesy of Dave. Because he loved to make me laugh.

Heavy sigh. We've lost so many heroes over the years that my heart breaks to think of it.

----

11   Dave Needle was key engineer and co-chief architect in the creation of the Amiga 1000, and one of the main designers and developers of the custom chips of the Amiga computer. Plus he had the biggest heart in the known universe.

I saw a pile of early Amiga documentation recently and then went strolling down memory lane for a bit as I remembered Rob Peck, our original tech writer, who worked so hard and created so many excellent descriptions – and who created so many headaches for our early developers because a few of the examples in the text were wrong!

Oh, I miss Rob so. He caught a lot of grief for the early documentation, but I remember him as a gentle giant among tech writers who had the skills to corral the wild Amiga story into something – anything – that was consumable by developers. With almost no help from us. Oh, I wish Rob had lived to see the full success of the Amiga he helped create.

And Dave Morse![12] The great Dave Morse. I learned so much from him, about business and grace under pressure, and how to be a mean-ass negotiator. He truly was my fearless leader, from the Amiga to the Lynx and the 3DO. Long live Dave Morse. I never did find out how he got that scar on his chin.

And Jay Miner.[13] Big, hearty, love-filled engineering god Jay Miner, who spent his retiring years creating medical equipment to help all of humanity. I miss Jay terribly. I wish I could hug him right now. In my mind's eye we're jumping into his hot tub and going underwater with only our faces exposed to the cool night air. We're telling jokes and laughing uproariously, drinking wine and dreaming together about the future of technology. Jay was the Father of the Amiga, and a hero to us all.

And Dave Needle. I loved him so. I always wanted to write Dave's story with him but we never got around to it, and now I can't.

One of the last meaningful acts I enjoyed with Dave was genuflecting before him onstage during the Amiga30 celebrations. And later I found a perfect moment to give him a kiss of recognition and

---

12   David Morse climbed the career ladder of the game/toy industry up to vice president at Tonka Toys, then leapt up to become president, chief negotiator and one of the cofounders of Amiga. Many an aspiring youth learned at the wise feet of Dave Morse.

13   Jay Miner – the 'father of the Amiga' – was an integrated circuit system designer who created the Atari 400/800 and the main multimedia chips for the Atari 2600, and who at last brought his spirit of love and engineering to its most fruitful days during his reign over Amiga.

appreciation. From the warm response that kiss got from the audience, I felt as if I was kissing Dave for all of us. I didn't know then that this was to be my goodbye kiss to Dave.

I loved those Amiga30 celebrations. It was superb to see the new inventions – all this new engineering for the Amiga! The dream lives on! So now we have new heroes – more and more of them every day – and they were on full display during the Amiga30 conferences. It was breathtaking!

But best of all for me was being with my Amiga family again, letting me bask once more in the company of my genius cohorts and in the glory of the magic we created together. I can't name all the family here but you know who you are: Glenn and Don, Jack and Sheryl, and Bob and Bob and Dave and Dave and Sam and Neil, and Diane and Gary and Mike and Mitch and Bill and Tracy and Jude and Nancy and John and on and on and … and I'm giving you all a big hug right now.

We made the Amiga. Yeah. An insane undertaking, you bet! But we didn't care – we were wild and carefree kids, the lot of us, gingerly stepping our way across the uneven stones that led to the future, ever the intrepid explorers. Like that night, threading our way through the darkness behind the scenery of that Peter Gabriel concert, determined to get what we wanted regardless of the rules. We were crazy with the fever of wanting to accomplish great things. There was no stopping us.

*

Once upon a time, Peter Gabriel had been part of a band called Genesis before he went off on his own. The concert we were about to see was his first solo concert. He had a song that was already quite popular by that point called 'Solsbury Hill'.

Here's a little-known detail: Gabriel wrote that song about his tortured soul-searching experience choosing to leave the band. 'You can keep my things, they've come to take me home,' he sang.

We Amiga people didn't know it, but when we went to see Peter Gabriel that night, most of us were about to 'leave the band' too. Some (like Carl and me) would hop off sooner than others. Many were about

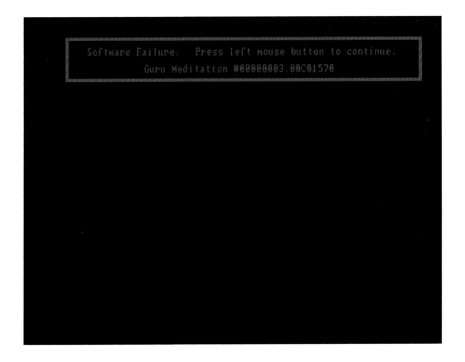

The infamous Guru
Meditation error screen

to lose their jobs in the forthcoming massacre that led to the Amiga Wake. Only a few (like Dale) would ride that Commodore train all the way to the terminal.

Caryn was pregnant with our firstborn, Alex, at that concert. The story of life was writing itself all around me, and weaving me into its fabric.

Inspired by Gabriel, I wanted to write a song about leaving Amiga behind me. I thought maybe I could write a song that would be my own little 'Solsbury Hill' way of saying goodbye. Sadly, I never finished it. But I sure wanted to. I thought about it a lot – even played it on the guitar. I was going to call it 'Lost Heroes'. I had a melody for the lyrics. But the words wouldn't come.

That night, sneaking through the shadows backstage at that Peter Gabriel concert, hoping to get a peek at the future of our little invention onstage, I thought again about my goodbye song to the Amiga. I hummed the melody to myself (which, on reflection, actually sounded

RJ Mical in 2010, signing
an Amiga for the 25th
anniversary of the computer

very much like 'Solsbury Hill'). And I thought again about that funny
mock commercial we had made, presciently pretending to slip away
into the post-Amiga darkness ...

And now we had finally found our way out from behind that curtain of darkness, where at last we could see the full display of our
Amiga 1000 computer onstage at the Gabriel concert. And what did
we find? You know the answer already.

There it was, the Guru Meditation message, blinking an angry red
and black at us, telling us that our beloved computer had crashed
yet again. This time it had crashed on the stage of a world-famous
musician. Would it crash during the live performance too?

'Uh-oh,' I thought, shuddering. 'What have we done?'

And it turned out to be a harbinger of the future, didn't it.

Indeed, our little machine had the *potential* to become a champion,
but it would never achieve the sales or recognition it deserved, or
even enough profit for its purse masters to keep the dream alive.

But that was OK. Yeah, the machine had its warts, and our relationships had their warts too. But, in the end, that was OK. Because …

What a life experience we had! We got to go on that whole wild ride together. Can you imagine it? *We made the Amiga*. And after the ride was over, we still had each other. In fact, we are still connected, many of us, to this day. We have our experiences and many fond memories to bind us together.

We had this vision, this fantastic dream, of putting powerful computing into the hands of everyday people, and we found a way to make that vision into a reality. We invented a new computer! That came to be known worldwide! We even managed to touch a few people on the way, to help them become bigger better versions of themselves. And this is what makes life most meaningful for me.

-2-

RUN

DAVE HAYNIE

When you drove up to the big Commodore plant in West Chester, Pennsylvania, from the south, you passed a tiny airport ... which made sense, being on Airport Road and all. There were other small corporate buildings in the area, but as you turned onto Wilson Drive and spotted the guard shack that lead to Commodore's manufacturing for North America – functional headquarters for business for the whole United States of America and world headquarters for engineering – you were pulling up to the largest building in Chester County at the time.

Once past the guard shack, you would have encountered the 'all-important speed bump network', which included not only speed bumps but a succession of signs and other countermeasures designed to keep the engineers' sports cars slowing for these road ridges, rather than seeking a way around them. This had been an ongoing process from the time the building opened in the early 1980s until the bad years of the 1990s, so if you worked there, you'd know just about when your TARDIS had landed by the state of the speed-bumps.

I first entered the Commodore building in the fall of 1983.

I had been working at General Electric (GE) in Philadelphia, Pennsylvania. In theory, I went there to work on the Space Shuttle, and while I wasn't there long enough to get a security clearance, it

The Exidy Sorcerer

was clear that most of their work was on weapons. I was working on software tools for hardware development in my four months at GE and had no interest in weapons.

So I had put out my résumé on a Tuesday and received a call that Thursday to come out for an interview. I was, that day, more or less rebelling against the slow disappearance of all the other college kids who had started that summer but one-by-one become indistinguishable from the other GE workers: new clothes, new haircuts, new behaviours maybe. Perhaps there was something in the air and I was immune; I knew I had to get out of there. That day I was wearing a home-made shirt, the least corporate thing I could have worn short of a few dirty, ripped t-shirts featuring punk or alternative rock bands ... I would probably have had to go there too, before long.

That interview put me in the lobby of a small 'headhunter', where I ran into a John Lennon-looking guy: longer hair, more casually dressed than I was. He asked if I was there for an interview ...

'Yup, just heard from them today. You?'

'Sort of,' he said.

We talked a little, and before long they called me in.

I met with a guy named Joe Krasucki, who was running the Engineering department at Commodore. I knew Commodore – heck, I had bought a Commodore 64 just that summer to replace my stolen

Exidy Sorcerer. I had used Commodore PETs owned by a few friends back in the 1970s.

Next up was ... that guy from the waiting room, who turned out to be Bil Herd.[1] He asked me technical things – the purpose of some diodes in an op-amp circuit, if I knew how to do Laplace transforms and so on. I started writing but he didn't need the example – it was good.

So they called me in to visit the plant that Monday and made an offer on the spot. I handed in my notice and so, in October of 1983, I started working at Commodore.

I was working directly for Bil, and the project I started on was called the Commodore 264. I was a bit surprised to find out it wasn't an upgrade for the Commodore 64, but was, in fact, something else, something incompatible. But ... whatever, I was working on computers! Other than spaceships and robots, this was pretty much top of the list.

When I was at Carnegie-Mellon University in Pittsburgh, I was already pretty certain that hardware and software, electronics and code were kind of different aspects of the same basic idea: the Computer. I had done both prior to college, learning electronics from kits and then books, learning computer programming basically by taking apart old programs, borrowing time on my dad's department computer at Bell Labs over a dial-up modem over the weekends ... I majored in electrical engineering, math/computer science and, for a while cognitive psychology – everything I would need for those robots of course!

GOTO 10

Working at General Electric, I was kind of shocked to find that they had erected a wall right out of Donald Trump's evil dreams between the software and hardware people. If you were in hardware, you did not write a line of code; if you were in software, you didn't touch a circuit. At the time I had been hired into a new group – Computational Design – that was the only group of people allowed to do both.

---

1   Bil Herd was the main engineer on the Plus/4, C16/116, C264, and C364 machines, and designed the Commodore 128.

The Timex Sinclair
1000 – the American
version of the ZX81

But when I got to Commodore, it was different. We had a 'cube farm' office, but this incorporated people designing custom chips, designing software, designing hardware – we all worked together! Why not ask the hardware guy how your chip would best go into his system? Why not ask the software engineer how they'd like their registers designed? Why did this never occur to people at big companies?

That fall in 1983, they had this office that looked like a computer museum: Sinclairs, Sol-20s, TRS-80s, calculators, all kinds of crazy stuff. But it wasn't any kind of museum – it was simply where they put all the gear that people sent in. Commodore USA was running an actual sales promotion: send in any kind of computing device and get $200 off the Commodore 64. It turns out they were planning to drop the C64's price by $200 anyway, but figured this would generate a lot of interest and bring in more cash during the all-important Christmas season.

The best outcome for us of this whole trade-in deal were the Sinclair ZX Spectrum computers – many were those imported to the USA by Timex as the Timex Sinclair 1000. These were ideal for use as doorstops around Commodore – just the right height.

I also soon found out that the Commodore 264 project was, in kind of a convoluted way, a response to the ZX. Commodore was run in those days by Jack Tramiel, who was a character if ever there was one. (You could rather imagine Jack eventually setting up a secret home in a dormant volcano surrounded by sharks – sharks with lasers, of course!) Jack had pushed hard on pricing – first with the PET series, then the VIC-20, and finally the C64. Commodore won when they had the upper hand on price, just as with this planned cut to the cost of the C64. Business is war.[2]

But the ZX was a $99 computer in the US. Sure, it was kind of terrible, but still, this was a threat. So the original plan for the TED chip – the all-in-one part that did video and sound in the Commodore 264 – was kind of a Sinclair clone, which was at the time called the Commodore 116. It even had a rubber chiclet keyboard, maybe a half step up from the membrane keyboard of the ZX in the US.

I wound up doing work on various aspects of the TED systems: I did the timing analysis (accurate to the nanosecond, but kept as a drawing, in pencil, on a huge sheet of drafting acetate) and I took over the CommodoreV364, which was a 264 with the addition of a version of Commodore's 'Magic Voice' phoneme synthesizer built-in, including extensions in BASIC that let it speak.[3]

Sadly, it didn't let you program phonemes – it used a library of about 260 words that had phoneme translations in ROM. Occasionally, while working on these in the lab, one of the lab guys would fire up 'SAM' (Software Automatic Mouth) on the C64 and basically start a game of 'The Dozens' with me, hurling an insult, waiting for mine to come back ... with my 260-word vocabulary. Ouch!

The TED era ended with a bit of corporate confusion. Jack left the company after the CES show in January of 1984, but a couple of his sons were still working at Commodore, and even more models of computers based on the TED chip were showing up as prototypes

---

2   'Business is war' was a motto of Tramiel and one that has gained some notoriety. In an interview with Fortune magazine in 1998 he is quoted as saying 'Business is war, I don't believe in compromising, I believe in winning.'

3   At Commodore, this was known as 'Tragic Voice'!

from Japan. I'm not sure anyone knew what to do with it, and Jack's sons weren't necessarily trying to avoid confusing Commodore. When the dust settled, the 264 had become the Plus/4, with one terrible 'productivity suite' replacing a couple of pretty useful option ROMs. And they also put out the Commodore 16, a 16KB version in a dark-grey version of the C64/VIC-20 case.

SYS 123, 45, 6

So I was asked to help out on a new project for a little while ... another engineer, Jeff Porter, was working on a new 8-bit computer, but it was battery powered. Simply called the Commodore LCD, this was 1984's answer to a laptop computer. It had a really nice display for the era as Commodore actually owned an LCD company in those days, and they were developing a very good suite of built-in applications – this was no Plus/4 fiasco. All seemed good with this project.

But before long, Bil called to say he needed help on another new system, which became the Commodore 128. This was going to be a first: an 8-bit computer with advanced features that would run C64 software and hardware.

I worked on timing analysis (in spreadsheets in the end) and on getting the system compatible with existing C64 hardware, trying out all kinds of add-ons, looking at what they did wrong, figuring out either how to fix their thing or, more likely, how to get the C128 to work with it. We actually had to make a few things as broken and bad-idea as they were on the C64, just to ensure compatibility.

And some of this was pure nutty, this compatibility thing. There was this idea that the C64 character set was a little ugly, so the software folks had put in a new font. It certainly looked better, but it also had a few unintended compatibility issues. We knew, for example, that the C64 as it existed was pretty unchangeable. When you put the C128 into C64 mode, it ran a real C64 ROM, for example, so programs that just randomly jumped into the C64 ROM would still work.

We loaded up this graphics painting software from Island Graphics, a pretty popular program on the C64. When it started up it presented a splash screen where it drew a nice island scene or something, then proceeded to write its name. The problem was that it was doing this by reading the character ROM and blowing up those characters to big graphics. Then it used its own painting routines to fill in colour, things like that, designed to show off a few features. But when it went to paint the dot in the 'i' from the new ROM it missed ... and wound up painting the background. This erased a bunch of stuff, so each new drawing operation messed up, and it would take 20–25 minutes to get this splash screen to go.

Because of that, we had to keep the C64 character set. But, it turned out, a double-sized character ROM wasn't much more expensive, so in every C128, there's a double-sized character ROM with the top address line driven by the C128/C64 signal, a hardware line that identifies which mode the system is running. Additional compatibility issues had the Z80 processor actually boot up first, look for the C= (Commodore) key to be held or a few other issues, and decide if it should boot the system into C128 or C64 mode.

I was asked to give the US marketing and sales people a presentation on the C128 and its hardware. This went pretty well, but I started to understand that much of what we did at Commodore was engineering driven. Maybe it was just corporate culture, but it made far more sense to me to have more sales and marketing involvement. I wanted to hand them a computer they could sell, after all. And if they want a feature and it can't be delivered, at least we've had the discussion and they know there's a good technical reason. I also flew to London and gave this talk to marketing and sales people from the UK, as well as from Italy, France and Germany, and perhaps a few other countries.

After the C128, Bil Herd left the company. He had put pretty much everything he had into that system and had no interest in doing it all over again. So, in 1985, I found myself as the lead design engineer on low-end systems at Commodore. Frank Palaia, the other hardware engineer on the C128, stuck around and tried to figure out what to do.

It wasn't as if Commodore Engineering got much marketing feedback back then. That was something I saw, in later years, as a structural problem at Commodore. Commodore had a central core organised under Commodore International that included Engineering and Production, but every country had their own marketing group. It was just a quirk of the era, even, that Commodore West Chester had Engineering, US Sales & Marketing, and Manufacturing all in one building. And of course, if you wanted to talk with a Commodore sales or marketing higher-up, it was probably not going to be one from the US. They basically only understood how to sell C64-class computers in Kmart. Commodore had long since lost their 'real computer' foot-print the US, and we had no real official channel or regular meeting with any of the sales or marketing folks from outside the company. Thus, much of what we did in Engineering was just what we thought might be a good idea.

So, we made a couple of prototypes of a Commodore 256 – mine had 256KB RAM, while Frank's version ran the Z80 twice as fast, in 80-column mode anyway. I also proposed a few other spin-offs, but there was really no management interest in an 8-bit computer beyond the C128 in those days.

KICKSTART

I first ran into the Amiga at the Consumer Electronics Show (CES) in Las Vegas, early in 1985. CES has always been a crazy show, even before we got there. It's always in January, which means if you're due to show something there and it's not quite working by Christmas or New Year, you're pretty much working through the holidays.

The C128's 80-column chip, the 8563, had a bug: its clock didn't synchronise correctly with the C128's independent bus clock. I found this out when we first got our hands on the C128s, and tried to pro-gram the chip from BASIC to make it do something. Sometimes when you wrote something to an 8563 machine register it would go there; sometimes, not too much. If you wrote it twice, it worked pretty well. Since the chip's designer was from Texas – and since we also saw somewhat similar behaviour in the 'Magic Voice' chips from Texas Instruments – we started calling this a 'Texas register'.

But even writing twice wasn't 100 per cent reliable, so Bil Herd and Dave DiOrio, designer of the C128's VIC-II chip, came up with a phase-locked loop 'tower'. A tower is a small circuit board – usually with a tall connector – that plugs into your main PCB in place of the chip that's supposed to go there, particularly back in the days of

DIP chips. It gives you more room to add extra stuff – whatever you need to force that chip to behave the way its intended, though some big towers actually deliver the whole function of a chip that's not available yet.

Bil's tower board helped, but there were still only so many 8563 video chips that really worked, even with the tower. So around New Year's Eve I was sorting through 1,000 or so of these to find maybe 25 that would work. In the end, we got to the CES show with just enough chips and towers to have every C128 we had made able to run.

Not every one was good for the 80-column 8563 display – some of them had shimmering pixels, indicating additional timing problems. These were carefully sorted and placed where the best ones would be doing the 80-column stuff – a fact that was naturally ignored by the sales and marketing folks at the show.

But it was a little worse than that. In order to reset a Commodore 64 you had to power cycle it. The 128 did have a built-in reset button, but most of the people demonstrating them didn't know about it, so they were power cycling them each time they went to show off something different on the system.

The phase-locked loop circuit was an analogue thing that had to be tuned to get its lock on any given C128, but that lock point also changed by heat. Once you were locked you were locked – but when you power cycled a C128, you lost the lock. I ended up running around the floor of CES with a can of freeze spray and a little plastic 'tweaking tool', getting C128s that the demonstrators had switched off to run again!

One night, we were invited to a hotel suite to see a presentation of this mysterious new Amiga computer that Commodore was buying. We saw the canned demos and it pretty much blew us all away – they did things that, pretty fundamentally, personal computers didn't do. Ever. Bil, of course, managed to talk up some of the Amiga people, and before I knew it I was tagging along and met RJ Mical and Dave Needle for the first time. They opened up what was then one of the first Amiga prototypes, and sure enough they had a tower board sitting under Daphne (later Denise), their video chip. One of us jumped in with, 'Hey, we have one of those, too!'

After CES, I really wanted an Amiga. That summer we got a few of the Zorro prototypes, predecessors to the Lorraine boards that would go into the Amiga 1000. We also got the first carefully controlled books about Amiga software, issued to individuals. Bil Herd got one of these, and within the week I had my own photocopy.

THE B-52

In the summer of 1986, Bob Welland and George Robbins had begun work on the Amiga 500 (code-named 'B-52'), based on an idea Bob had to further integrate the Amiga chipset. The original design had used quite a few external buffers and PAL devices.

The original Amiga team at Los Gatos weren't big champions of this idea – some didn't even think it would work – but there was a big push by the engineering management team, particularly Jeff Porter, to get an Amiga that Commodore people, and particularly Commodore sales and marketing, could deal with. And one that spoke to the company's low-cost strengths.

I started helping out on the Amiga 500 project that summer and pretty much never looked back to 8-bit systems. I already knew the overall architecture – how to use and write Amiga programs and so on. But it was pure fun to finally get paid to work on the actual hardware.

Bob and George were refugees from the Commodore 900 project, a 16-bit computer system based on Zilog's Z8000 project, which had been in the works for several years across several different engineering teams. These guys actually made it work. It ran a UNIX clone called Coherent and offered either a multi-terminal card or a megapixel display, with a custom windowing system. In short, the C900 was a pretty high-end system, as things at Commodore went. Unfortunately, it was cancelled when the Amiga came along.

Meanwhile, in Commodore's office in Braunschweig, Germany, some engineers had come up with a new Amiga they called the Amiga 2000. This version used the original Amiga chips and essentially mated the Amiga 1000 design to the expansion bus dubbed Zorro (also the name of one of the early motherboards). However, they decided to abandon the original Zorro card form factor – which looked like little VMEbus cards – in favour of an IBM PC card form factor. This was to enable the 'Bridge Card', a pet project of Henry Rubin's.

The A2000 design was essentially seen as a prototype and they wanted to get the new A500 chips added. Jeff Porter had formulated a plan to hand the new A2000 design over to George Robbins and put me in charge of finishing the A500 – only George didn't want to hand over the A500. So it became mine.

THE BOSS

So, I took on the Amiga 2000 and set to basing it on the A500 chip set. The original design had, along with the Zorro slots, an expansion slot that was basically the A1000 expansion edge, used for a 512KB memory card in the German version. The plan was always to include 1MB of memory on board the new A2000, which everyone started calling 'B2000'.[4] To me, this extra slot was to attach faster CPU cards – except the original design didn't really allow that, so I came up with a new design that added that feature.

The German system also had a slot that was basically the Amiga 23-pin connector put into a card-edge connector, to allow internal genlock.[5] I figured we ought to bring out all 12-bits of digital video – 4,096 colours means 4 bits each of R, G and B. I just doubled the original connector – so all we needed was an extra part – and wound up with lots of free space. I talked over the changes with George and he suggested running the parallel port there as well, which would allow the slot to control things. And so we paved the way for flicker fixers[6] and the Video Toaster[7] in an amazingly casual way.

---

4   B-52 + A2000 = B2000. The main board also said 'A2000-CR' (the CR stood for 'cost reduced'). I dubbed the board 'The Boss' after Bruce Springsteen (and also after the fact it was pretty much controlling my life).

5   A 'genlock' is a technique for maintaining the synchronisation of two different video signals, or a video signal and a computer/audio signal, enabling video images and computer graphics to be mixed.

6   A 'flicker fixer' is a piece of hardware that de-interlaces video by adjusting the timing of the interlaced signal to suit the requirements of a progressive display, such as a VGA monitor.

7   The Video Toaster was a famous editing suite created by NewTek that came in the form of an expansion card and accompanying software.

The Amiga 2620
accelerator

Around this time there were a couple of rounds of lay-offs at Commodore. They had been hit with various expenses and lower sales and who knows what else – I wasn't yet paying attention to much of that stuff.

Terry Fisher, who designed the PCB layout on the Amiga 2000, managed to put an inscription on the underside of the Revision 3 board that said, 'The Few, the Proud, the Remaining', and then listed the initials of pretty much everyone left in engineering. Tragically, management discovered this little 'Easter egg' and required that it be removed by the time the very next PCB revision came out, so it never made it into production.

But the Amiga 2000 did get out the door, on the heels of the Amiga 500. My first computer as a project lead ... and in fact, a big chunk of the project.

32-BIT ADD-INS

While I was finishing up the Amiga 2000, Bob Welland had been working on a thing he called 'the 68020 card' – or, more formally, the Amiga 2620. This had a Motorola 68020 processor, memory management unit (MMU) and floating point unit (FPU) on a CPU-slot card. It also had 2MB of 32-bit-wide 'fast' memory, which was more than four times faster than the chip RAM on the main Amiga 2000. We had coordinated some of the CPU-slot protocols but it wasn't completely working yet, so I agreed to help out.

Bob's main goal for this was still the same as for the C900: build a UNIX-compatible system. UNIX systems always used MMUs for virtual memory, which is why the Motorola unit was on the board. And of course, an FPU made rendering spaceships many times faster, so that made complete sense. I took on the job of ensuring the A2620 and its UNIX boot ROMs would be invisible if you were running AmigaOS. I found a few bugs but we got it working pretty well. Bob was amazing at computer architectures, but Bil had taught me some pretty serious debugging chops, at least back in those days. It was a good match, but Bob eventually left for work at Apple.

One day, Jeff Porter, director of new product development at that time, mentioned to me that we would have a 68030 prototype chip in about a week or two. That's all he said. About three days later, I was handing over schematics for a 68030 add-in for the Amiga 2000. This one also ran from its own clock, not from the Amiga clocks as the A2620 did. So I could run it at 25MHz rather than 14MHz, plus it had a connector for an add-on memory board, allowing even more full 32-bit 'fast' memory.

THE LAST GOLDEN AGE

By 1989 or so, it was pretty clear we would need to build a whole new system architecture, rather than leveraging off the A500 once again. Before this started, I began working on an expansion upgrade to the Zorro bus. I had some ideas about making the 16-bit bus much faster, and decided to run them by a few people. Hedley Davis, who was working on strange monitor ideas at the time, gave me some feedback and enough push to scrap that and figure out a full 32-bit protocol that worked entirely on the original connector in conjunction with the old 16-bit bus. Since the PC-ified version of Zorro had been dubbed Zorro II, this became Zorro III, and possibly the first time anyone at Commodore had written a complete bus specification for any add-on slot or socket.

As we moved on, the full 32-bit project brought me together with Hedley, Greg Berlin, Scott Hood and Jeff Boyer. We had Herb Mosteller make a new case design and, of course, Terry Fisher working on PCBs. Along with the full 32-bit expansion, the system got 32-bit chip RAM,

32-bit fast RAM, and a 32-bit CPU socket. As with the A2630, the A3000's 'fast RAM' was designed specifically to meet the demands of the 68030, rather than being slowed down as the 'chip RAM' always was, being shared between the CPU and the custom Amiga chips. Scott designed a built-in flicker fixer using digital video-buffering chips that were more efficient than the SRAM used in Pete Silverstone's original 'flickerFixer'.

This was a great project – not just because we got to make the best Amiga computer of all time, but because we had a real team. It was possible to do quite a bit of what we actually wanted to do.

The Amiga 3000T tower (040 variant)

We debuted the system at ... well, technically at Margarita's restaurant in West Goshen, Pennsylvania first, but formally at the 1990 Developer's Conference in Paris. Developers were pretty happy with the design, as well as the fact it was very compatible with the existing systems and expansion cards and so on.

It seemed management were also happy with this system, even hosting a splashy introduction party at the Palladium in New York City. We were able to bring in 68040 processor expert Scott Schaeffer, who had managed to get a high-end 68040 processor board running by the time of the launch of the A3000 in 1990.

In fact, we wanted to show the 68040 off at the debut, but initially Motorola wouldn't let us. It seems no one else had yet shown a 68040 running in public except Motorola themselves, and they were concerned. At the last minute, they gave permission and sent over a 'golden' 68040 for us to use ('golden' meant it was one of the few 68040 chips Motorola had fully tested and found to be bug-free). But Commodore management decided to nix that showing. It was still a fun time, but there was a big question – that 68040 board, which had its own external L2 cache, never shipped.

After the A3000, Greg went on to build the tower version, the Amiga 3000T. I helped out a little, but I was already working with George Robbins and two chip designers, Bob Raible and Victor Andrade, on the next big thing: a new Amiga chip set we had dubbed 'Pandora'. George had been working on some of the chip details and the system interface with lower-end computers in mind, while I was ensuring it did what I wanted for an A3000 replacement. Then I started working on that replacement.

We called it the Amiga 3000+, though that was not necessarily a product name, more of an in-house name like 'B-52'. Along with the new Amiga chips, Jeff Porter had given me some information on a digital signal processor (DSP) from AT&T, the DSP3210. This chip could run at twice the clock speed and 10 times the floating-point performance of the 68040, but after some of my applied cleverness, it could also share the Amiga 3000+ main bus. That was critical, because prior DSP systems had often needed expensive static RAM. Those chips also did not have direct memory access to main CPU memory, so they were restrictive. Not so with this design.

Jeff and I went to meet with AT&T about this processor. They had the idea that a DSP was something they could sell to a company that would replace a big pile of old-fashioned analogue hardware, and they priced their hardware – but particularly their software – based on that. We said we were adding this as a system resource, replacing nothing, and wanted pretty much all the software for $5. We eventually came to a deal and while we didn't get everything, we were pretty close.

So, to go along with the DSP, the Amiga 3000+ got one 16-bit stereo codec for high-quality sound input and output, and a special modem codec with phase correction capable of supporting a 9600 baud modem! Hey, that was pretty good for 1991! At this point it still used the 68030, but I was hoping to revise a bunch of chips and make it a 68040 system. However, it was critical to get a system up as fast as possible to find chip bugs and put software development into high gear. The first prototype was up and running on AmigaOS in February of 1991.

NIGHT FALLING IN WEST CHESTER

Ever since Jack Tramiel left Commodore for Atari, Commodore's chairman, Irving Gould, had been playing musical managers. He would bring in a guy to run Commodore, give them a tiny fraction of the time needed to actually make any changes, and then fire them and hire the next guy. This was happening both at the top level, with Commodore International, and at the Commodore Business Machines in the US. This practice had not previously affected us, but that wasn't to last.

While the Amiga 3000+ was something I was working on for the high-end, we had another system as well. A formerly junior engineer, Joe Augenbraun, had taken on the task of building a true mid-range Amiga system, code-named the Amiga 1000+. This was a separate box and keyboard concept, not based on the A3000 chips, with a 32-bit CPU (probably a 68020) and fast memory that planned to sell for under $1,000. We all pretty much believed these could be as popular as the A500-class machines, and of course, we had an A500-class machine in the planning as well, which became the Amiga 1200. Meanwhile, George Robbins was working on a thing he called the Amiga 300, which was an even lower-cost home/gaming version with a built-in genlock.

One of the big investors in Commodore at the time was the insurance company Prudential, and they had not been happy with the company's performance. They decided to send over a guy called Mehdi Ali, who had a reputation as a hatchet-man and bean counter – his job had been cutting costs at a company long enough for Prudential to get their money out at a profit. And so apparently, while Ali was at Commodore, old Uncle Irv, as he was known, decided to hire Ali as president of Commodore International.

One-by-one, Ali went around messing with parts of Commodore and putting in his own people – but this was not a guy who put the

The infamous IBM PCjr

best people in place. In fact, he didn't even make much of an attempt, as far as anyone knew, to learn anything about the computer business – he was the sort of narcissist who already 'just knew everything'. And so, naturally, he installed 'yes' men at various positions at the company – and that spring, he turned his eye towards engineering.

Henry Rubin was immediately out as vice president of engineering, and an IBM guy, Bill Sydnes, was put in place. Now, it's fairly amazing what an idiot this Sydnes was, and given his history, this should have been obvious even to Ali.

There was a computer company in New Jersey called Franklin Computer that had decided to make a clone of the Apple II, a project Sydnes had been in charge of. They made the big mistake of simply copying Apple's ROM along with the hardware design – you can't copyright a hardware design in the US, but everyone knew software was copyrighted.

Franklin's claim was that as the software was in ROM form there was no copyright. They lost in court and the case helped establish the legal foundation for not stealing other folks' ROM code.

Another Sydnes project had been the 'Peanut' – better known as the IBM PCjr, perhaps IBM's greatest failure up until that point. The Peanut was IBM's effort to build a home computer, and it was an amazing flop. It sold for nearly $1,300 in 1984, but came with a chiclet keyboard and only 128KB of memory. Even the VIC-20 was easier to type on! It was off the market in just over a year.

So this was the guy that Ali had brought in to run engineering. Commodore had been more or less getting out of the PC-clone business before Sydnes and Ali, but Sydnes wasn't sure about that and promoted former PC engineer Jeff Frank to director of new product development, pushing Jeff Porter aside to be director of multimedia (or one of those titles that basically meant that they wanted you out).

The primary mission of the new Sydnes team, for the first six months or so, was to just grind engineering to a full stop. Sydnes was so insecure he basically had to sabotage or cancel just about every ongoing hardware project. The A1000+ was no more.

They effectively did sabotage the next revision of the A3000+, forcing us to build a very large surface-mounted PCB without a solder mask. That machine was so full of short circuits, even after working on it for a month I could never find them all. Eventually we did a scaled-back Revision 2 board that went back to through-hole parts and eliminated most of the analogue section.

Sydnes's big promise to Mehdi Ali was a replacement for the A500 that would cost $50 less to make – which, luckily for him, basically amounted to exactly the A300 project that George Robbins was working on. But Sydnes wanted a bunch of additional stuff added to the A300 – a PCMCIA slot, an IDE controller and so on – and it ultimately cost $50 more to make than the A500 or A500+.

It released to poor reviews, so in order to get them to sell, management cancelled the still-selling Amiga 500+ – a move I had never before seen at Commodore. So customers took the A600 or nothing.

Sydnes also ordered two scaled-down versions of the Amiga 3000 – the real, original Amiga 3000, the one with ECS graphics chips. The new management were apparently hell-bent on making the Pandora or 'AA'[8] chips sit on the sidelines. Only the A1200 project was still moving forward.

The first of these scaled-down A3000s was a computer officially called the Amiga 2200, which was a two-slot, Zorro II-only, IDE-not-SCSI version of the Amiga 3000. Everyone at Commodore dubbed it the A1000jr in 'honour' of Sydnes and as a memorial to the demise of the actual A1000+.

The other was a stripped down, four-slot A3000-like system with only Zorro II slots and IDE. Greg Berlin and Scott Schaeffer were mainly in charge of these, and no one particularly thought they were a good idea other than Jeff Frank and Bill Sydnes – and I do mean no one!

If you recall my description of Commodore, I mentioned that our sales and marketing companies were not really closely tied to the central company, and that each region had its own marketing and sales people with their own plans and advertising campaigns and so on. That's how you could have a failed sales and marketing company in the US and still sell a million computers a year in Germany or the UK.

And so, when this A1000jr/A2200 and the larger A3400 were introduced to the international sales companies, nobody ordered any. None. They were not fooled – everybody knew about Pandora and wanted it.

THE LAST GASP

Naturally, we did not get the A3000+ or A1000+ back, but we moved fast. Even before this, Greg Berlin knew that the A2200 and A3400 were not what people wanted – not with 68020 or 68030 processors two years after the A3000. So he asked Scott Schaeffer to make 'the cheapest 68040 board known to mankind'.

And so we had those – the A3640 boards – already up and running when the A2200 and A3400 were cancelled, and Sydnes was in a tizzy trying to figure out what to do about it. Berlin and Schaeffer took my A3000+ Pandora design, mixed it with some of the cost-reduction

---

8   We had a longer-term project in development: the Advanced Amiga Architecture or AAA. Being a bit less than AAA, pretty much everyone started calling it 'AA'. Commodore's marketing team only dubbed these 'AGA' when they decided to ship some new machines.

The Amiga 4000

bits of the A3400, upgraded the expansion to Zorro III, and only a few months after the original date we had hoped the A3000+ would ship to consumers (around April 1992), the Amiga 4000 was born.

I had a few things going on then. For one, I was working on a huge computer system called 'Nyx' – a test and development system, not even close to being a commercial prototype, for the AAA chips. It was a six-chip AAA system that could deliver 64-bit graphics, but that could also be built as a 32-bit version. This machine also had Amiga ROM on a SIMM (single in-line memory module) card, chip RAM on plug-in modules, a third 8520 chip, a built-in network ... I had built up a few ideas, and as many as possible landed here.

I had also designed a SCSI board for the A4000 dubbed the A4091; I had a multiprocessor card in development dubbed 'Gemini'; and I was working on the next-generation system chips to replace 'Ramsey', 'Gary', 'Buster' and so on (i.e. the A3000 architecture), a design dubbed Acutiator, with much better modularity than we had in past systems. I felt for quite a while that Commodore spent too much time reinventing the same wheel for each next computer we made.

All of these projects were essentially 'skunkworks projects',[9] and progressed under-the-table if at all. I could use the CAD systems all I wanted to design circuits or write machine code for Acutiator, but to actually make anything required money.

Meanwhile. Jeff Porter, still hanging around, had, to an extent, come to lead a shadow engineering department: Commodore's very own 'Order of Leibowitz'. Jeff had kept development going on the A3000+ DSP project throughout 1992. He helped get some of these things made, at least to the point where I could begin debugging hardware.

And the thing is, all this time, I was pretty sure Commodore was doomed. Ali was an idiot and just kept making stupid mistake after stupid mistake – we shouldn't have expected anything else.

Here was a guy who didn't watch television, didn't use computers, and had no idea why putting the two together was useful. Moreover, he didn't have the natural curiosity even to want to learn about things important to his job. A good manager learns as much as possible about his new business; a great manager understands his new business well enough to speak 'engineer' to engineers, 'sales' to salespeople and so on. The kind of manager who runs a billion-dollar company into bankruptcy in three years is the kind who thinks he knows it all and doesn't want to hear otherwise.

Maybe there are others to blame here, but given how so many of the bad people at Commodore in the early 1990s were brought in by Ali, they're not the root cause. They might not be able to help being terrible at their jobs, but Ali was the guy who knew that. He was the guy who read their résumés and hired them anyway. I guess their main job qualification was the ability to always say: 'Yes'.

That last flurry of activity was my engineer's response to troubles that have no engineering solution. In good times, great engineering can launch a company to new levels, to new business, to new prosperity. You want to think that you can do that in any situation, but ultimately, you can't. And it took me some years after Commodore, reflection and so many 'what ifs' before I really became to accept

---

9   Skunkwork projects are usually developed by a small, often loosely structured group of people primarily for the sake of radical innovation.

that. I had hoped that Irving Gould would wake up one morning, bump his head on a clue-by-four, and suddenly realise that Mehdi Ali didn't have the slightest idea how to run a computer company, even if Gould's kids did call him 'Uncle Mehdi'. He'd bring in someone and all those projects would come alive.[10]

Commodore had a terrible Christmas season in 1992. There was demand for A1200s and A4000s, but Sydnes had spent so much time sabotaging the Pandora project before he figured out he needed to support us that parts were in short supply. The Lisa chip was being made in 0.8 micron CMOS at Hewlett-Packard, not at MOS Technology like the other chips, so supplies had to be contracted in advance. There were plenty of Amiga 600s, but they did not sell very well.

Sydnes was fired some time around then – I don't recall if he made it into 1993 or not. It started with his missed target on the price of the A600, which absolutely everyone and their houseplants could have told you was a problem back in 1991. In fact we all did – some people are just too stupid to listen.

Sydnes was replaced as vice president of engineering by Lew Eggebrecht. I didn't really know much about Lew coming in. He had been a primary member of the original PC team at IBM, which I gather impressed Mehdi Ali. In fact, Sydnes's presence was the reason Ali was able to get Eggebrecht in. So yes, a former engineer, though if you had ever inspected the design of an IBM PC, it looked like something some kids cooked up in their garage with parts from RadioShack.[11]

Eggebrecht did at least want to do engineering, so many of the shadow projects became a bit less in the shadow. But even if Eggebrecht had been a superstar – which never happened at Commodore at least – too much damage was already done. The one major project launched in 1993 was from the low-end folks, who essentially merged with the CDTV people to make the CD32 game console, which I thought was

---

10   I later learned that Jean-Louis Gassée, former Apple engineering lead and eventual founder of Be Inc., had tried to get a gig running Commodore Engineering.

11   Well, some kids who were not Steve Wozniak – the Apple II was way, way more elegant in design than the PC, and built by just one guy (though I hear he got a bit of help from Chuck Peddle, the Commodore chip engineer who designed the 6502 used in the Apple II, the Commodore PETs, and the early Ataris).

a fantastic idea. However, Commodore had lost so much money that they basically owed all of their suppliers. So in order to build something, they had to pay in cash, they had to buy chips expensively on the spot market and so on. In short, that meant only a relatively small number of CD32s – less than 100,000 – were made available for sale, and they all cost way too much to make.

What we had here was the final circling of the drain of the company, all thanks to Mehdi's bad management and, in my opinion anyway, his meddling with things he was incapable of and uninterested in understanding in engineering. You don't waste a year with intentional product delays and expect to just start again without consequence.

Commodore lost something like $350 million in the Christmas 1993 season. And so, on the 24th of April 1994 – at the close of business, in the usual fashion – Commodore declared bankruptcy.

THE SEASON OF ZOMBIES

Just prior to the bankruptcy, all but about 30 of us in West Chester were laid off. I left in June to go work for Scala, mostly because they were local and full of a bunch of Commodore folks, such as Jeff Porter, Mike Sinz, Randell Jesup and a few others. The bankruptcy people were trying to sell Commodore all summer, and the few who stuck around were paid double salary to hang out and give a dog and pony show usually about once a week.

Ultimately, ESCOM of Germany, one of the largest PC companies, bought all of the Commodore assets. They set up a division called Amiga Technologies, brought in some recently former Commodore people to discuss the future, and put the Amiga 1200 and the Amiga 4000T back into production.

In the autumn of 1995, they contacted Andy Finkel, the former head of software development, and me, offering us a trip to Germany to talk Amiga. I had basically decided to help out any Amiga buyer in any way I could, so I made the trip.

They were interested in building an A1200-style computer using the PowerPC RISC processor and porting the whole operating system over as well. As I recall, they were actually talking about doing it right, both in terms of the hardware and the OS. We had IBM and Motorola

'I documented the last few days at Commodore
in a film called "The Deathbed Vigil and other
tales of digital angst", available to buy on DVD
from Amazon (or to watch on YouTube for free)'

in-house to discuss some PowerPC options and some graphics/multi-media chips as well. I had pretty much finished the architecture for a custom PowerPC chip for low-cost home computers, but at the time, neither IBM nor Motorola had synthesizable cores, so something like that would be a few years off, but possible.

We had a small developer meeting early in 1996 that went pretty well, all things considered. It was probably a few weeks after that when the bad news hit.

ESCOM had made some stupid product projections for their Christmas season – their PCs hadn't sold well enough and they were in big trouble. Amiga Technologies soon fell apart.

The ESCOM bankruptcy went on for a few more years, and eventually the Amiga assets alone were sold to US PC company Gateway 2000. They initially announced all sorts of plans to build computers called 'Amiga' that really had nothing much to do with the Amiga, but that didn't last long. They eventually licensed the rights to a tiny outfit in Washington state that emerged as Amiga, Inc., and initially promised to ship an operating system for phones that also had absolutely nothing to do with the Amiga.

A little more time passed and they sublicensed OS development to Hyperion, Inc., a gaming company in the UK – because everyone knows that game developers, working only part time on a new OS, make the best OS developers. Or perhaps not. After about twice as long as it took to originally write AmigaOS 1.0, 1.1, 1.2, 1.3 and 2.0 combined, Hyperion came out with AmigaOS 4.0 for the PowerPC processor ... which had been a complete non-starter as a choice of desktop platform ever since Apple killed the future of the PowerPC in 1997 with the end of MacOS licensing.

In 1996, I started another company, PIOS Computer AG, with Andy Finkel and two German businessmen, Stefan Domeyer and Geerd Ebeling, basically from the ashes of Amiga Technologies. Our original intent was to license AmigaOS – assuming we could figure out who owned it – and do a port ourselves. But after the various post-ESCOM scrambles for AmigaOS, we could not get that licence.

So we decided to start making Macintosh clones. That worked well for a while – we had introduced the world's fastest Mac-compatible computer at 300MHz in those days. Then Apple cancelled MacOS licensing, but we managed to bounce back by making small computers for internet browsing on your TV, then one based on low-cost PC technology that could do low-quality digital video as well, and finally an in-house design that slowly feature-crept to do just about anything, including playing digital television and DVD, with the right video module. This ran on a ColdFire microprocessor at 144MHz and ran an in-house developed operating system called CAOS – Carsten and Andy's Operating System, as I recall. If you were an Amiga fan, it would have felt familiar.

The company fell apart in 2000. Management was over-spending on the wrong things and stock prices were falling, as they were pretty much everywhere. Without going into too much detail, I'll just say I still have the scars from the knives placed squarely into my back by supposed friends. They say in the start-up business, 'You have no friends on the way down' – not entirely true. I've never turned on my partners – neither did Andy. Some things are more important than money.

Dave Haynie, today

WHAT IS DEAD MAY NEVER DIE

So that was my adventure with Commodore and Amiga – or so I thought. I caught back up with David Pleasance at a 30th anniversary party for the Amiga in Amsterdam in 2015. I suppose I had been following the various attempts by individuals or companies to bring back some form of Amiga, or at least some computer running AmigaOS that reminds one of the Amiga. Electronic nostalgia is more often than not no more than a useful tool, and I was not particularly interested in playing with any of these attempts.

But more recently, at shows in the past few years, I've seen a change. There have been more new Amiga-like computers – some even recreating the classic Amiga and some delivering performance only dreamt of in the Amiga's golden age – and they are getting more real every year. Better hardware, lower cost … I suspect I'll have one of these for myself before too long.

Am I ready to make my own yet? Not sure about that. But it does, after a few decades, give me a reason to – as RJ says – 'Keep the Faith!'

3

COMMODORE UK – THE EARLY DAYS

TIM CHANEY

It was late 1981. Back then there was no internet and *The Grocer* was essential weekly reading for job postings. If you were looking for work in the fast-moving consumer goods (FMCG) industry, the best jobs were there.

It was odd, then, to find an advert from Commodore Business Machines for regional sales managers to help introduce to the UK its new home computer, the VIC-20.

I bought a few magazines to buff up on what a home computer was, applied, and was offered an interview to be held at the Spider's Web Motel in Watford. After the usual wait, I was introduced to Commodore's sales manager Paul Welch, a fiery northerner. As interviews go, it wasn't a good one.

Paul dismissed much of my CV and accomplishments, and as I began to think I wasn't going to get the job anyway I started to defend myself, telling him he was wrong. By the time I'd left the interview I decided I had no chance, so my brain erased the whole episode.

A couple of weeks later I was at home in Newport Pagnell when the phone rang.

'Hi Tim, this is Paul Welch,' came the voice.

'Who?' I replied.

'Paul Welch. From Commodore? We met a couple of weeks ago in Watford.'

'Oh, yeah?'

'I'm calling to offer you the job.'

'The what? The job? But it was a terrible interview. You thought I was crap!'

'Not at all – you were the only one who fought your corner and came back at me. My interview style is always like that. So ... the job is yours if you still want it?'

And so a few weeks later I was dropped off at Ajax Avenue in Slough (incidentally home of TV show *The Office*) to pick up my Ford Cortina – the sales rep Ferrari of the day.

*

After receiving the quick tour, Paul took me to the office of Bob Gleadow, the managing director.

'Hi Bob, this is Tim,' Paul said, pointing in my direction. 'He's joining us for north London and the home counties.'

Bob looked up and, to Paul, said: 'OK ... Is that it?'

We continued the tour.

At that time, CBM was two animals: there was a full Business Division selling the Commodore PET, and there was this 'toy computer' group – the Consumer Products Division – to launch the VIC-20.

Paul and the rest of his team in Consumer Products – John Baxter, Aileen Bradley, Brian Reed, Keith Langley and six or so others – would ring up John Lewis, Boots, WHSmith, Toymaster and all the other UK retailer powerhouses of the day to ask if they wanted to sell Commodore's home computers, and there would be about 50 leads each week from independent retailers who wanted to stock the product too. Everyone received a visit.

Inside Commodore we were the lower classes compared to the CBM upper classes, but on the streets we were pioneers with a great product. But we really had little idea what the masses wanted to use it for. Learn BASIC? Do your accounts? Check your horoscope? Write? Play games?

During my first week, Paul, Brian and I were stationed in the Post House hotel at Heathrow. We would meet up for drinks and dinner, then I would head back to my room to go through *Introduction to Basic Vol. 1* until midnight. The first meeting the next day was at 9am no matter where it was, so if it was in Cardiff, we had breakfast at 5am. And back then there was no M25.

But the most significant part of this beginning was the induction into the culture of Jack Tramiel and Commodore. There was a 10-point code for working at Jack's Commodore which came in a little booklet that included such gems as, 'We don't have competitors, only enemies. Respect them but crush them', and the fairly obvious 'Treat every penny as if it was your own.'

There were others, but Jack Tramiel's favourite mantra was 'Business is war', and was intended to seep into every brain and blood cell – we were not there to take prisoners, we were there to rip the wristwatches off the dead. And over the next few years, we did: Atari's Lynx, the Dragon, the Grundy NewBrain, the Jupiter Ace, Memotech, the Oric, the Sharp MZ, the Thomson T07 – all fell by our hands. RIP.

Only Sinclair, who had already had some success with the ZX80/ZX81 kit computers, gave us a run for our money with the Spectrum and the QL, while the BBC Micro and the Amstrad CPC shared our shelf space for more than a few months.

That first year at Commodore was spent signing up independent stores as Commodore-'Approved' retailers and training the staff of large retail chains. To become a Commodore stockist, the retailer had to buy an initial stocking order at £3,500 for each location (it was usually one but many had small chains). As well as the essential VIC-20s and cassette players, a gaggle of very average and expensive cartridge games (and a few cassette games) and copies of *Introduction to Basic*, the order had to include a Commodore 1541 disk drive (which was just about unsaleable) and some RAM expansion cartridges.

'Business is war' breaks down to the minutiae on a daily trading basis of course and manifests itself many ways. Take a retailer I signed in Greenford, Middlesex. He signed up for the order, posted his credit check, and the truck duly dropped off the stock. Even though

The Commodore 1541
5.25" floppy disk drive

he displayed it in his shop window he didn't sell much of it at all, and after 60 days or so he couldn't afford to pay the bill.

Commodore were gearing up to issue a winding up order. Back in the office, Paul cornered me.

'What are we doing about the guy in Greenford?' he asked.

'Well,' I said, 'he's tried hard to build up local business by advertising and he's put us in the front window.'

'So? He can't pay the bill!'

'We should show some goodwill, Paul.'

'Goodwill? When I want fucking goodwill, I will pay for it!'

*

The home computer training of retail managers and staff for Dixons, Rumbelows, Currys, Wigfalls, the Co-op and others either took place in hotels or at the retailers' training offices. A truck would drop off between 25 and 50 VIC-20 packs and staff would open them, go through the contents, cover all the sales features and then, as a finale, be taught how to perform simple BASIC code, like GO TO and RUN.

The strangest training day I can recall was one where we taught some Hoover vacuum cleaner dealers how to sell the VIC-20.

Paul had made a deal with around 170 Hoover stockists in the UK to sell the VIC-20. They came in over the course of a week to a purpose-built and rather plush training room in the Skyline Hotel near Heathrow Airport to learn the fundamentals. In the space of a day the attendees went from 'This model has great suction along the skirting boards' to 'This model has 5K of RAM, 3.5K of which is usable while the rest runs the system.' I don't know if they managed to sell any as I moved up into the role of national accounts manager.

*

In 1982, in the lead-up to Christmas, the first deliveries of the Commodore 64 arrived. I spent that week going to Slough, loading my car up with C64s with help from Kelly Sumner (who, like me, would go on to work in video games) and then delivering them – one per shop – for display purposes only, to show during the Christmas season.

If the VIC-20 was a game changer, the C64 turned the game on its head. Positioned as a hybrid business and casual computer, it was market-designated as a games machine in less than six months. It was very successful in the US, leading to a significant uptake in the development of games there, while the UK forged its own ecosystem, stealing a lot of development resources from the Sinclair Spectrum and BBC Micro, who had a difficult task in keeping up.

At Commodore, in my new position in National Accounts, I had a plethora of 'B' accounts (such as The Co-op (CWS) and The Co-op (CRS) – as confusing as it sounds). There was also Rumbelows, Wigfalls, Terry Blood, Our Price, Virgin, Littlewoods and others. Many of these were based in the north, so most weeks I would stay at the Post House in Manchester and attend Grab-a-Granny nights for some local colour (I was 28 at the time and the 'grannies' in question were only a bit older, maybe 30).

In late 1983, I was offered a sales director job by Camputers in Cambridge. The company had launched three versions of its Lynx

Z80A-based home computer (48K, 96K, 128K) and was based in a quaint office overlooking the River Cam. The job came with whatever car I wanted – so I left Commodore and took the position, opting for a Saab 900.

Getting UK distribution was difficult – a new competing home computer was launched every few months, our margins were tight and our games were Z80/Z81 rehashes. So I focused on export and we found distributors in France, Norway, Belgium, Italy and South Africa. But Camputers had run out of money, and most of my time was spent helping shareholders try to raise more capital. In the end, we had £3 million of orders that we couldn't build.

I saw the writing on the wall and called Paul Welch to see if there was anything available back at Commodore despite the company launching two shockers – the Commodore 16 and the Commodore Plus/4 – in the interim. Both products bombed, but the following year would see another milestone launch: the Amiga.

In the summer of 1984 I met with Paul at Newport Pagnell Services one Sunday morning and gave him my Camputers hard-luck story. He said there was a role for me as head of software sales – I wasn't aware we had any that warranted selling, but I accepted and it was back in the fast lane with another new car: a Ford Granada Ghia Mk2. Now that was a sales director car!

Around that time, Commodore had built a large facility at Corby in Northamptonshire. Corby was a steel town that was now without steel. The £20 million building was originally announced in May 1983 and was built with the assistance of UK government grants. It included facilities for marketing, sales and administration, and an assembly line.

Within eight months of the announcement, the factory – one of four Commodore production sites worldwide – was turning out 5,000 VIC-20s and Commodore 64s a day. By this point, Jack Tramiel had left Commodore along with Bob Gleadow, and Irving Gould had stepped in as the new president.

Returning to Commodore at its new Corby office was a strange experience. Most of the familiar Slough faces had been swapped for new ones, and the cottage industry of 1982 and 1983 had made way for the home computer gold rush, spawning an entire industry out of nothing.

Meanwhile, 1984 gave rise to Alan Sugar's Amstrad CPC, a new Z80 machine that would go on to sell some 3 million units, a fraction of what the C64 sold.[1] And there was talk of 14 hi-fi manufacturers creating a common PC format called the MSX – which transpired but was dead and gone soon after.

Back at Commodore there was a new face I didn't like much and vice versa – your author, David Pleasance. Although we were segregated by the hardware/software divide, there was natural tension between us: from my perspective he had the job I should have had had I not left; from his perspective, Paul treated me as a favourite, promoted me a few times and then, despite originally having left the company, brought me back into the fold. It was like we were playing for the same team but refused to pass to each other.

Selling – or at least trying to sell – Commodore software introduced me to a whole new sector: indie distributors that were becoming a major factor in the games retail chain. Firms such as Microdealer, CentreSoft, Websters, Leisuresoft, Terry Blood Distribution, Tiger Distribution and others loomed large as publishers started to bid for attention and shelf space in the independent retailer and national chains.

One of my customers for software (and hardware before that) was Lightning Records, based in NW10, London, and run by Ray Laren and Loretta Cohen. They were far too savvy to buy our software, but Loretta liked me and offered me a role as sales director at the company. This represented a move into records and video alongside home computers, and came with a Rover SD1 as my chosen company car. I accepted and handed Paul my notice.

Come the afternoon of my final day, as I was packing up my office, Paul came to see me and offer me the role of national sales manager.

---

1   Nobody doubts that the Commodore 64 was the greatest selling single computer model of all time – it even made it into the *Guinness Book of Records*. But nobody knew quite how many it really sold. Some sources said 17 million and Jack Tramiel of course claimed it was 30 million. But according to David – who, along with Colin Proudfoot, had scoured Commodore's sales records as part of their due diligence process when trying to resurrect the company in 1994 – volume of sales were at least 23 million.

I accepted, and rang Loretta to tell her and to send the car back. She was very gallant about it.

This new role put me in charge of your author, Mr Pleasance. So I set about teaching him how to sell ... haha, not really! But I did do training days with him and would send him and Paul my subsequent report.

I kept on working in software part-time, but the software itself was getting weaker and weaker. One day I visited CentreSoft at their new offices in Birmingham and Geoff told me that as he didn't know much about Commodore's software I should just send him what I thought he should have and could sell. Well, the 'Business is war' part of me said I would do that – so, I cleared the Corby warehouse and relocated it in Birmingham.

At Christmas that year, I was given a budget to take my best software accounts clients for a meal, so I took Geoff and his wife, the fiery, feisty Anne. Towards the end of the meal, Anne asked me if I would like to join their games software label, U.S. Gold, as managing director – basically, employee Number 1. I asked Anne, 'Why me?'

'You're the only salesman who has ever stitched us up, and we want you on our side.'

And so I joined in January 1985, the day the CND protested the U.S. Gold offices over the pending release of *Raid Over Moscow*. I got the first quote of my career comparing *Raid Over Moscow* to a modern-day Cowboys and Indians – CND campaigner Monsignor Bruce Kent referred to me a 'horrible little man'.

I never did get to sell any Amiga hardware, and David would go onto greater things once I, and later Paul, had left the company. The rest, for me, has been a life in games.

Within four years of joining U.S. Gold, the company became the largest games publisher in Europe, primarily due to the amazing catalogue of US product we had, especially Epyx's *Summer Games* and *Winter Games* series. We were also a major player in coin-op conversions, such as *Street Fighter*, *Gauntlet*, *Road Runner*, *RoadBlasters*, *Thunder Blade* and *Out Run*.

I left in 1989 to start my own games label TecMagik in conjunction with International Development Group in California, to launch

The title screen for
Raid Over Moscow

games for the Sega Master System. Then in 1991 I was approached by Robert Devereux and Frank Herman to take over as president of Virgin Games, which had been spun-out of Virgin Mastertronic following the acquisition of the hardware business by Sega.

Virgin Games' European business, worth $1 million in 1991, was built to $200 million in three years, and the global company was sold to Blockbuster for $250 million in 1994 following investment from Hasbro. By 1995, Virgin Interactive Entertainment, as it was renamed in 1993, was running neck and neck with EA for domination over Europe. I have always been gratified by a quote from David Gardner, executive vice president of EA Europe, that he 'spent the 90s trying to catch up with Tim Chaney'.

Viacom bought Blockbuster in 1996 and, having taken a bath on its own Viacom New Media in the games business, didn't want a games company and so sold key assets, including Westwood Studios, creators of the popular *Command & Conquer* series, to EA for $130 million. I engineered a management buyout with Mark Dyne (of Skype,

Tim Chaney, today

among others) in 1998 and we sold the company to Titus Interactive the next year.

I had a two-year golden parachute, moved to Madrid, and bought Virgin Interactive Entertainment España from Titus in 2002. The company became the largest independent distributor in Spain and in 2006, after raising venture capital funding, moved into publishing, securing the rights to Real Madrid and Pocoyo. I left the company in 2008 following a boardroom battle with the company's then venture capital shareholders who couldn't see beyond the Nintendo DS and the Wii.

I temporarily retreated to London and started Zattikka plc, which became the first social games company to go public on the UK's AIM market in 2012.

Since late 2015 I have been an agent for games developer funding and representing major digital platforms on boarding games IP.

4

MEMORIES FROM THE SOFT SIDE

GAIL WELLINGTON

When I look back at my time at Commodore, I remember the good times, the great people, the interesting experiences, the funny stories ... Was it all like that? Absolutely not. There were many frustrations, including product failures – but the good memories come to mind first.

Even my hiring was an interesting experience. I am an American but was living in the UK because of my husband's job. One day, I saw a sign in an employment agency's window about a technical writing position for a computer company. I knew that if it was a hardware position I was not qualified, but it was in software. I got an interview at Commodore but not an offer. However, I thought – no, I knew – that this was my job. A few weeks later, I received a phone call saying that the man who had accepted the position had not shown up on his first day and was unreachable. The job was mine. The year was 1981.

At that time, Commodore relied heavily on independent software publishers to provide applications to generate sales of its PET business computers. My first assignment was to create a 'Software Manuals Standard' delineating how quality manuals should be written. Soon after, I was reassigned to oversee user manual writing for third-party software, to be published under the Commodore label.

The writers were struggling because the software was buggy and constantly changing – we would work hard on a manual only to have the features and user interface change at the eleventh hour. My direct supervisor (known to all as 'Bird Man' because his surname was Pidgeon) didn't understand the problem created by these last-minute changes. I proposed a vertical integration approach to Pidgeon's boss, in which the person writing the manual had responsibility for all aspects of the product, from design to production. It would either fix the problem or I would be out of a job. Unfortunately, it sat on his desk, unread. Frustrated, I told John Baxter, the marketing director, about my dilemma.

Bob Gleadow, general manager at the Commodore UK office in Slough, kept his finger on the pulse of the organisation by walking through the entire facility almost every afternoon. One day, he knocked on a closed office door and said he was looking for someone, although he had just seen that person in the hall – Gleadow wanted to know what was going on in that office and used the ruse to have a look. Baxter had tipped Gleadow off to my proposal, so when Bob walked by the desk where my proposal was sitting, he spotted the document and walked off with it. The next day, I was head of software applications for Commodore UK.

The UK applications software team was smart, dedicated and self-motivated. Many came from a jobs retraining programme in the north of England. Most noteworthy was Steve Beats, who had been an apprentice boat builder. After joining Commodore UK, Steve went on to work for Commodore in the US as a programmer. Unfortunately, the US would not give him a green card because he did not have a college degree. Commodore lost a talented employee when he had to return to the UK.[1]

The team's work environment in the Slough office was unique. Commodore occupied a large warehouse with two floors of offices along the front and one side. However, the software group and the mail-order sales group were relegated to a part of the warehouse

---

[1]   My office nickname was 'Mother' – although I was a tough boss. However, people like Steve and the rest of the team knew I cared about them and their success.

that had been cordoned off from storage and shipping. We were the ultimate in open-plan – just desks and computers on tables in the middle of all that space. This had the advantage of flexibility because the desks (and occupants) could be easily rearranged to create project teams as assignments changed. However, there were disadvantages, including the lack of privacy. We solved this by declaring a meeting table as 'private space' – anyone sitting at the table was considered to be sitting in a closed-door office and not to be disturbed.

Open plan created another challenge. One staff member had a very young son who visited occasionally. The son discovered that when you turned off a computer and turned it back on again it made an interesting noise. When the toddler visited, we soon learned to put a hand over the switch on the back of our computers so that we would not be the victim of an unwanted reboot.

VIC-20: THE FIRST TRUE HOME COMPUTER

Soon we were working on software for the VIC-20, the first true home computer. However, delivery of the hardware was delayed. The press were hounding Commodore for dates as Christmas was fast approaching. We joked about releasing some packaging into the sea and spreading the rumour that the shipment had been lost overboard.

In the UK, people first bought the VIC-20 because they wanted to learn about computers. The best-selling software, *Introduction to Basic*, taught the fundamentals in an easy-to-understand way. John Colin, a university instructor from the north of England, was the author, and Commodore the publisher. *Introduction to Basic* was translated into 10 languages, making Commodore UK software a global market force.

Of course, games were also popular for the Vic, although, due to little RAM, a 22-character wide screen and limited 'horsepower', they were primitive. The games – such as one with snakes that crawled across the screen eating bugs and avoiding bombs – were unsophisticated but fun.

To encourage software development, we accepted and reviewed programs from the public. They arrived at a rate of over 100 per week. The team evaluated them using specific criteria and a rating system, and comments and suggestions were then sent to the author. The top 5 per cent were considered for further development and publication under a licensing agreement, or recommended for inclusion in a direct mail software catalogue that Commodore UK distributed. It didn't matter who or how old you were – one game we published, *Maggotmania*, was designed by Jason Perkins, who was only 16 years old at the time.

The most challenging submissions came from educators. Many were appealing ideas, but the educators' timelines for

Gortek and the Microchips, 1984

development were set in years – at this point in time, home computers would change in a matter of months. Educators' timelines and ours just didn't align. (In retrospect this makes sense, since educators take 12 years to deliver their 'finished product'!)

One successful idea that arrived in the post was *Gortek and the Microchips*. This was developed into a colourful glossy book about space-age critters that was aimed at teaching those as young as 7 or 8 the basics of programming. We were challenged on the name because of its similarity to the trademarked name for the fabric Gore-Tex, but we prevailed.

THE COMMODORE 64: A WHOLE NEW SOFTWARE WORLD

The Commodore 64 opened up new possibilities for software developers, who now had access to more memory, higher resolution, faster processing and sprites.

Sprites – programmable, movable objects – really changed game potential. At our request, Andrew Spencer created *International Soccer*, which took advantage of those sprites. It was a state-of-the-art

Entrants into the Young Computer
Brain of the Year 1984 competition

Showing Prince Michael of Kent
how to use a Commodore 64

game ahead of anything else published for a home computer at that time in 1983. Although only seven-a-side, two players could each control their team simultaneously. It was released on cartridge and sold very well.

Easy Script, by Simon Tranmer of Precision Software, was another outstanding program. This word processor – originally written for the PET and enhanced for the VIC-20 and Commodore 64 – was ahead of anything similar on the home market.[2]

The idea for another of our bestsellers just walked in the door one day. (Well, they had made an appointment, otherwise my very protective secretary, Ruth Briner, probably would have marched them right back out!) John van Til, a charming and handsome Dutchman from London-based Music Sales, proposed a product called *Music Maker*. Richard Watts, a technical magician with all things musical, did the implementation. He created an eight-voice synthesizer with backing percussion rhythms, which was controlled the computer keyboard of the Commodore 64 using a piano keyboard overlay. The product was very popular in many countries and was used in retail bundles.

SOFTWARE PRODUCTION

Initially, software was published on a ROM cartridge or cassette tape. Cartridges required anticipated software sales of 100,000 to make the manufacturing costs practical. Cassettes were slow to load and inherently unreliable, yet they proliferated because they were quick and cheap to make and could be produced in small quantities.

Later, a disk drive was introduced that allowed for larger games and faster load times. In the early days of disk drives for the VIC-20 and Commodore 64, floppy disk production in the UK was all done in-house, using 20 Commodore PET computers connected to Commodore 4040 disk drives. Commodore titles such as *Easy Script*, *High Flyer* and *Introduction to Basic* were produced this way. We

2   *Easy Script* did not need all the ROM in the cartridge, so rather than having random 1s and 0s in the remaining space, Tranmer programmed it to play 'Land of Hope and Glory'. The music, accessed by a secret keystroke combination, was played every hour at a trade show while the British Navy was on its way to retake the Falkland Islands.

could make up to 16,000 disks a week, which was adequate to meet demand since sales of the drives started off slowly. One man was hired to spend all day, every day, moving from machine to machine, removing disks, inserting new ones and typing 'copy' ...

PUBLIC RELATIONS HELPED CREATE THE MARKET

Commodore's approach to selling in the UK combined public relations with advertising. Some of the public relations activities were designed to get people to think about how computers could help them. In conjunction with *The Sunday Times* of London, we ran a competition called 'The Young Computer Brain of the Year'. Entrants submitted not programs, but ideas for how computers could be used.

One winning entry came from a young man whose idea was to benefit old-age pensioners by monitoring their daily activities. If the pensioner did not follow the usual routine, there would be an alert that help was needed. The submission included a hand-drawn illustration with labels on the loo, the kitchen and the TV. The alert on the TV said: 'Did not watch Coronation Street'.

By 1984, the Commodore 64 was selling at a phenomenal rate, outselling all other computers in the world. Its market share in its price range was 38 per cent, and it was voted 'Home Computer of the Year' for the second year in a row by a panel of computer magazines from seven different countries. The Corby UK factory had produced its millionth computer in just 15 months.[3]

THE INTERNATIONAL SCENE

By the time Commodore UK had moved offices from Slough to Corby, the need for the company to work closely with programmers was gone. Independent developers had formed publishing companies because of the success of the home computer market and especially

---

3   Not long before Christmas 1983, I was a guest on a UK radio phone-in show. The host asked me to answer the callers' questions generically, rather than be Commodore specific. The first caller started his question with, 'I own a Commodore 64 and was wondering ...'. The next caller hoped for a Commodore 64 for Christmas. After the fourth call began in a similar fashion, the host threw up his hands and shrugged. For that night, the show became 'The Commodore Hour'.

the Commodore 64. I was transferred to Commodore Electronics Limited (CEL) in Maidenhead to support Commodore's international distributors. The experience taught me that it is governments and not people that cause international tensions. For example, at distributor meetings, the Greeks and Turks always sat and talked together. Despite their governments' dispute over Cyprus, they had the most in common.

While working for CEL, I spoke at an education conference in Israel and, on another trip there, at a dealer meeting. The Israelis had classrooms full of Commodore 64s for students in primary schools, which led to many developers of education software for them. After a meeting at a hotel in Kiryat Shmona, near the Lebanese border, a developer invited us to dinner at his home, which was on the hillside above the fertile Hula Valley and looked across at the Golan Heights. They had three children and the home had four bedrooms. One was the parents' office, one the parents' bedroom, one the children's playroom and the fourth, which was built into the hillside, was the bedroom for all three children, chosen because it was bomb-proof. Despite living in a state of constant war-readiness, the Israelis were warm, friendly and forward-thinking.[4]

LAUNCHING THE AMIGA

Each year, Commodore participated in CeBIT, a technology exhibition that is still held today in Hanover, Germany. On the lower level of our two-story booth, the latest technology and applications were exhibited. The upper level was where the corporate executives held meetings and generally 'hung out'. (There was a full-service bar so there was a fair amount of 'hanging'!) At CeBIT in the spring of 1985, less than a year after Commodore acquired the Amiga, Gleadow asked me to go to Los Gatos in California for a few months to work with the development team for this new computer that would become the Amiga 1000. I welcomed the new challenge and the opportunity

---

4   Tensions in Israel were relatively calm during my two visits. However, while I was in the country, there were several bomb scares and an explosion in a bank in Jerusalem only 24 hours after I was in the area.

to get out of the Maidenhead office, where the man in charge was heavy-handed and a misogynist.

The company that developed the Amiga envisioned it as a games machine, while Commodore recognised that it would be too pricey for that market. The California-based development group worked day and night, seven days a week to get all the bugs out, while the East Coast management pressured them to be ready for a summer launch. This resulted in some friction, and I was to be a 'neutral party' liaison between the two.[5]

One of the key independent software developers for the Amiga was Sausalito-based Island Graphics, creators of *ProPaint*. Jeff Bruette of Commodore USA had been assigned to their office to ensure they stayed on target and to learn the ins and out of the program. Their product was critical to a successful launch event because it would be used in two of the most impressive on-stage presentations. Jeff went back east in June to teach Andy Warhol how to use the software since Andy was to do an on-stage demonstration of the Amiga.

By then, Carabiner, a production company in New York, was planning the Amiga launch event and I was making weekly cross-country trips. If it was Tuesday, I was sleeping on an American Airlines plane. The launch date was set for Tuesday the 23rd of July 1985, at Lincoln Center in New York. The invitations were out and the press kits prepared, but the hardware still did not run reliably and the software was fragile. At the tech rehearsal on the 22nd, three Amigas were connected to large rear projection screens on the stage, using prototype hardware called Genlock, of which there were only five in existence at that time.

When it was time for the morning dress rehearsal, only one of the three onsite Amigas would work. No one knew what had happened in our absence. Eventually, the engineers were able to solve the problems – which were discovered to have been caused by Genlock failures – and the final run-through went on.

---

5   I describe it as the summer when I 'tiptoed through the vice presidents', still reporting to Gleadow and officially employed by CEL, but seconded to the head of Amiga and to two Commodore VPs based in the West Chester headquarters in Pennsylvania.

COMMODORE BUSINESS MACHINES

presents

The World Premiere of

AMIGA

Tuesday, July 23, 1985

VIVIAN BEAUMONT THEATRE BUILDING

at Lincoln Center

New York, New York

Cocktails at 6:00 p.m.

Presentation begins promptly at 6:30 p.m.

black tie optional   R.S.V.P. by July 19

Please present

invitation for admittance.

The invitation to the industry launch
premiere of the Amiga 1000

Commodore staff at the
launch of the Amiga 1000

I resolved not to let those three Amigas out of my sight until the launch event was over. It would not have made a difference, but in my mind, I had to be there. I sent someone to the hotel to get me a change of clothes and waited out the afternoon by pacing around in the Vivian Beaumont Theatre at Lincoln Center.

The Amiga and projector operators and I communicated via headsets. The plan was that if any operator suspected he would need to reboot his computer, we could direct the projectionist to shut down that screen and switch to a working one. The curtain went up and all went impressively well. Although a few reboots were needed, no one in the audience was aware of the glitches. Most importantly, we had no computer or Genlock crashes.

Amid the speeches and technical presentations, there were two key demonstrations. The first was done by Andy Warhol, who used *ProPaint* on-stage to create a portrait of Debbie Harry. The second, the finale, was a Degas-inspired short ballet performance by Star Danias of the Joffrey Ballet Company. She then did a perfectly synchronised duet with her animated Amiga likeness projected on the screen behind her. The animation was made by Island Graphics from a video of the ballerina.

I cried when I saw the dance, but I suspect they were tears of relief as much as tears of joy. The Commodore Amiga had had a successful launch event.

THE AMIGA COMES TO EUROPE

With the launch and the first round of trade shows behind us, Commodore USA offered me a position in the US headquarters at West Chester. I convinced management that I would be more valuable where my European contacts could be used to recruit developers to write software for the Amiga, and went back to the UK.

By early December 1985, we had organised the first European Amiga Developer Conference (DevCon) at a Victorian hotel in Eastbourne on the coast of England. Over 300 developers from 100 different software companies representing 18 or more countries attended the three-day event. The Amiga gurus from Los Gatos and West Chester arrived in their silver Amiga baseball-style jackets with the red and white checked 'boing ball' motif on the back, ready to share their knowledge.[6]

The hotel in Eastbourne was extremely accommodating and helped us plan two memorable conference dinners. The first was a Victorian night at which the Commodore staff wore Victorian outfits. Following the cocktail hour, a butler formally invited everyone into the dining room. The printed menus included dishes named for Queen Victoria, Prince Albert and other notables of that period. The staff wore tuxedos or maids' outfits and served from silver platters.

The second dinner was a 'futures night'. Green cocktails with stirrers featuring the boing ball were served, and this time it was the Amiga's computer voice that announced dinner. The waiters entered the dining room dressed in silicon clean-room suits and carrying domed silver servers. They opened these to reveal tiny 'food pills' – Smarties candies – which they served to each guest. The real dinner consisted of dishes named for key members of the Amiga team. The centrepieces were red, white and silver balloons held down with red and white checked cubes. Soon a spontaneous challenge developed to see which table could get the balance just right so that their centrepiece would hover just above their table.

By the new year, Commodore's European subsidiaries were planning Amiga launches, the largest of which was in Germany at the Alte Oper opera house in Frankfurt. The production company for the launch event had hired actors to be a 'typical' family using the Amiga. It quickly became obvious that not only did they know nothing about computers, but they were unrealistic as a family. They were sent on their way and an interview with Commodore's German marketing director was substituted. The last-minute change meant that when the curtain went up before the live audience, we were running the complete show for the first time. Thankfully, it went smoothly.

---

6   The screen saver designed into the Amiga had the boing ball bouncing in random fashion on the screen. The checked ball was to be the Amiga logo, but shortly before launch Commodore decided it was 'too gamey' and changed the logo to the rainbow check mark. However, the ball remained the favourite of the original Amiga team.

Surrounded by friends and colleagues from
the Maidenhead, West Chester and Los Gatos
offices at the first European DevCon in 1985

In Basel, the Swiss tried to outdo the Germans with their launch,
while other countries simply held press events. I was asked to speak
in Belgium, and of course my talk and demonstration had to be in
English. Since it is a bilingual country, all the other talks were in
Flemish and French. I prefaced my remarks with an apology for using
English, but explained that at least they would only have to hear my
speech once.

One of my most memorable presentations was in Moscow in the spring of 1986, when Russia was still part of the Soviet Union. The main demonstration was to key engineers at GKNT, the Soviet State Committee for Science and Technology. Their official translator was sick, but our hosts, a company involved in British–Soviet trade, were able to get permission to use another translator. Every sentence was translated into Russian, but the translator often used the wrong words for computer terms. Each time he made a mistake, the audience called out the correct Russian word. It quickly became obvious that they all spoke excellent English.

In the belief that incorporating a few fun lines into a talk helps keep an audience's attention, whenever I did a demonstration, I varied the colours on the Amiga desktop and said, 'I always change the orange, because it is my ex-husband's favourite colour'. This translated into any language and always got a laugh.

CATS

In 1987, I was given the position of general manager of worldwide software and support based in West Chester, Pennsylvania. The group, named CATS (Commodore Application and Technical Support), was tasked with motivating third-party software and hardware add-on development, and providing technical support to those developers.[7]

CATS was a group with unique talents. The team understood the technology and the marketplace, and, most importantly, had good communications skills. Like the Amiga itself, they were often required to multitask, juggling several projects at once. Key leaders in the department were Carolyn Scheppner, who headed developer support, and John Campbell, who was responsible for Commodore-branded applications software. As more independent software companies began to write for the Amiga, we expanded our team and, of course, continued to hold DevCons.

---

7   One of the CATS team made me a letterhead that said, 'Chief in Charge of Miscellaneous and Assorted, Worldwide', joking that this was a more accurate description of what CATS was asked to do.

THE DEVCONS

These three-day long events were an opportunity for attendees to learn about hardware, operating system and user interface upgrades. They also provided feedback to the Commodore engineers regarding needed and desired improvements and enhancements. Sessions about marketing and distribution plans were also included and were attended by the owners and managers of independent software companies. Trip Hawkins and Bing Gordon of Electronic Arts, Kailash Ambwani of Gold Disk, Bobby Kotick of The Disc Company and Reichart Von Wolfsheild of Silent Software were among the most vocal in criticising – and sometime praising – Commodore.

With as many as three concurrent sessions in most time slots, organising these events was a large undertaking and was all done in-house by CATS staff. Lauren Brown, CATS' administrator, worked out the details. Pages of documentation and disks of examples and tools were given to each attendee. Incorporating relaxing and fun times was also essential to a successful DevCon – it was like planning a long-weekend party for 300 close friends.

Over the years, the atmosphere at the DevCons evolved. In a 1989 article in Amiga Plus magazine, I likened the conferences to musical styles. The first few were like folk music – friendly, happy and sponta-neous, with simple melodies and unsophisticated harmonies. By the sixth conference, they resembled big bands, fully orchestrated with close harmony brass and wind sections playing a swing rhythm. The analogy came to mind because those attending were all in tune and moving to the same drum beat.

Each conference introduced unique information about creating products for the Amiga and each had memorable moments.

For the May 1988 DevCon in Washington, DC, each member of the CATS group wore a red polo shirt with a small black cat painted on the left front. Even conservative John Campbell wore one. This was the conference at which the phrase, 'I'm hardware, she's software. No remarks,' was coined by Jeff Porter, Commodore's chief engineer, when introducing me – we were referred to as 'Father Hardware' and 'Mother Software'.

The hotel for the June 1989 DevCon in San Francisco had a pool

GOLD DISK
P.O. Box 789, Streetsville
Mississauga, Ontario, Canada
L5M 2C2
Phone (416) 828-0913
FAX (416) 828-7754

UNIVERSAL
ARCADE

'GAIL'
Diana 88
COMPLIMENTS OF
GOLD DISK.
DEC. 2. 88.

A cartoon drawn by an artist
at the Gold Disk booth at the
World of Commodore event

on the roof of a three- or four-storey wing, which seemed like a fun place to have a luau. No one had told us that San Francisco had the coldest summers in the US, but the developers went along with the request to wear their craziest beach attire. It was so cold and windy I considered putting on all the clothes in my suitcase, but settled on a Commodore hockey jersey. Willy Langenfeld of Jet Propulsion Laboratories won a prize for his outfit combining a Hawaiian shirt and shorts with cowboy boots, hat and belt. Kite flying was planned, but when the wind grew too strong, the engineers put helium-filled balloons on the ends of the kite strings.

Probably the most memorable DevCon moment was the live enactment of DMA Design's game *Lemmings*, published by Psygnosis in 1991. Bryce Nesbit, Amiga software engineer, aided by Carolyn Scheppner, acquired the costumes, props and 'actors'. Dressed in green yarn wigs and wearing pale blue bedsheets, the group came down the escalator single file into the area where the cocktail party was being held. Lauren Brown had the *Lemmings* theme music playing loudly as we proceeded into the room, up onto a chair and across a countertop, only to 'fall' into the imaginary abyss. To complete the image, balloons were popped so confetti could fly. The attendees cheered our performance. We were prepared to give the hotel staff a tip because they had to clean up the confetti, but they refused it, saying that they too had enjoyed the show.

When I got to the end of the counter and prepared to jump, I remember thinking, 'My, this is higher than I thought it would be.' In true lemming fashion, I went over the edge, saying, 'Oh, No!' as in the game.

THE CDTV: THE IDEA THAT DIDN'T SELL

In January 1990, wishing to be more business-oriented in its marketing, Commodore appointed Jeff Scherb to head CATS. Scherb's background was in database and data communications software.

When Scherb took over CATs, I was appointed director of special projects. I was responsible for applications for the CDTV (Commodore Dynamic Total Vision), an offshoot of the Amiga that ran CD software and could be controlled with a remote like a VCR. The focus was on applications for the family: education, information and games. Don Gilbreath was tasked with the hardware design.

Developers were excited because they saw the CDTV as an expansion of the home computer market, but without a huge start-up investment. The Amiga development tools could be used to create

Pretending to be
a Lemming at the
1991 DevCon

CDTV titles so their technical teams only needed to master the user
interface differences of the remote control. Whether it was a trailer
outside the West Hall at the Consumer Electronics Show (CES) in Las
Vegas or a suite down the street from the Olympia Exhibition Hall in
London, they lined up at the door to see this new hardware.[8]

The CDTV was launched at CES, Las Vegas, in January 1991.
Commodore was able to demonstrate 30 titles at its booth and
announced that there would be 100 titles available before Christmas
that year. Publishers of Amiga software such as Virgin Mastertronic,

8   Irving Gould, Commodore's major stockholder and chairman of the board, was a proponent
    of the CDTV. He said that it was the first Commodore product since the calculator days that
    he would be able to operate.

Mirrorsoft, Psygnosis, Spectrum HoloByte, Discis, Music Sales, Domark and Xiphias were joined by names such as Disney, Grolier, LucasFilm, Guinness, Cinemaware and Accolade. I had accomplished my task.

Nowadays we think nothing of saving files, music or videos to CD or DVD, but in the early 90s it took elaborate and expensive equipment to 'burn' a CD. Producing multiple copies, once a master was created, was inexpensive, but one-offs for testing purposes were costly – about $100 each, after the equipment was purchased. Commodore invested in the necessary equipment and made test and prototype discs for third-party developers.

The CDTV had come out of nowhere to rival Philips' CD-i. Executives from Philips visited the Commodore stand personally because they did not believe we could have so many titles so quickly. Their software development was hampered by a Hollywood mentality of big names, expensive licensing rights and costly production budgets. Having a unique platform without the development tools and experience available to Amiga developers meant that bringing a CD-i title to market was an expensive and slow process.

Neither platform succeeded. Commodore never put the marketing money behind the CDTV, and soon Commodore itself ceased to exist. Philips was the only dog in the hunt and failed to create the buzz necessary to have a new electronic device in universal demand. Perhaps if Commodore had continued then the competition between the two platforms would have created the market, just as the Commodore 64's competition with Sinclair and Atari during the home computer wars did. But perhaps we were both misguided about the appeal of the concept and it would never have been popular.

THE MEN AT THE TOP: JACK, IRVING, HENRI AND MEHDI

Up until his departure in 1984, Jack Tramiel, Commodore's founder and CEO, was the company's guiding light. A smart businessman, he wasn't afraid of a gamble. He was tough (his management philosophy was 'kick 'em or kiss 'em') but he had a sense of humour. Once, at a press conference, he announced that there were two forces in the computer industry, IBM and Commodore – 'big blue and the little fat Jew'. At another, he said, 'Commodore makes computers for the masses, not the classes.' He visited the UK every few months, and on one trip, at the end of a senior staff meeting, Jack asked if we had any questions. The director of finance said that it looked like Commodore UK would be making a big profit that year and wanted to know what Jack wanted him to do with the extra money. Jack reached over, picked up the paper bag that lunch had come in, smiled, and held it open in front of the man.[9]

Jack's departure, after a management dispute at the Winter Consumer Electronics Show (CES) in 1984, was the beginning of the end for Commodore. A succession of top managers who did not recognise the company's strengths outside the USA and who underestimated the marketing costs of getting back into the business market bled money away from Commodore's efforts to build on its strong positions in home computing and computers for the vertical markets (graphics, video and music). Moreover, most did not recognise the significant differences in Commodore's reputation and market position between the US, where it was seen as a low-end opportunistic company, and Europe, where it was recognised as a major quality technology player.

Some reports say that the problems in the US stemmed from the historically bad treatment Commodore gave its dealers as far back as its days in the calculator business. Others believe it was because the VIC-20 and Commodore 64 were distributed in toy stores in the US. This established a low-end reputation for Commodore that prevented it being taken seriously as the provider of a computer for productivity applications. Since the European subsidiaries operated in ways that meant these problems were not present in their markets, perhaps both are correct. Whatever the reason, Commodore reported in its own publications that 76 per cent of its sales were outside North America in 1989. By 1991, it was 85 per cent.[10]

---

9   The VIC-20 was called the VC-20 in Germany because 'vic' is a rude word in German. When it came time to name the Commodore 64, Jack directed the management team that the name was to 'start with Commodore, end with a number and have nothing in-between.'

10   Generating sales in other currencies but reporting financials in dollars made Commodore's balance sheets vulnerable to exchange rate changes.

Irving Gould with Commodore's
Mexican distributor and Kalish
Ambwani of Gold Disk

I never counted how many people occupied the top post after Jack Tramiel left Commodore. However, between the heads of the parent company Commodore International, CBM USA and CBM North America, management turnover seemed constant. Some of the changes were executives moving within the company – managers from Canada and Australia were transferred to try to shore up the USA operation, for example. Other changes brought in new people from outside the company. None stayed in their position long and none solved the problems. It may have been because of the lack of a plan, or the lack of patience to stick with a plan. It may have been unwillingness to put resources into a solution long enough for it to work.

Despite his privileged lifestyle and his private plane (flying to NYC from Toronto to land after midnight, spending two days in the Park Avenue office, then off to The Bahamas for the weekend and back to Toronto), Irving Gould, chairman of the board, was kind, down-to-earth and approachable. While in Mexico City to meet with our local distributor, he was not above riding in a minibus with the rest of the group. Rain prevented a planned trip to see the Aztec ruins, so we went to a bar to listen to a mariachi band and drink tequila slammers. Irving joined right in, even wearing a sombrero. At one point, he claimed he was a hypnotist and then demonstrated with one of the young women in our group.[11]

It is said that Irving was responsible for saving the company when it had financial troubles in the 1980s, but he was blamed for Commodore's eventual downfall as well. I believe his weakness was that he was a nice guy who knew that he did not understand the computer industry. As a result, he listened to and relied on others who told him what they thought Commodore needed to do to grow. Unfortunately, they thought the answer was business computing and did not have the global perspective that might have saved the organisation.

One of Irving's choices was Henri Rubin, who had been the Commodore distributor in South Africa and was brought to the USA to head technology. Henri believed strongly that IBM PC compatibility was essential to the success of the Amiga and backed the development of the Sidecar, a hardware add-on consisting of a PC compatible computer that shared the user controls and display of the Amiga.

Henri had two challenging management quirks. When he thought of something he wanted done, he assigned the task to whomever was sitting in front of him. As a result, I was given hardware tasks and engineers were given software or marketing tasks. We overcame this by passing the assignment on to the appropriate person.

Henri's second quirk related to time. He would say he would get back to you in a few hours, but it always turned into days, or more. We joked that South African time must be different from USA time, but we never found a solution to this and had to live with the frustrations of 'South African time'.

---

11   While in his New York office, Irving introduced me to the United Nations ambassador for The Gambia. I later found out that Irving was an unpaid business development adviser to that country and had invested in ventures to promote tourism there.

If Jack Tramiel was the beginning of the end, Mehdi Ali was the end of the end. After he was appointed head of Commodore International, the real downward skid set in. Working for Ali meant that we went to his office on Park Avenue, New York for meetings. The trip (by car, train and then taxi) took well over two hours from West Chester. Sometimes I would sit around the office in New York waiting to be called into the meeting, only to be told at mid-afternoon that Ali was not coming back from lunch and no meeting would be held. One has to wonder if it was a power game.

At first, I felt that Ali was a misogynist, although to be fair he seemed to dislike all of us at Commodore, male or female. He belittled some people and terminated others. For example, one of the key software engineers Andy Finkel, a quiet and hard-working guy, respected by the other engineers for his expertise, was summarily escorted out of the building one Friday afternoon. The axe fell in other places and morale dropped lower with each chop.

At the 'death watch vigil' party at the beginning of the summer of 1993, when they knew that the end of Commodore was inevitable, the engineers from West Chester burned Ali in effigy. My toast to the effigy was: 'Here's to the only warmth ever received from the man.'

HOW IT ENDED FOR ME

My 'reward' for recruiting so many to write applications for the CDTV was to be moved to a small office down the hall from my former CATS office and given nothing to do. By the end of July 1992, after 11 years with Commodore, my employment was terminated. Ironically, a few months later I was hired by OptImage in Des Moines, Iowa – a Philips-owned company that made an authoring tool for CD-i based kiosks.

In retrospect, I know I was one of the lucky ones. I left with a nice severance package and many happy memories. I had travelled to Israel with the Commodore 64, to the Soviet Union with the Amiga and to Australia with the CDTV. I had appeared on TV and radio in many countries, been interviewed for multiple publications, written my name on the wall of a restaurant in Braunschweig, Germany, been a superstar to young UK programmers, played broom hockey with Commodore Canada, and been a lemming. Along the way, I met

With the rest of the CDTV team: (L-R)
Louise Carroll, Mike Kurasawa, Roy
Strauss, me and Ben Phister

many interesting people, some who remain friends to this day, and had a few love affairs. While I wish the outcome had been different for Commodore and for the many of us that gave so much sweat and tears for it, I do not regret any of my time there.

Memories often are imperfect – especially after so long – but these are my personal recollections. The opinions and conjecture are also mine. Filter them through the sieve of your own experiences and knowledge. I apologise for any errors or omissions, but mostly I thank David Pleasance for giving me the chance to remember so many good times.

5

MY TIME AT COMMODORE GERMANY

PETER KITTEL

It was the mid 1970s, while working at a physics institute on my thesis, when I spotted the announcement of the Commodore PET in an electronics magazine. An all-in-one device, it was everything you needed at a very competitive price. Yet it took two more years before the first products shipped.

At that time, I had a few opportunities to try out some of the other computer models the PET would have to compete with, but none of them were really attractive to me – they were too confusing or too expensive, or you had to fight with some ugly line editor on a command line.

Then one evening, shortly after I had arrived home from university, my telephone rang and a colleague of mine shouted: 'I got it! It has arrived! My PET!'

He really had one! I immediately jumped in my car and drove the 30km to his home. There it was, as promised: all-in-one, everything waiting for me to take command.

And that screen editor! No tedious and ugly command-line commands – just walk around on your screen with the cursor keys, change a bit here, correct something there and then hit return. I immediately fell in love.

Plus it let you put cursor actions into a PRINT statement. So I instantly started putting together a small graphics demo program – OK fine, really it took me hours to get it working while giving the other guys their turns on the machine. But late in the night, at about 4am, they had to pry my tired fingers from the keyboard and send me home, as we all had to go back to work the next day.

The Commodore
PET 4016

I began to lobby for a purchase of a PET for our physics institute and eventually we got one. Then some years later, I got my first own PET – it was a 'fat' CBM 4016 model, used, which I instantly upgraded to a CBM 8032, a process that meant I was intimately experienced with the hardware and firmware of the machine.

While at university in Braunschweig – which happened to be the location of Commodore's production and engineering facility – I had my first contact with Commodore staff when the boss of the Engineering department visited some seminars. I tried to join them as soon as I finished my education – there was an open position in engineering – but some guy from our competing university institute was a few weeks faster than me and got it. Still, I went along for an interview and the Engineering boss asked me if I would join the Support department in Frankfurt – 'They need reasonable people there, too.' Up until that point, I had never even heard of the term 'support'. Nevertheless, a couple of days later I was part of it.

The knowledge I had gathered in my previous years with the PET helped me greatly at Commodore. My first task was to replace a leaving staff member who had done support for peripherals in the Systems area of Support. Systems dealt with the bureau computers of the CBM series, whereas the other part was called 'PC' – yes, PC! – and covered the home computers up to the C64. (The PC name had definitely been coined prior to the first IBM PC.)

So I would dive into the mail with questions about our printers and floppies. Manuals were a significant part of the job as there were new models of printer being released fairly regularly. That said, most of them were variants of existing models, so the manual only needed a few changes to existing text. The editing was done strictly on CBM 8000s and printed on our daisy wheel printer for the best printed look.[1]

Soon more manuals were needed for the PCs, the Commodore 16 and its sister models, and later for the Commodore 64's GEOS OS. I volunteered for that task and did most of the work. So, over time, my focus moved more and more onto manuals and documentation in general.

Those were the mid 1980s, a very active and developing time. People came and went and my bosses would change sometimes as often as every three months. (On average, in my time at Commodore, my boss changed once a year.)

Around that time we had our first try at UNIX systems (well, UNIX lookalikes) with the Z8000 prototype; then the Commodore PC, which ignored UNIX altogether; and some months later, news about the upcoming Amiga first arose. These were exciting times.

When we put together the manuals for the PCs I would be assisted by other staff members at Commodore – but when it came to the Amiga, I did most of the work alone. (Though I did not do the writing or translating all by myself – that aspect of the job was far too big for one person.) Raw translation was done by external companies, but nevertheless I reviewed every single word.

And boy did they have their struggles with these high-tech issues. Communication with the translation companies was put in the hands of our European headquarters, which was in the same building in Frankfurt, so I had to cooperate with them.

Our Support department was also responsible for demonstrating the Amiga at fairs, as well as at the big presentation in the old opera house in Frankfurt. And as I said, it was very exciting.

---

1   We also had an OEM plotter to generate PCBs, using software developed by my Braunschweig colleagues in Engineering. They used this to design the PCB for the first Commodore PC (a fact I only learnt much later).

Times were great, and the Amiga opened up more and more new areas, but the first model didn't sell that well. That was not such a big problem – at least Commodore in Europe also had its PC line, which sold like hotcakes. The sales statistics in Germany showed that during some months Commodore even outsold IBM, obviously because of the more attractive price and a reputation for solid and highly compatible (well, more compatible than newer models from IBM!) products.

The Amiga side finally gained more momentum with the introduction of the Amiga 2000 and Amiga 500. As I was still more part of the Systems side of Support, the manuals for the A500 were made by other people and I did those for the A2000. I repeated the same procedure years later for the Amiga 3000, and even later for the CDTV and Amiga 4000.

At that time, I was the longest surviving staff member in the Systems part of Support. I did not fight to become Support boss because I had realised early on that it was, as we say in German, a 'Schleudersitz' – an ejection seat – where you get fired for the tiniest issue, serving as a scapegoat. I had no interest in such a fate.

I once had some very serious insight into the communication style at Commodore. For some harmless issue, I was talking in a room with our German boss, when his telephone rang and *his* boss, Mehdi Ali from Commodore USA, was on the line. I began to leave the room, but my boss told me to stay to overhear their phone call. My ears probably turned red – every third word was a four-letter one when he talked about some other person. It was unbelievable. Yet it was fitting with the rumours I had heard about Ali and his 'style'.

In late 1993, news came up that Commodore USA was about to fold. Well, in Germany, and in Europe generally, we had done fairly well over the past few years thanks to very stable trading in business and home computers. Both were still alive and well here. They both had their problems, but generally when one part was struggling the other one had some money to earn and vice versa. Yet in the US they had totally lost their grip on the business sector, so every slight variation in the market shook them completely. There were also rumours about our top boss Mehdi Ali and his personal conflicts with business partners, which made things even worse.

Peter Kittle, today

So, Commodore Germany also had to call for liquidation, with a big amount of money in its bank accounts. But when you don't have a product to sell because your mother company has broken down, you can't continue doing business for long. (About that remaining money – there were fights among all the trustees for many years following. I don't know who got it in the end.)

For us employees, this meant we had to drive our business down. The liquidator did not fire us all at once but one by one, and the building became emptier and emptier over the days and weeks that ensued. Eventually I was the last remaining guy in Support, until in early 1995 it was my turn and I had to leave. Bye Commodore.

And that is the sad end of my Commodore tale!

6

DESIGN MANY, SHIP FEW

BETH RICHARD

COMING TO COMMODORE

I graduated from college in the middle of the Reagan years. There were plenty of jobs in the defence sector but hardly any in the commercial sector, so once I'd earned a degree in electrical engineering I got a job at General Electric (GE) Aerospace in upstate New York.

I'd had access to computers in high school and college, but once I was out of the academic environment I needed to buy a computer of my own. A college friend of mine had bought an Amiga in December 1985 and he showed it to me in the summer of 1986. Soon I was saving some of my pay cheques and investigating the best place to buy an Amiga of my own, which I finally did in December 1986.

In 1989, I joined a group within GE that made custom computer chips called application-specific integrated circuits (ASICs), used for networking hardware in the sonar systems of Seawolf-class submarines.

To build an ASIC requires significant investment to set up the tools used in the factory, but after that each ASIC is inexpensive to produce. That means the ASIC design must be as close to perfect as possible because of the expense of making a new design.

We were doing a large number of ASIC designs for the project, all with digital logic engineers who had minimal-to-no experience designing them. We worked with LSI Logic as our silicon ASIC fabrication factory (fab), and instead of sending dozens of engineers to their design centre to learn ASIC design using their processes and tools, they sent Dan Deisz, a field applications engineer, to train us.

Once we had completed the project design in winter and spring 1991, GE started laying off design engineers. I'd made it through several rounds of layoffs, but decided I'd rather control my own destiny than have GE's management control it for me.

I saw an ad in *EE Times* magazine for an electrical engineering position at Commodore to work on Amiga board and system ASIC design. I was a passionate Amiga user and decided I'd like to turn that passion into being part of the engineering team. Around that time I was on an internet mailing list with Linda Thomas, an engineer in the Product Assurance and Test group at Commodore, and we'd become friends. So I asked her what she thought of working at Commodore and she gave me some coaching about the interview and hiring processes there. My résumé reached Jeff Porter and I was invited in for an interview in the late spring of 1991.

I travelled down to West Chester on a Sunday afternoon to spend a full Monday of interviews with Jeff Porter, Hedley Davis, Dave Haynie, Greg Berlin, Joe Augenbraun and probably one or two more people who I can't remember. I should have learned something about the level of organisation at Commodore that day as no one had given me a time to arrive. Thus, I learned that Commodore was a bit more laid back than a defence contractor.

A week or so after the interview I received and accepted a job offer, so I gave my two-weeks' notice at GE. During that two-week period there was another round of layoffs – the list was made before I'd given notice, but my name wasn't on it. When I started at Commodore Engineering in July 1991, I found out that the next round of layoffs included my manager and the remaining team members. I'd left the defence sector just in time.

When I arrived, I joined the Multimedia Projects Team led by Hedley Davis, with Scott Schaeffer as the third engineer in the team. Our team reported to Jeff Porter.

CDTV-CR

Don Gilbreath's Special Projects team was put together to design small projects and do research into concepts that could be put into the Amiga. They came up with a machine based on the Amiga 500 that incorporated a CD-ROM drive when they were still very new, and this became the CDTV.

The machine they demonstrated to upper management was what I would call a proof-of-concept machine. Proof-of-concept means that it works but is not really designed to be a product. Typically it's an existing design that has things hacked onto it to give you a working machine and may also carry a lot of unneeded baggage from the previous design. You generally give a proof-of-concept machine to a product team whose job it is to come up with a design that's easy to produce in volume that incorporates all the hacks natively, leaving out the unnecessary baggage. A proof-of-concept is not intended to be a prototype for a product.

Apparently, the demonstration went so well that Mehdi Ali decided it should be made into a product and sold 'as is'. But since the design wasn't optimised for sale, it was costly to manufacture and had several daughterboards with bits of logic here and there that made it difficult to build.

CD-ROM drives were still very new at that point and were expensive, so Ali pushed Gilbreath for ways to reduce costs and the method they settled on was to buy the parts in volume to get them at a discount. As such, they built a lot of CDTV machines! Even then, the high materials cost meant that their sale price was also high. It was designed to look like a piece of stereo hi-fi equipment, so most of the expansion ports were on the rear of the machine, which weren't easy to access. With all those factors combined, it didn't sell well.

The CDTV concept was a good one, though, but it needed to be a purpose-designed product. So, Jeff Porter took on that project under the name CDTV-CR (with 'CR' standing for 'cost reduced').

The new version was designed to cost quite a bit less by having only a minimal number of boards and using a CD-ROM drive intended for use in audio equipment to save cost. It comprised a motherboard and an isolated board for the CD-ROM drive electronics, as well as a front panel for the user display and controls, and a video board that could be customised for either NTSC or PAL/SECAM video standards. The separate video board meant you could switch it out for different regions instead of having to support both on the motherboard, thus saving space. Space was at a premium on the CDTV-CR.

As with the CDTV, the primary input was an infrared (IR) remote control, and in fact the CDTV's optional IR keyboard and mouse were compatible with it. But there was also a front-mounted keyboard/serial port behind a small swing-down door, space for a floppy disk behind a pop-off cover on the front panel, an internal expansion card for more RAM and an IDE port to access a laptop-sized IDE drive that mounted to the underside of the bracket that held the floppy drive. Together with the Enhanced Chip Set (ECS) and Workbench 2.04, this was a pretty solid Amiga for 1992!

Hedley Davis was lead engineer on the entire project, as well as on the board and ASIC designs. Amiga system architecture includes a bridge to the custom chips (Agnes, Paula, Denise and their successors) from the rest of the system. This bridge is made up of a pair of chips whose initials are G and B, such as Gary and Buster, and later Gayle and Budgie. In the CDTV-CR, these were Grace and Beauty.

Scott Schaeffer and I backed him up on board design, and I did most of the design on the Grace ASIC while Scott did most of the design on the Beauty ASIC. The ASICs were designed to be emulated in field programmable gate arrays (FPGAs) and mounted into sockets on the prototype boards. Each FPGA cost a lot more than each ASIC, but an FPGA can be reprogrammed many, many times, and mere minutes can have elapsed between completing the schematic and programming the design into the FPGA. Using FPGAs as prototypes for the ASICs allowed the software developers to have systems working on hardware much sooner than waiting for full production ASICs, and also meant the ASIC design team could find and solve issues with the designs before committing to have the ASICs built in silicon.

We built the CDTV-CR prototypes with the FPGAs and got them working, and then went on to build a pilot production using ASICs fabricated by Commodore Semiconductor Group in a run of about 64 units. In order to enter pilot production phase, the design has to have been debugged and deemed production-ready. Then the manu-facturing process is debugged during the pilot phase in preparation for setting up full production lines at the factory.

At this point, Mehdi Ali decided to suddenly halt progress because there were too many original CDTV machines in stock in the ware-house that had not been sold, and he refused to let the CDTV-CR go to production until the older units were out of the warehouse. The efforts of dozens of hardware, fab, software, board layout, and mechanical engineers, along with all the other teams at Commodore, were put on hold.

I wasn't the only one who thought that the best thing to do was donate all those CDTVs to elementary schools across the country with an educational software bundle. Then at least all those kids would be asking for CDTVs for Christmas 1992, ready for us to sell the parents the better priced and more capable CDTV-CR.

But Ali wouldn't hear any of it. And in the end, the CDTVs sat in the warehouse for years and the CDTV-CR never went into production.

MOTIVATOR

Chris Coley had been working in the PC group at Commodore and was interested in graphics, so along with Joe Augenbraum he came up with an idea that would allow the Amiga to drive a very high-resolution colour monitor using a board plugged into the graphics expansion slot. They called it 'The Motivator', after the bits of technology in the *Star Wars* saga that were always the reason things failed to work.

The Hedley Hi-Res system at the time used a modified high-resolution greyscale monitor with a frame buffer added. This frame buffer had a scan converter to drive the monitor at full frame rate, and the Amiga would write into a portion of the frame buffer at full frame rate. The portions of the frame buffer that were not written were played back from the previous frame.

The Motivator did the same sort of thing but the frame buffer was on the expansion board, instead of requiring a custom monitor. The Amiga was set to a resolution that was very large, but even at the fastest pixel clock rate the Amiga could support, the frame rate was too slow for any monitor to sync to the graphics. So the slow frame was written into the frame buffer and played back at a high frame rate out to the monitor.

Joe and Chris built a wire-wrap proof-of-concept board and asked Spence Shanson in the software team to make a modification to the software to support this mode. Spence had told them it would take a couple weeks – but the next day he came back with a floppy disk in hand and said: 'Try this.'

It worked. But the proof-of-concept wasn't built for very high speeds. We would have to convert our wire-wrap design into silicon to really get the speeds needed. That's where I joined the story.

Given silicon speeds, we targeted a video output resolution of 1600x1200 at 12-bit colour (4 bits for each colour per pixel) or 1200x800 at 24-bit colour (8 bits for each colour per pixel). We figured out that we would need five ASICs on the board to load the frame buffer in, read it out, and handle the synchronising between everything. But rather than spend the money on five relatively small ASICs, I bundled the designs together into one mid-sized ASIC that had five config-urations depending on how the ASIC was connected. I created all the schematics and put together a simulation to verify that it would work. Meanwhile, Chris and Joe had completed the schematics for the board design. We were ready to go!

The ASIC also needed to be very fast! It was beyond the capabilities of the Commodore Semiconductor Group, so I reached out to Dan Deisz at LSI Logic, who was now the design center manager at the Bethesda Design Center in Maryland. I wanted to see if they would be interested in working with Commodore to build this ASIC. He put together a quote, which I passed over to Jeff Porter.

Jeff pitched the project to upper management, but never was able to get it approved for funding. Another cancelled project.

MPEG-4000

Jeff Porter was affiliated with the MPEG CD standards committee and came up with the idea of making a plug-in card that could decode MPEG video streams on an Amiga – this proof-of-concept was called the MPEG-4000.

Hedley was busy doing preliminary architecture work for the CD32 so he turned the project over to me. It was my first project as lead engineer at Commodore.

Jeff worked with LSI Logic to supply the audio decoder and with C-Cube Microsystems for the video decoder. The board had to take a data stream of MPEG-encoded video and output video and audio streams that could be mixed into the Amiga's video and audio, and it had a small FPGA that interfaced with the Zorro III bus on an Amiga 4000 to coordinate the decoder chips.

At the time I expected this proof-of-concept board to become the basis for a product for the A3000 and A4000. But once again, Jeff pitched the project to upper management and they declined to produce it. Another cancelled project ... for now.

PLANNING CD32 – AKIKO

Games consoles had a big boom in the early 1990s, and by early 1992 the trend was moving from 8-bit to 16-bit machines.

The Amiga was a 32-bit machine, and the CDTV and CDTV-CR demonstrated that it could exist in a form other than a typical desktop or tower. CDs had also gained enough popularity as a storage medium that it was clear the optimal way to store the OS along with the game content would be on a bootable CD. And so the CD32 was to be Commodore's entry into the gaming console market.

But to make an Amiga with a CD-ROM drive fit into a form factor as small as a typical console there had to be some changes. Jeff and Hedley proposed a new system ASIC that would incorporate the Grace and Beauty ASIC designs as well as both 8520 Complex Interface Adaptor (CIA) chips. This ASIC hadn't yet been named, but we had to get started on the design, so Hedley wrote 'Mehdi Gate Array' on the title block of the schematics, with perhaps just a little bit of irony.

Late in the development there were some connectors within the CD32 design that needed to be miniaturised as much as possible. Jeff worked with a supply chain manager in Commodore Japan to find the perfect connector, who asked that we name the ASIC after his wife 'Akiko' if he could find it. He found it, so we did. However, most of the

ASIC schematics were done by then, so 'Mehdi Gate Array' remained in the title block for most of the design.

Hedley was team lead: I integrated the Grace logic, Scott Schaeffer integrated the Beauty logic, and an engineer who had been working on the PC systems ported the 8520 CIA from a full custom design to a gate array design, and integrated that as well.

The top level of the schematic was drawn with four large blocks, one for each of the major blocks. Chris Coley and I had been working on a generic library of schematic elements that let us target different vendor's cell libraries by simply changing a parameter to the compiler and so we were able to compile each of the top-level blocks, individually specifying that the output netlist be compatible with the tools for loading the designs into FPGAs.

Hedley took that top-level schematic and turned it into a board schematic with four FPGAs on it that were connected in exactly the same way as the top-level blocks in the top-level ASIC schematic. The edge of the board had connectors with all the same signals as the pins on the Akiko ASIC. Although early CD32 prototype boards had an empty footprint for Akiko, all the signals matching the Akiko pins were brought to connectors to match the FPGA board. This was a new method because the Akiko design was too big to fit into a single FPGA, so the board allowed for four FPGAs to emulate a single ASIC.

CHUNKY TO PLANAR, CORNER-TURN MEMORY

Sometime in the summer of 1992, Chris Coley, Ken Dyke and I were eating sandwiches bought from a nearby deli at a picnic table near the Commodore offices at lunchtime.

Ken, a software engineer, had been looking into methods of porting programs from the IBM PC architecture to the Amiga. He explained that this was difficult because of the very different ways the PC handled the graphics compared to the Amiga.

Amiga graphics operated on several parallel image frames (planes), each plane containing a single bit of colour for each pixel on screen. So an 8-bit colour image would take up eight planes, and extracting one bit from each plane made up all eight bits for the colour. In the

IBM PC at that time, the colour of a pixel's bits were together in a chunk. So for an 8-bit colour image there is only one frame, but it is eight times larger than an Amiga plane.

Computer processors prefer to work with larger pieces of data. The Motorola 68020 used in the Amiga in 1992 and the Intel 80486 used in the PC clones of the same era were 32-bit processors, and they work efficiently on 32-bits at a time. But to convert software written for the PC clones' 'chunky' architecture to run in the Amiga's 'planar' system involves reading many chunky pixels and then rearranging bits within the 32-bit pieces so they can be written out as planes, which is very inefficient for a processor.

So Chris posed the idea of creating a small piece of logic that could reorder pixel chunks as pixel planes in hardware. And since it was in hardware we could make it do all the pixel rearranging at once, instead of the software having to reload the pixel chunks every time for each plane it worked on.

We came up with the idea of a small piece of logic that could be arranged in an array. The software could write pixel chunks into the array from one side edge of the array and then read out pixel planar data from the bottom edge. To do 8-bit colours, all the software needed to do was make eight writes, then eight reads. 12-bit colours were 12 writes, then 12 reads. It was a flexible design! I sketched it out on the back of a paper napkin and we pitched it to Hedley when we got back to the office. It could be added to the Grace portion of the Akiko logic. Hedley said he'd think about it.

The next morning, we came in to the office and, overnight, Hedley had designed the entire thing and the schematic page for it was done! This is the 'chunky-to-planar converter' or 'corner-turn memory' that was in the CD32, but not in other Amigas.

THE ARIZONA

By late 1992, we had the designs in the FPGA daughterboard and the system as a whole working well. One particular benefit to the FPGA daughterboard was that it was designed to fit inside the plastic case of the CD32, which meant that prototype CD32s could be built in a mechanically identical way to the production version.

The plan was to demonstrate the CD32 at the January 1993 Consumer Electronics Show (CES). Ali insisted the demonstrations be done with the actual ASICs and not the FPGA daughterboard. But ASIC design needs to be basically perfect when sent to the fab, and tests need to be developed for the factory to be able to sort out good chips from bad.

The ASIC design team was scheduled to deliver the design and test to the fab in something like March 1993. Ali's request to move things up the schedule in time for the January CES meant that the fab had to get started in early December 1992, and even then it was a rush order. We were fairly confident that the design of the top-level logic blocks was correct due to successful tests with the FPGA board, but what we hadn't tested was the single unified design of the top-level blocks and the connections between them. It was suggested that we send a release to the fab with no tests, just the design.

The deadline to send it to the fab was the 7th of December 1992. Hedley decided to name this version of the Akiko project 'The Arizona', after the famous US battleship that was sunk in the battle at Pearl Harbour, exactly 50 years earlier to the day in 1942 – it was a complete gamble that we'd get anything working back from the fab without testing, and he figured the project would be sunk.

The parts were delivered in the last week of December and they worked ... sometimes. We were most sceptical about the top-level connections since they remained untested in a system, and after a thorough review we discovered that the critical timing signal for the 8520 CIAs was connected to the FPGAs via an interface block that changed the phase of the signal (which was against a design rule we'd all agreed on when we decided to do the FPGA board). Since the ASIC didn't use these interface blocks and connected all the top-level block signals directly, the timing signal on the ASIC version was shifted compared to the FPGA version.

To get them to operate reliably, we needed to find a way to fix just two signals in the whole chip. Ideally we would have fixed it in the schematics, resubmitted the design to the fab (along with a lot of money) and waited several weeks for the corrected design to come back. But that wasn't going to happen.

Instead, the plan was to take the lid off the top of the chip package, cut the bad signal and replace it with a 'wire' connected to the good signal. Sounds easy? Well, inside a premade chip it's not!

In the end, a laser was focused on the place where the bad signal was being sent to each of the 8520 CIAs and carefully pulsed to knock off just a tiny bit of metal at a time until finally the signal was cut. Too little and the bad signal was still present; too much and the signals on the next layer down get cut. And all of this was done under a scanning electron microscope.

Adding the new 'wire' was done with focused ion beam (FIB) deposition. The FIB melts and evaporates metal into a gas that has been given an electric charge. The stream of charged metal gas can then be controlled into a beam that is focused where the new 'wire' needs to go. When the hot metal gas hits the surface of the cold silicon, it cools into solid metal again. The 'wire' was made by slowly moving the beam along a line from the good signal to the end of the cut that goes to the 8520 CIAs, leaving metal behind on the path.

The odds of getting both the cut and the 'wire' correct are very much stacked against you, but we managed to rework several chips in time to have a couple of working units at the January CES, and in the end, the CD32 was received extremely favourably by all those who saw it there.

After CES, myself and the rest of the design team went back to doing our job. We fixed the design error then built the tests and proved them in the simulation system. Akiko was then sent to the fab only a bit later than the original schedule (due to the time it took to deal with The Arizona). We were back on track for an autumn release.

CD32 FMV

While I was working on Akiko, some of the other engineers took a look at my design for the MPEG 4000 and used it as a reference design to create a full motion video (FMV) card that could be plugged into the CD32 to allow MPEG-encoded Video CDs to be played on the platform. It was basically the same design as mine but repackaged to fit on a plug-in card for the CD32 instead of the Zorro III bus.

'FUCKING OFF'

We used VLSI Technologies to fab Akiko. They charged a fairly high price to manufacture each chip, so by the summer of 1993 I suggested we look into LSI Logic as a second-source fab to see if we could get a better price. I called up Dan Deisz again and gave him the information he needed to know to make up a quote. He came back with a much better price than we were paying – about $10 less per chip! And with the volumes we were hoping to see on the CD32 this would have added up fast, so it didn't take much convincing to get management buy-in to agree to work with LSI Logic. I built out the netlist for Akiko using the LSI Logic cell library and shipped it to Dan along with the timing requirements.

A day or two later, Dan sent me back the actual timing information that was going to be in the chip. I looked it over and found an error, and then dug into it a bit and discovered a line in a timing file was off. But it was easy to fix! I could just talk Dan through it over the phone instead of having to resend everything. He said it wasn't a problem and would have it back to me the next day.

Well the next day came and went. Then the next. So on the third day I called him.

'Hey Dan,' I started. 'What are you doing with my design files?'

'Fucking off,' he replied.

'What? But working with you guys is going to save us a lot of money on every CD32 we ship! We need that stuff, and the sooner the better!'

'Oh, you haven't heard. Well, when our chief financial officer found out I was working on this for you she called up your chief executive officer to tell him she was happy Commodore was working with LSI on this chip, but asked if you could pay for the Budgie chips we made for the Amiga 1200 last year before we start manufacturing a new one. Your CEO told our CFO to "fuck off", so she told me to "fuck off" on your design ... so now I'm officially 'fucking off' on your design.'

What a wasted opportunity to save the company a lot of money! Suffice to say, it also destroyed our relationship with one of the most competent fab houses in the world at the time.

CD1200

For a while there had been talk of building a plug-in card for the Amiga 1200 to connect to an external CD drive that shared a lot of the electronics of the CD32, the idea being to allow the A1200 to run CD32 titles. In the late summer of 1993, I put together a pitch on exactly how we'd do that. Jeff Porter approved it and the CD1200 project was born.

Normally, this is something Hedley would have been in charge of. But by this time, Hedley had already left Commodore. There were many engineers leaving around this time as it had become clear that major changes were coming – whether it was reorganisation under new senior management, being acquired or the company being folded. With Hedley gone, that left me as lead engineer on the project.

My motivation for building the CD1200 was to show either a buyer or a replacement management team that Commodore's Engineering department still had a roadmap into the future, and indeed Dave Haynie was doing a similar thing with the higher-end Amigas.

The things that needed to be added to the A1200 for it to run CD32 titles included the CD-ROM drive logic and the corner-turn memory from Akiko, and a ROM with the software to drive them.

As we were also going to use up the big expansion slot, I thought we should include a Fast RAM expansion SIMM and a socket for a Motorola 68030 processor upgrade expansion. We planned to make a small ASIC on the expansion card that included a bus interface to talk to the A1200 through the trapdoor expansion connector, as well as the logic needed from Akiko, a RAM controller and the logic to let the 68030 take over as the expansion processor.

But there wasn't any money to make an ASIC, so instead we used the Akiko as is. We really didn't need most of the Grace, Beauty or CIA portions of Akiko because Gayle and Budgie and the two 8520 CIAs were already on the A1200 motherboard. Also, Akiko expects to be the chipset ASIC on the CD32's motherboard, so I had to create a design to make it think it was still in charge of the system. In reality, about 80 per cent of Akiko was wasted on that card.

I built the design into an FPGA along with the bus interface and the RAM controller, but because we had to fit Akiko *and* an FPGA, we lost the board area that I wanted to use for the 68030, so that feature had to go. A custom cable was attached to the board and it came out of the back of the A1200 and into an external CD-ROM drive.

The case for the first version of the CD1200's CD-ROM drive unit was made by cutting up prototype CD32 units and gluing them back together – I think we made four of those for our proof-of-concept. Later, we got some nicer-looking prototype units that were made by modifying the tooling from the CD32, and we made about 12 units from these using a whiter plastic to match the colour of the A1200 case.

Two of these prototype units were sent to the 1994 CeBIT conference in Hanover, Germany. But as all that was going on, signs that Commodore was coming to an end were becoming more visible.

All of the CD1200 units were lost to history, until one of the units that went to CeBIT was acquired by the Retro Computer Museum in Leicester, UK, in June 2017.

DONE

We all received an email on Monday the 25th of April 1994 from the Human Resources department asking everyone in the company to meet in the cafeteria at noon that Wednesday. I wrote back and told them that I couldn't be there at that time, so they asked if I could come to the HR office the next day. I said I could if it was in the morning.

That's when I received my layoff package from Commodore, just shy of my fourth anniversary at the company. The rest of the company received theirs on the next day, except for a few people who remained to manage the dismantling of the 40-year-old business.

I left the building to go to the airport for a house-hunting trip in Houston as I had just accepted a new job with Compaq Computers – I had intended to give my notice to Commodore upon return from that trip. But as ever, Commodore had other ideas.

Given the merits of the machine and the system, the Amiga could have been the front-runner in the PC wars of the late 1980s. The technology was superior, but upper management had no idea what they had in their hands.

COMPAQ

After Commodore, I worked at Compaq in the Consumer Multimedia Systems group. Another former Commodore engineer, John Barker, had gone to the same group. Compaq was palatial compared to the very industrial feel of Commodore towards its end.

I was hired to make a VGA controller that could output directly to NTSC or PAL, to be used in a computer designed for the living room – the 'Compaq PC Theatre'. At least, that's what they told me when they offered me the job. But by the time I arrived, they'd found a VGA controller that almost did the job. It needed some software help though, so my job was changed to write a 'hook' that let the graphics interrupt run, then go back and adjust all the registers in the VGA controller to get the timings compliant with the NTSC or PAL standards.

One day we got a visit from Ajay Bhatt and Bala Cadambi from Intel who were looking for people interested in their proposed 'High Speed Serial Interface' (HSSI), which was at revision 0.3. They designed it to replace dedicated keyboard and mouse connections, as well as printer and modem connections. This version was targeting a data rate of 1 Mbps.

From my experiences with the CDTV-CR and CD32, I knew that the data rate of a 1X speed CD-ROM drive was 1.5 Mbps. I suggested that they try to increase their data rate to support that in order to get audio and even MPEG video off of a CD, and they agreed. Then I mentioned a new standard was under development for something called 'Digital Versatile Disc' (DVD) that was going to use a data rate of 10.5 Mbps, and that it would be able to support high-quality video long enough for feature films. They agreed that this was important, but a harder problem to solve.

In the end they decided to support the different speeds using two slightly different protocols. They went home and worked on their spec for a while then sent us the 0.8 revision of the spec to review. By then, they'd changed the name of the system from HSSI to Universal Serial Bus – or USB. USB 1.0 has a Low Speed mode of 1.5 Mbps and a Full Speed mode of 12 Mbps. Such was my contribution to the forming of USB.

USB was very cool but beyond our delivery schedule for the PC Theatre. So I came up with a way to reprogram the keyboard and mouse controller in Compaq systems to allow for a new kind of peripheral bus, which we called 'Q-Port'. Compared to USB it was slow and clunky, but it had hot-plug support for both hardware and software, and devices could be added to the bus either by daisy-chaining from other devices already plugged in or via a hub device. It was inspired by some of the concepts of USB but could be rolled out by early 1995. It was useful for a living room environment, but USB would make it obsolete within a few years. My first patents were from the Q-Port and the PC Theatre.

I worked in Multimedia for just over a year before being given a chance to join the Enterprise Chipset Group. I liked designing ASICs so this gave me a chance to return to doing that.

Our group was very active in creating the PCI Bus specification. The chair of the PCI-SIG (Peripheral Component Interconnect Special Interest Group) sat just down the hall from me. I was part of the team that developed the PCI Hot-Plug standard and later the PCI-X standard. We were building system chipsets for large server machines that didn't have to be turned off to replace PCI cards, and with the PCI-X standards those cards ran at a very high data rate!

Later, I was involved in the designs for very large symmetric multi-processor servers with huge memory spaces. All of it was built with redundant backups so that repairs could be made without shutting down the machine – power supplies, cooling fans, hard drives, network cards, processor cards and even the memory systems had failover redundant support. A few more patents came from there. One of the two fab houses we consistently worked with was LSI Logic, where Dan Deisz had now become the vice president of Worldwide Design Centers. This industry is a small place!

I remained in this group at Compaq until after its merger with HP, who let us complete our project to work out the architecture for an even bigger multiprocessing machine which was some way finished at the time of the buyout. The machine was going to use PCI Express to connect processing, memory and I/O nodes in a large shared resource pool – but then HP cut the entire chip design group in Houston in 2003. HP had chip designers in California and Colorado and didn't want more in Texas. Compaq had a very large market share of the high-end Intel-based server market due to features and performance that only Compaq provided with custom chips delivered by the chipset group. The decision to cut the chipset group meant HP would use the same commodity chipsets that all the other server manufacturers were using. The consequences were that HP's server market share dropped to match the rest of the market.

TEXAS INSTRUMENTS

I landed a job at Texas Instruments in Dallas working in the Connectivity Group to build PCI Express products, although we were also very active in the USB specification process and contributed to the USB 3.0 spec. Our team was working on a mixed-signal USB 3.0 Physical Layer interface chip – I did the digital logic and worked with analogue engineers to build the design. Several more patents came from my work on some tricky bits in implementing data integrity checking in USB 3.0.

By 2009, the economy was in bad shape and Texas Instruments decided to do a round of layoffs. Their targets meant our group had to lose two people. They seemed to follow a 'last in, first out' principle, and as there was only one person in the group newer than me, we were the two who had to go.

INTEL

I applied to Intel at their Austin office, but with my background in chipsets, PCI Express and USB 3.0, they sent me to work at the company's Folsom Design Center near Sacramento, California.

I came to Intel to be the microarchitect and designer for the USB 3.0 port and Link Layer (the next two layers higher in the stack than the Physical Layer I'd worked on at Texas Instruments). Intel was *way* behind because the team that had been contributing to the USB 3.0 spec was just a research group and hadn't been sharing their progress with the design teams (conversely, at Texas Instruments, the design team was directly involved in the spec development). My designs were in the first generation of chipsets with USB 3.0 support and are still the basis for the USB 3.2 ports in Intel machines even now.

In 2013, I met Tom Piazza, senior fellow in Intel's Graphics Group, and he recruited me into his Graphics Architecture team. I was the junior architect on the Execution Unit (EU) team. The EU is the small processor inside the GPU that is laid out in an array and does parallel processing of the graphics shader programs.

Intel decided to cut costs by cutting employees in June 2015. Once again, I suffered the 'last in, first out' principle. This was two weeks prior to the Amiga 1000's 30th Anniversary celebration at the Computer History Museum in Mountain View, California.

CASTAR

I'd known of Jeri Ellsworth as creator of the C64 Direct-to-TV, a joystick with a Commodore 64 implemented in FPGA built into it that came with many games that was able to connect directly to a TV. She was selling it via QVC, which by 1997 had moved into the building where Commodore used to manufacture the original Commodore 64.

When I reached out to her to let her know she was very excited! We stayed in touch very sporadically over the years and finally had a chance to meet face-to-face at the Amiga30 event.

Jeri had started a company called castAR that was developing a set of augmented reality glasses. She was demonstrating her latest prototypes at the anniversary event – the same prototypes she was showing venture capitalists to get her series A funding for castAR. Luckily for me she was hiring, and so I joined castAR in August 2015 to work on the design of the chips for the camera pipelines. There were 12 people at the company when I got there – quite a contrast from Intel with its staff of 105,000!

The team got the technology to a point where we felt we were within a few months of being ready to go to production. We were growing quickly to get it all done, with the team reaching about 110 members at one point. The tech worked well and the app store and developer support community infrastructure around it was also coming together nicely. The only thing that didn't come together was the funding – castAR never closed the series B funding round, and operations ceased on the 26th of June 2017.

Beth Richard, today

FACEBOOK AND OCULUS VR

Facebook recruiters contacted me within a few days of castAR's closing to work on Silicon for Oculus. I started in August 2017, joining the Facebook Silicon team just at its very beginning. There is a lot of work to do as VR and AR products continue to push the boundaries of high performance and low power. I can't wait to see where we take the technology!

*

I've been quite happy with the trajectory of my career over the past few decades, but Commodore was instrumental in forming my maturation as a silicon design engineer. I credit people like Jeff Porter for his leadership and Hedley Davis, who always told me when I did something wrong but would make me figure out how to do it right. In fact, the entire engineering team at Commodore was something quite special and rare – if only the management had understood the capabilities of the team and the place they could have held in the industry. The entire computer industry would look very different today.

7

MEMORIES OF A YOUNG RECRUIT

MIGUEL DE GRACIA

I was fortunate enough to have the opportunity to work at Commodore Business Machines twice – initially as a summer intern in 1987 after completing my junior year in college, and later on as a young recruit, having finished my business administration degree at the university in 1989. I am originally from Madrid, Spain, so the opportunity to work at a foreign entity in an area that truly fit my career aspirations was a wonderful challenge.

My father used to be the managing director of the Commodore's Spain subsidiary and was a good friend of the managing director of the subsidiary in the UK, and it is thanks to this relationship that I secured my first internship. I guess I must have done well for them to want me back two years later!

What I recall the most about both experiences was the welcoming attitude of the team at Commodore. Here I was, a young intern from another country with a strong foreign accent, yet they welcomed me with open arms and made both of my stays truly unforgettable.

During my first phase as an intern I worked in the sales department, where my work consisted mainly of sales support, both from the office as well as out in the field. I often think that the company contributed more to my own learning of the business than I did to them, given my limited time there and the fact that this was my first work experience.

I was fortunate enough to be put up in one of the houses the company would rent out to executives staying in the area while their families were in another part of the country. That allowed me to engage more with members of the team and get to know them better. Imagine being a young person, fresh out of college, and being offered a job with a company car and a house to stay at, and all in a foreign country! I will always be grateful for what Commodore UK and its management did for me.

Those were during the years of Commodore's great successes with the Commodore 64 and the Amiga 500 – but it was during my second tenure in 1989, having completed my college degree, that I would truly experience how the company was flourishing.

I was fortunate enough to be assigned to the Key Accounts section in Sales. The department was working at its full potential – orders, activity, shipments, objectives being met ... You could sense the enthusiasm! We had an impressive Christmas holiday season of sales.

The great thing about Commodore is that its employees worked hard but also found the time to celebrate and make the most of those moments of brilliance. We would have conferences in London, group dinners, meetings, evenings out with customers ... It was very busy, but it was a lot of fun.

On top of that, I got to know the beautiful United Kingdom, learn its culture and understand the lives of its citizens. I would regularly go out in the field with other team members and travel to the Midlands and the North, and even to Scotland and Northern Ireland. We would visit customer after customer, but also find the time to dine out, and to meet and get to know many great people. I learnt about sales, about the importance of negotiation and knowing your numbers – and above all, how to hit those targets. I felt like part of a truly wonderful team.

In January 1990, I had to return to Spain for compulsory military service and leave my great friends at Commodore. They threw a good-bye party for me just before leaving, and I will always remember those last moments with my team. I had a true sense of pride, of belonging

Miguel De Gracia, today

to a family and of being part of a successful group of people – good friends such as Steve Franklin, David Pleasance and Kelly Sumner.

I have been fortunate enough to stay in touch with some of those people, and when we recall those years it becomes clear how a well-unified team with a common purpose can drive incredible results – and have a fun and family-oriented atmosphere at the same time!

My experience at Commodore UK played an important part in me being admitted to the Simon School at the University of Rochester for an MBA. And as a result, I subsequently joined SC Johnson and had an international career across Europe, the US, Caribbean, Africa and Asia. I am now based in the US as the CEO of Root Candles, a leading manufacturer and producer of candles.

I will always remember my wonderful experience at Commodore UK, its team, and the values of courage, the drive for results and the passion to achieve.

8

COMMODORE MEMORIES

JOE BENZING

In 1980, having developed an interest in computers, I sent off for my 1K Sinclair build-it-yourself computer. A few Sinclair Spectrums, Sinclair QLs and BBC Micros later, my wife and I attended a Commodore Amiga open event on a beautiful summer's evening in 1986.

The event was sponsored by Hobbyte/Busbyte computers with support from Commodore UK. It was here that I met Kieron Sumner and other members of Commodore, as well as the owners of Hobbyte/Busbyte, Linda Craig and John Jux.

I had a very strong artistic background (I attended the School of the Art Institute of Chicago before taking computer and business studies in the UK) and I turned up fully intending to purchase a graphics computer, with my choice being between an Amiga or an Atari ST.

Having watched the presentations – finding myself hooked by the bouncing boing ball graphics and sound demo – I decided on an Amiga 1000 with a 1081 colour monitor and 256k memory pack, plus Electronic Arts' *DeLuxe Paint* and *Aegis Animator*. When I approached my bank to prepare the draft to Busbyte, they thought I was crazy to spend over £2,000 on a computer – but it would turn out to be the best investment I ever made, and when my Amiga finally arrived, I was utterly enthralled.

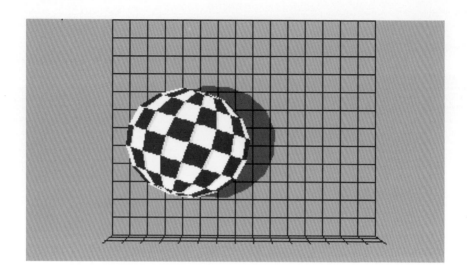

The famous boing ball demo

In 1986, Hobbyte held their second open day. At the time I was working for a multimedia company and was delighted to be invited along to demo for the Amiga. The product I was demonstrating was the DigiView, a colour scanner from NewTek (NewTek went on to become better known for their 3D animation package LightWave). It was at this event that Commodore invited me to do my first official show with them at a major UK computer event.

The relationships I was building within the industry were growing (I had formed strong relationships with NewTek, Aegis and Sunrize Industries too, among others), and during my stay with the Amiga Centre Scotland, I recognised the importance of good relationships with Commodore developers.

I was offered a job as a demo Amiga employee closer to home at Hobbyte that also involved selling other computers. The job kept me close to Commodore, which turned out to be very beneficial when the company's technical support manager, Barry Thurston, contacted me to ask if I would be interested in a position at the newly established Commodore Marketing International.[1]

---

1   Setting up Commodore Marketing International was one of Mehdi's bigger mistakes – see part 1, chapter 10, 'A comedy of errors – Our Industrious Leader, Mehdi Ali'.

I visited the new offices and was offered a job as an Amiga consultant, offering my opinion and seeking software applications for the Amiga.

One particular application I spent a lot of time on was *Amiga Vision*, a multimedia presentation solution. It was script-based, meaning you had to have some programming skills to use the software to its full capacity. Then along came *Scala*, an excellent multimedia solution for interactive presentations that allowed you to include animations, video, sound and photos.

Commodore president Mehdi Ali soon realised he had made a mistake as the International Marketing Division was not delivering on its promise to unite the marketing activities of the subsidiaries, so he closed it down. However, as I had been doing well, I was offered the opportunity to apply for a position within Commodore UK.

My interview was with Dawn Levack, Commodore UK's marketing manager for both business systems and consumer products. The position on offer was product marketing manager for business systems products, which at the time included PCs and the Amiga 1000. I was offered the position the same day, and it was a role that mostly only really required common sense. I reported to Dawn and worked with Terry Cooke, who was business systems sales manager.

I retained this role in the marketing department until June 1987 when Mehdi Ali appointed Steve Franklin as managing director of Commodore UK. When Steve arrived he brought with him an entourage of salesmen who had no experience with the Amiga, only PC compatibles, peripherals and software. He proceeded to dismiss all prior business system salespeople with the exception of Kieron Sumner, who was left responsible for the Amiga 1000, and Peter Talbot, who continued to head up Education.

I was transferred to the tech support department where I reported to Barry Thurston, who had recruited me into Commodore Marketing International in the first place. I was very happy about that move; I had immense respect for Barry.

It was a special day when the Amiga 500 was launched in the UK as it offered much of the Amiga 1000 capabilities but at a much lower and more affordable price point.

Amiga 500 sales had been amazing and the UK was the number one market for Commodore worldwide – successes that had much to do with David Pleasance and his team, of course.

*

One highlight from the many demonstrations we gave potential customers was a presentation for McDonald's that required an interactive workflow where the McDonald's menu would be shown, and I was given the responsibility of putting something together.

This brought some issues as the food had to look on the computer screen like it did in their stores and advertising, which of course were real photographs and therefore much higher quality. I was supplied with photos of the food, some logos and, of course, Ronald McDonald.

The first thing I was required to do was determine how to put the presentation together, but this was made considerably easier using *Scala*. Management at McDonald's briefed me on what they wanted – a slide show of products and an interactive ordering system incorporating the menu of meals – and I set to work.

It took me two weeks working flat out to put the demo together back at Commodore, and in the end I was finished just two days before I was due to present in central London. The scans of the various artwork they provided were particularly tricky to capture as I was limited to just 16 colours, even on an Amiga 2000 with a high-resolution monitor.

When I found out all the heads of McDonald's were due to attend the presentation, I was nervous to say the least. On the day of the meeting, I walked into the boardroom to find all the global heads of McDonald's, including the president.

I kept the equipment simple – just an Amiga, the monitor and some speakers. I started up the Amiga, launched *Scala* and let the demo run, showing off the interactive menus that displayed the various meals.

The whole room was very impressed that a computer could do this, and after the demo their technical folks wanted to know how it was done. They were impressed with the Amiga and *Scala*, and although they sadly decided not to go ahead, to my delight the demonstration led to several more trial runs of Amiga and *Scala* in the London area.

*

I've always been interested in being able to record video and sound together on a computer and edit in real time, and the Amiga had some rather crude solutions. Then, in late 1993/early 1994, Digital Processing Systems sent me their Personal Animation Recorder (PAR) expansion card. This piece of hardware could record frames rendered in an Amiga animation package onto a hard drive for the user to play back in real time and in broadcast quality.

This solution created sales for the Amiga in London's West End. I had the pleasure of demonstrating this solution, and customers would enjoy building an animation and rendering to the hard drive. Then it occurred to me that it would be nice to record video to the hard drive, so I setup a LaserDisc player, the PAR card and a Madonna music video, and began to record. It was fabulous when playing back, but there was no audio. So I installed a Sunrize Industries audio card inside the Amiga and, using ARexx,[2] I wrote a script to have the audio card and PAR card work together to record the video and audio in real time.

I was blown away as I watched Madonna singing 'Like a Virgin' in real time. Sure there were some audio sync issues, but this was a first on the Amiga, and it later led to sales for this exceptional computer in the video studio market.

I remember going to the BBC around this time to show this off and, impressed, they said: 'Get the editing and sync of audio and video sorted and we are interested.'

Sadly, by the time those solutions were due to be developed, Commodore went bankrupt, and Apple and the PC moved into that space.

In 1990, when David Pleasance left Commodore UK having been promoted to general manager of Commodore Electronics Ltd based in Basle Switzerland, he would come regularly to the Maidenhead offices for meetings with his international customers (he would

2   ARexx is an Amiga variation of IBM's REXX programming language, and was written in 1987 by William S Hawes.

Joe Benzing, today

occasionally ask me to do graphics work for him, which I enjoyed immensely). Meanwhile, Kelly Sumner took over the running of the consumer division in his place.

In 1992, shrouded in all sorts of allegations, Steve Franklin unexpectedly left Commodore. Around that time, David was appointed to vice president of Consumer Products at Commodore Inc, the US sales company, which he had been chasing for some time.

Eventually, Kelly Sumner took over as managing director of Commodore UK and remained there until early 1993, at which time David came back to become joint managing director with Colin Proudfoot.

I recall a time of great pressure when I was writing and doing many of the graphics for the CD32 launch presentation at the Science

Museum in London in July 1993. The event had suddenly been brought forward from its intended launch in late spring/early summer the following year.

The show was a veritable who's who of top retail buyers and software developers, and involved the Amiga press as well as TV and radio. Chris Evans, who at that time was an up-and-coming TV/radio DJ, was co-presenter with David.

The launch was a huge success, mainly because we had managed to keep our development of the world's first 32-bit CD-based games machine a complete secret, so the retail buyers were blown away that we had product that would be in their stores in time for Christmas.

The tragedy that transpired later is well documented – despite selling 100,000 units in Europe, Commodore International went bankrupt in April the following year. David and Colin did their best to keep the UK operation running, and I helped them with their presentations to potential partners to save the Amiga platform. But finally, after 14 months, they had to shut it down.

Commodore, and particularly the Amiga, are directly responsible for the career successes I've had in the computer business – in the end, Digital Processing Systems offered me a position in Europe, where I ended up building a number one sales market for them in Russia.

The Amiga truly was an amazing computer. Thank you, Commodore.

9

HOW THE AMIGA CHANGED MY LIFE

FRANÇOIS LIONET

Computers fast became a passion for me in 1981 when I got my first machine, a brand new Ohio Scientific Superboard II. Finally, I could create my own video games just like the simple tennis games of those early consoles that my brother and I had spent so much time on, or the fabulous tank game I built as an electronic kit.

It was goodbye Fischertechnik, scotch tape, soldering and wires; hello spaceships, meteorites, *Star Trek* and moon landers.

I must have programmed six different games in that first year with the Superboard II – in BASIC at first, and then, once my own assembler in BASIC was completed, in machine language. With its 6502 microprocessor and video memory of 32x32 letters, on the Superboard II I was free, and I had all I needed to create the *Star Trek* ships, tanks and cars I wanted to include in my games.

I began attending classes for my prep year of vet school in 1981, mostly to please my mum. But when I wasn't in class I was programming – I would program in the evening, in-between exams, in Maths and in English courses.

People would come to my room to play my games and have so much fun, and seeing someone play and enjoy my creations made me incredibly proud. I would watch with delight as they fell into the traps I had set … and with dismay when the program crashed as they encountered a bug.

The prep year passed quickly. I passed the exam with flying colours and joined the Lyon vet school for four years of study – which, of course, meant four more years of programming. Courses were not mandatory, so I dedicated all of my afternoons to my passion.

As a result of not attending the courses I of course didn't learn anything. But I knew my mother would have been so disappointed if I did not get my diploma – so I cheated! (Apologies to any honest vets I stole a job from!)

By the end I was a real pro at cheating. In my final year I created an FM radio system complete with microphones and ultra-discrete headphones – wires the breadth of a hair – that I and some of my friends used to pass the exams.

For written exams, I hid a microphone with an FM transmitter behind the blackboard of the amphitheatre to transmit the subject from the exam room to an accomplice in a car outside. He would then look up the answers and speak them into his own FM transmitter, which would transmit into our invisible headphones.

It even worked for the dreaded meat inspection orals, which we passed with flying colours. Oral exams being public, the accomplice would just sit in the amphitheatre, listen to the subject and transmit the answers via an FM transmitter hidden in a folder, as if he was rehearsing lessons. It was quite an experience to stand in front of your teacher while someone whispers the answers in your ear.

My first commercial game, *Driver*, was programmed on an Oric-1, a nice little machine with 48k of ram, eight colours and a 6502 processor. A replica of an arcade game, I programmed it in the afternoons of my first year at vet school.

My brother used to say that it was the only good game I made, and I tend to agree with him. It had movement and nice scrolling, it was progressive and fun, and it even had entertaining music that I composed myself.

I sent the game to a couple of publishers and the response was positive – one of them offered me 'four games to choose from their back catalogue' in return for the publication. Clearly sensing the geek

The Oric-1

in me they thought I would be easy to exploit. I should have kept the paper ...

In the end I decided to publish with Dialog Informatique, who offered me a 15 per cent royalty rate and a publication contract. The game sold at more than 2,000 copies, which was very respectable, and paid for a whole summer of skydiving, my other passion at the time.

I programmed various other games on the Oric-1 and the Commodore 64 over the four years of vet study, but one game in particular was very special.

Every September, the 4th year students welcomed new students – or 'poulots' – with a full week of parties and games. One of the games was a treasure hunt with challenges that sent you all over school.

I made one of the challenges on a Commodore 64 – a game I called Urinary Survey. The poulot was tasked with implanting a probe into the urethral canal of a moving cow on screen. The Commodore 64 was hidden under the table, and with my feet on the F1, F2, F3 and F4 keys I could make the cow move and react. F4 made the cow piss at the student, which happens in real life. Welcome to vet school!

After I left vet school I joined JAWX, 'France's first game creation group' – a big title for such a small team. The group logo was a shark.

JAWX was started by Jacques Fleurance and Frédéric Pinlet, two young businessmen, fresh out of school, who wanted to make video games. And although we did not speak the same language, we got along well. They would come up with the basic idea for a game and I would implement it – Frederic or I would make the graphics and music was provided by Jim Cuomo, who composed the music for Defender of the Crown.

I am quite a clumsy person who tends to speak with large gestures, and as a result things often seem to fall down around me. Each time I visited them in Paris I would always make something fall, including a whole shelf that fell on Frédéric's glass desk. Then one day when I visited them they had removed every object from my reach and kept a constant eye on me while I was there!

I programmed *Cock-in* for the Oric-1 (renamed *Chicken Chase* in England as the title was considered far too rude for the English market), and *Katuvu*, *Serenade* and the bullfighting game *Olé* for the Commodore 64, which was fun but arguably too complicated. I was particularly proud of the routines of the bull, who I programmed to get nervous among other things.

At one point, JAWX decided to port *Olé* to the Amstrad CPC 464. Jacques and Frédéric, whose knowledge of computers and programming didn't stretch far beyond what they had learned at school, chose two polytechnicien engineers to do the port, who wanted to cover the cost of their summer holiday with the job.

I was impressed at first, and they seemed perfectly suited to the job – until they explained the method they wanted to use for the conversion.

According to them, the simplest method would be to create a C64 emulator on the Amstrad CPC 464 and run the original source code on it. Well of course, such a method was doomed to fail. *Olé* was a large program that used most of the memory of the C64, and it would have been impossible to host that plus a C64 emulator on the Amstrad.

I tried to explain that it would be impossible, but they held fast. It is well known in France that the mind of a polytechnicien does not work like a normal mind, and that they always choose the most difficult approach. Well, this was a perfect example. I was laughing inside, thinking about their future next months in hell.

It would have worked fine initially. After a couple of months' work on the 6502 emulator, they would have seen their first pixel move across the screen (although there were no hardware sprites on the CPC 464 so they would first have had to program a sprite engine as well). They might even have had a bull on the screen. But that would be all. A complete video game – particularly this one – is a mountain of intricate complexity, and their poor emulator, which might have worked on the mainframe computers they were used to, would fail miserably in real life.

There was no news for a month, but then came the confirmation I was after: 'They were late; they had to choose another algorithmic approach.' I thought it was hilarious.

Eventually they finished the adaptation, but it was very late. I don't know if they went on holiday in the end or if they had to stare at the green monitor of the CPC 464 all summer instead of the blue sea ...

STOS

At the end of 1986, Jacques and Frédéric introduced me to Constantin Sotiropoulos, a Greek programmer with a heavy accent, for a 'secret project' they had in store.

At the time I needed to be close to Paris for my work, so I had moved into a first floor flat in Maison-Alfort with three of my friends from vet school, who were studying a tropical medicine specialisation course. Carine, my girlfriend (and future wife), would visit on the weekends from Lyon.

The secret project was for the Atari 520ST, a new machine that was gaining popularity in France at the time (the Amiga was not yet available), and sought to replace the graphical interface of the ST – that I hated for no real reason – with a DOS-like command line system, and add a coding language similar to Microsoft BASIC. Constantin was hired to program the DOS environment and I was hired to program the coding language.

I was in my element.

The first tasks you had to achieve on a new machine at that time were always the same: create a sprite generator to display graphics, create a sound generator that runs under interruptions, create routines to move the sprites and animate them and so on – in other words, you have to create the engine. Then, with game-oriented instructions driving the internal sprite engine, music and sound instructions, you had everything you needed to do what I loved: create games.

This new ST operating system – or *STOS* – was taking shape as the first real language to create games. It contained many features that seem normal to programmers today but were new at the time. It had a memory bank to store game resources, a sprite editor and a music editor, and support for extensions: machine language-coded libraries that added new instructions to the already huge instruction set.

The product was finished by the end of 1987 and published by WIFI International. It was a total flop, selling less than 10 copies. But the failure was mainly due to the packaging, which was too serious, and the basic imbalance of the product – the DOS command line is

An advert for *STOS*

quite complicated whereas BASIC is quite simple. You cannot sell a product that claims to be complicated and simple at the same time.

But Jacques and Frédéric did their job well. They took *STOS* to England and shopped it around several publishers, eventually coming to Mandarin Software in Manchester. There they met Christopher Payne, the CEO, and Richard Vanner, who was to be my project manager for many years and became a good friend.

They were both amazed by our demonstration of the BASIC, with sprites flying under interruptions over an editable source code, and immediately saw the potential of the product for the English market. But it had to be revamped and presented as a game creator only. England was far ahead of France at the time in terms of personal computing thanks to the BBC and its computers – people wanted to make games and they wanted to program, and *STOS* was the perfect tool.

Mandarin removed the DOS part of the product, helped me redesign the interface and reprogram the sprite editor and the major accessories to make them more user-friendly, and assigned a real author to write the manual. Throw in some well-produced graphics for a fun-looking box, and *STOS* was reborn.

And it was a big hit. It was launched at a computer show and you could see people sitting in the hallways reading the user manual and discovering all the cool things you could do with sprites and sounds. User clubs were created, public domain games were released and a whole community of *STOS* users were born.

But while my product was a success over the channel, I barely knew it, isolated as I was in France in front of my computer. The only thing I received were good royalties and bug reports – kilometres of faxes from Richard Vanner!

I carried on my freelance work – such as a port of the brilliant *L'Arche du Capitaine Blood* (aka *Captain Blood* in the UK) on IBM PC and Commodore 64, during which time I met Yves Lamoureux (with whom I later formed the software company Clickteam – and after *STOS* came *STOS Compiler*, which increased the speed of the games by a factor of three.

Then the Amiga arrived on the market. Although it was very expensive in France at first, it was nevertheless heralded as a 'dream machine', and in England of course it was a massive success. So in 1988, as the popularity of the Atari ST started to wane in the UK, Christopher Payne asked me to port *STOS* to the Amiga. I accepted immediately.

It was a big jump from the Atari ST, and with delight I started to learn how to use the Amiga's custom chips – Denise, Paula, Agnus and the Copper coprocessor. It had real sampled sounds in four voices, and sprites filled the screen in brilliant colours. The Amiga was a revolution.

AMOS

I programmed *AMOS* during my year of military service in 1989 in my hometown of Metz, in the east of France. I had been assigned as a vet and my job was to visit the kitchens of the regiments to inspect their cleanliness. In truth, I had to pretend to know my job a lot better than I did, but if it became too complicated or serious for the animal I would admit I knew nothing and suggested calling another person!

Metz was a military town and had many barracks in the suburbs, but as it was my hometown, I spent much of my time at my mother's house. I had Amigas both at home and at the barracks so I could continue programming in the evenings and at the weekend. Every day at 7am I would ride on my moped in uniform to the barracks with the last modified code on a set of floppy disks in my pocket.

AMOS took shape in-between the many German Shepherds I tended to and the many dirty kitchens I had to report, each time making the cook furious. I ported all the cool features of *STOS*, rewriting the code instead of copying it, making it work better with more possibilities. One of the major features of *AMOS* was the interrupt driven animation language (AMAL), which was an enhanced version of the ST routines.

The product was released at the end of 1989 and was the big hit of my career. But again, I did not know it in France. It taught programming to thousands of kids and many of them thank me today. Even my current boss Hogne Titlestad, the founder of Friend Corporation in Norway, learned to program with *AMOS*. A massive amount of games have been published in the AMOS PD library and the AMOS club had several hundreds of users. It was a real success.

AMOS Compiler was the next product I coded, this time in Paris where Carine and I settled for two years. Then came *Easy AMOS*, *AMOS Professional* and *AMOS Professional Compiler*, all programmed entirely in pure machine language.

I was also a journalist writing about *STOS* and *AMOS* in various magazine columns (up to 18 pages per month). My dog Daisy even had her own column in *Amiga Dream* called 'Daisy Demos', which were simple and impressive effects in *AMOS* 'programmed by my dog'!

But every good thing comes to an end. In 1993, the Amiga was on the decline in the UK and I had to move onto the PC. Writing software was my profession and not a hobby – I could not stay on an abandoned machine.

So I contacted Yves Lamoureux and asked him if he wanted to make a game-creator system for Windows 3.1. He accepted, and *Klik & Play* was born – but that is another story.

The Amiga changed my life, as it changed the lives of millions of people. For the first time a computer could display real colours,

François Lionet, today

real full-screen animations and produce TV-quality content. It was a glimpse at the future of computing, a future where things could be both simple and powerful.

And indeed, the Amiga keeps on changing my life. I now work at Friend Software Labs with Hogne Titlestad and David Pleasance where we are making the computer of the future. It won't be an Amiga but it will contain the same spirit of simplicity, creativity and power.

I will finish this chapter with a thank you. Thank you, David Pleasance, for making the Amiga a success in England, thus allowing me to write *AMOS*. The butterfly effect this machine has had on the entire computer industry will become more and more apparent as the years pass. The Amiga spirit will never die and computers will once again be fun and simple – this is the promise we have made at Friend.

In the meantime, Hogne and I have made the decision to program *AMOS 2* on our spare time. It will be compatible with the original

AMOS programs, offer all the power of Friend in a 'future mode' and run inside a comfortable development environment. Watch this space.

I am now living my dreams in Norway as part of a fabulous start-up company with the potential to really change the world of computers. For the first time in my life I am part of a team and I am really happy. And all this I owe to the Amiga.

Thank you Amiga, my Friend!

10

DEATH BY MANAGEMENT, CUSTOMERS AND USERS

WIM MEULDERS

Like everyone else growing up in the eighties, I knew Commodore thanks to the Commodore 64, which was by far the best home computer in those days. It was a huge success, but that success inevitably went away, and by the time I had started at Commodore the C64 was a memory from the past.

Unlike with the C64, there was significant competition for the PC range. But nevertheless, Commodore Belgium had moved successfully into the PC industry, and by the time I joined in 1990 they had made it into the top-three PC vendors, competing with the likes of IBM, Compaq, Olivetti and Philips (none of whom, you may notice, are still active as PC vendors today).

How I got hired by Commodore is a story in itself.

A couple of months prior to joining, I was finishing my international marketing bachelor degree at Antwerp Business School in Belgium and managing a student newspaper. I was called up by Commodore asking if we could search for a student to present the Amiga multimedia computer at the Bureau'89 fair.

So we placed an ad in our newspaper looking for student presenters and received quite a few replies, but no one was good enough for Commodore. As we were working on a 'no cure, no pay' basis with

Commodore, I finally applied myself, and to my own surprise (I had never presented anything before) I was hired to do the job.

It was crazy. Every half hour I would show the capabilities of the Amiga to a flabbergasted PC audience blown away by the graphics, sound and video possibilities, which were miles ahead of any PC at that time. At a time when PCs were running white text on a black screen in MS-DOS, DR-DOS or other DOS, there we were with a multitasking graphical power PC. The slogan 'Only Amiga makes it possible' was no lie.[1]

Right after the fair ended, ComputerLand approached me and offered me a job as their marketing assistant, to which I agreed. Then some months later, I received a surprise phone call from a headhunter asking me to come and talk with Commodore.

Apparently I had made a good impression on the managing director of Commodore Belgium and he wanted me for a permanent position at the company. Well they didn't need to ask twice – though the fact that they were offering double what I was earning at ComputerLand helped a bit!

Those early years for the computer industry were marked by fast cars, big parties and a fortune to be earned if you hit your targets. Commodore was no exception, and after a year I was making over €5,000 a month and driving a Saab 9000 Aero, living life in the fast lane – all in my early 20s.

Although by outward appearances all seemed to be well with Commodore, internally it was a different story. These days I work as a business consultant and interim manager, and I often look back on my time at Commodore as an example of how even a well-known company with good products can be ruined if they don't adapt fast enough to a changing market.

Instead of adapting to new market rules, management were concerned mainly with increasing their own personal profits. Meanwhile our customers were abusing the products for tax evasion and users

---

1   The 'Only Amiga' song from the movie we played during the presentation still plays in my head to this day. You can listen for yourself here: https://www.youtube.com/watch?v=PWeO5IkCssk – but watch out; you won't get it out of your head!

were pirating software, which resulted in independent software vendors turning their backs.

In those early years at Commodore, every quarter was the same: the first month would be spent cleaning up the problems from last quarter; the second month was party time; and the third was heavy working to get the numbers in. I had built up a channel of resellers and every quarter they would happily buy their stock for the next quarter.

But then came the first clone PCs and dealers could buy them at much lower prices. At first this didn't pose a problem because we were Commodore and our quality was much better – up until the day it emerged that our keyboards were manufactured by Mitsumi and our monitors were made by Philips, while of course components like the CPU and hard drive came from Intel and WD or Seagate. So the only real differentiator was the motherboard, but that wasn't really much better than some Taiwanese products.

Finally, in June 1993, Commodore hit big trouble again. The clone PC industry had really taken off, and we just couldn't compete on price and specifications anymore.

To give you an idea of how fast it went, we had set up a travelling roadshow on an NMBS (National Railway Company of Belgium) train going to all major train stations so their employees could buy a PC at reduced prices. It was an enormous success with many thousands of pieces sold – but two years later people were still paying off their by-then outdated PC, and by that time you could already buy a much better PC for half the price.

But Commodore International didn't have an answer. And even though sales in Belgium were still going strong, one day in June 1993 we were all called into the managing director's office and, one by one, fired. Our team of more than 30 people was reduced to around 10 and we were going to leave the PC industry completely.

As I was by then in charge of the Amiga product line and had received extensive leadership training, I was promoted to sales and marketing director for Belgium, and as a young rookie at 24, I inched closer to the powers that were.

This is my story of why Commodore as a company went out of business on the 29th of April 1994.

The infamous *X-Copy*
piracy software

PIRACY

A big problem with the incredibly successful Amiga – aside from the fact that the guys at the head of Commodore didn't know how to position it, leading to an Amiga 3000 designed for high-end video being positioned next to an overpriced but underspec'd Amiga 600 designed for games – was that game and software copying was rife.

In the short-run this was good because it drove sales of the hardware – why spend €2,500 on a PC when you could go out and buy an Amiga 500 for €699 and – provided you knew someone who could copy them for you – have all the games you wanted at your fingertips. But as a result, while the install base for the Amiga was high, software and games sales were not in-line.

Professional software vendors like Scala Computer Television (a company I worked at after Commodore) tried to prevent piracy by selling dongles – hardware that you would have to connect to the serial port to get a piece of software to work. Commodore also tried to fight back by offering Amiga packs that came bundled with software, but the problem remained huge. But for most Amiga software vendors, piracy was taking away profit and making development for Amiga less interesting.

Piracy was an issue on IBM-compatible PCs too but the install base there was much bigger, and in the end software developers would bring out their games on the PC before the Amiga and other platforms.

DISTRIBUTION TAX EVASION

Another big problem was that the distribution channel back then was full of cowboys trying to make a quick buck, and that sometimes led to hilarious situations.

I remember one day we were completely fed up with a small retailer who owned four stores. Every couple of months they were selling Amigas at ridiculously low prices, and we assumed it was stock coming from Germany or another big country that was dumped on the Belgian market.

One day they were again selling Amigas to end users at prices that were too low, but this time they had priced the A500 lower even than the price at which we were buying them internally. Our managing director decided he'd had enough of it and ordered me and three colleagues to go to the four different stores to each buy an Amiga 500 each so we could check the serial numbers and start building a case against the subsidiary that was dumping the products on our market.

I remember the day I came returned to the office with an A500 in my hands as if it was yesterday.

I entered the managing director's office. He took the box from me and typed the serial number into the AS/400[2] system on his desk. His face turned white.

'This ... this can't be! It's one we sold ourselves!'

When my colleagues came to him with their A500s, the same thing happened – they had all come from our own stock.

Our managing director picked up the phone and called the trader who had bought the 500 pieces that included these models 'for export

---

2   The AS/400 was a popular business computer from IBM. Introduced in 1988, it survived until 2000, when it was replaced by the IBM eServer iSeries.

to Poland' and subsequently claimed he didn't know how they had ended up back in Belgium.

Poland was not yet part of the EU back then, and many Amigas from Western Europe were sold to end-users in Poland – but certainly not this batch. It had ended up back in Belgium at cheaper prices than we had sold it.

How was this possible? A tax fraud now known as 'VAT carousel'.

VAT carousel fraud – or missing trader fraud – occurs when a company sells goods to a foreign country and then recuperates the VAT. In a 'VAT carousel', this VAT recuperation system is abused to recuperate the VAT by 'officially' exporting the goods when you are in fact keeping them inside the country or bringing them back in illegally. It was a time when borders in Europe were still closed and customs could be bribed to look the other way.

In this specific case, the Amigas were exported and illegally reimported more than once in order to recoup enough VAT to get the price down so low. We never found out if the trader was involved or not, but the system had also been used to bring down the cost of CPUs and flash memory, and many Belgian wholesalers and traders were caught.

Of course, this price difference caused honest resellers and retailers a lot of problems as end users didn't understand why a big official retailer was more expensive than a small dodgy retailer. As a result, serious resellers began selling alternate brands and mass retailers were getting very low margins, even on an exclusive range like the Amiga.

MANAGEMENT

End user piracy and corrupt distribution channels were not the only – or even the main – factors that caused Commodore to file for bankruptcy in April 1994. There was something very wrong with Commodore's management.

Commodore Belgium was dependent on Commodore Benelux in the Netherlands, and after my promotion to sales and marketing director in June 1993, I was put in regular contact with my Dutch counterpart Tjeerd-Jan 'TJ' Smit.

One day we were both called by Mehdi Ali to come to New York to discuss the business in the Benelux. Just two days prior to our trip the meeting was moved to London, so we booked new flights and arrived in the UK office for a meeting with the big boss.

I have worked with many CEOs in my career but none have been quite like Mehdi. As anyone who has met him can attest, this small man (he can't have been much taller than five feet at a guess) was something special.

As we were waiting to be seen, an Australian colleague who had just had a meeting with Mehdi told us he was going straight back to the airport for his return flight having only flown in that morning – although Mehdi had changed the meeting location to London he had decided not to pay for anyone's hotel room. The poor guy had to travel half the world and back to meet Mehdi in the space of about 48 hours.

Finally, we were called in. Normally when you meet someone you start off with some sort of introduction, but not so Mehdi Ali. Instead what we were greeted with was a half-sitting, half-lying man behind a desk, with a cigar poking out of his mouth.

'Which of you is from the Netherlands?' he shouted.

Neither of us had even sat down yet, but nevertheless TJ replied, 'Me?'

Mehdi suddenly erupted, furiously shouting, 'WHERE THE FUCK ARE MY MILLIONS?!'

Bewildered, TJ replied, 'I don't know.'

'You have to know! Everybody in Holland must have known Bernard was stealing from me!'

'I really don't kno—'

'LIAR!'

This went on for several minutes until Mehdi finally changed the subject and got back to business.

It turns out that shortly before our meeting, the managing director of the Amsterdam office, Bernard van Tienen, had been kicked out of Commodore, as Mehdi had just discovered that he had been creating fake Commodore companies to invoice from one company to the other, creating false turnover and shipping the goods to his own warehouses elsewhere.

There was not just one fake company but an entire series, and when van Tienen had run out of names like 'Commodore Computers', 'Commodore Holland' and 'Commodore the Netherlands', he just called them 'Commodore Alpha', 'Commodore Beta', 'Commodore Gamma' and so on. As a result, he was able to reach his targets and get bonuses on 'pre-sold' sales that were basically done to another Commodore company.

A year later, when Commodore went bankrupt, the liquidator in The Netherlands sued van Tienen personally for 300 million guilders (around €150 million).

Having employees on his side was probably the reason van Tienen had been able to hide his scheme from Mehdi, whose reaction and anger towards TJ was so real I'm quite sure he wasn't aware of it. But by the time van Tienen had been found out, he had already left and started up a retailer called The Champs.

This soon entered into its own difficulties and was later taken over by Escom, a computer company that was founded by Manfred Schmitt, ex of Commodore Germany. Escom of course went on to buy the Commodore and Amiga brand names in 1995.

THE END

In a last attempt to avoid bankruptcy, Commodore's loss-making PC division was closed in June 1993 and all bets were placed on the Amiga CD32, a revolutionary 32-bit game machine. But it was too little too late.

I remember going to the European Computer Trade Show in London in September 1993, where Sony was showing the first PlayStation behind closed doors. Yes, we had a lot of software titles at launch, but most of them were old A500 titles burned onto a CD with little or nothing new. Nevertheless, we went all-in on the CD32, with large store displays, a TV commercial and so on.

But at the launch event in Belgium – shortly after I had done a TV interview talking about how great the CD32 was – I received a phone call from Mehdi telling me it was over for the Belgium office and we were to close the office in April.

If you take a look at Commodore's figures, you can see what a roller coaster it was:

Year	Turnover (US$)	Profit (US$)
1990	$887,300,000	$1,500,000
1991	$1,040,000,000	$48,200,000
1992	$911,000,000	$27,600,000
1993	$590,800,000	-$356,500,000
1994	$70,100,000	-$17,500,000

Source: https://dfarq.homeip.net/commodore-financial-history-1978-1994/

After the closure of Commodore Belgium in April 1994, Mehdi asked me to stay on board as he had a plan to found a new Amiga company in Belgium with the help of Daewoo, and he needed me to keep the Belgian market 'alive' in the meantime. This was rather difficult without new products to sell, but Mehdi was quite sure it would happen. So I moved to the Dutch office, which was still open, and spent quite some time in Amsterdam with a couple of colleagues who didn't have a lot to do either.

Soon after I started in Amsterdam I had an insight into how Commodore International worked. Alongside Bernard's series of companies under the Commodore name was a strange company called Commodore Air – an airline company owned by Commodore. Commodore Air had bought a new private jet to fly Irving Gould between The Bahamas, Canada and the US (if he spent more than three days in a country he would have to pay taxes). It was sold only a year later for just 15 per cent of its value … to himself.

Commodore did pay well but no one can explain why in 1990 Mehdi Ali earned $2 million and Irving Gould earned $1.75 million while IBM chairman John Akers earned $713,000. IBM was already a much larger and more successful company back then – it made a profit of $6 billion in 1990, versus Commodore's profit of $1.5 million.

It's a good example of what happened to the money when Commodore was still very profitable. While the margins were being reduced for the reasons mentioned above, management weren't able to resist using the company as a money machine and continued to leech funds at a time when Commodore needed the cash to answer the changing market.

And they weren't the only ones; some people earned a lot of money privately with Commodore Amiga. If only some of that money had stayed in the company and we had had a CEO with proper vision, the history of Commodore Amiga might have been much longer.

Even now, more than 20 years after the bankruptcy, the names Commodore and Amiga are still alive, and I am very proud to have been involved with this part of computer history.

-11-

IT'S ALL IN THE VALUE

KIERON SUMNER

I was quite happy in my job working for Hattori UK, the Japanese giant behind the Seiko and Pulsar brands. My job was to plan, implement and oversee projects involving computer systems design, so I would work with mainframes and minicomputers, and when the PC was launched I quickly became involved with that powerful new office tool too.

But I was unsettled one day in 1985 when the sales director suggested that I should be in sales. This was a career path I had not really considered, but it got me thinking. He was hinting for me to apply for a job in his team, but instead I looked for an opportunity outside Hattori, and when my younger brother Kelly – who already worked at Commodore – pointed me towards an advert in the *Daily Telegraph* for someone to join Commodore Business Machines to sell an exciting new product called the 'Amiga', it seemed like the only option. Of course, it helped that my brother already worked there, and he lent me an Amiga 1000 for the weekend so I could learn all about the product. I was hooked.

After an interview with the totally eccentric Chris Kaday (who was acting managing director at the time), I was offered a role looking after the south of England. Armed with the Amiga 1000 and a few brochures

I hit the road, visiting every likely computer dealer in my extensive area. But selling a computer with no peripherals and no software was hit-and-miss at best – and in the early days, more miss than hit.

It quickly became obvious that what the Amiga needed was software, as apart from the powerful *Deluxe Paint*, *Deluxe Music* and *Deluxe Print* trio from Electronic Arts that were bundled with the computer, there was very little else. These products were powerful but left the user feeling frustrated, because at the time we had no medium to save any projects or files onto. As a business tool, the Amiga had little support from the mainstream software community, who saw it instead as a bit of a toy and so focused all of their efforts where they would see the greatest return – on the PC platform.

It was incredibly frustrating trying to sell a product that had amazing power and versatility, but fell just a little short owing to the lack of software and peripherals.

Of course, Commodore also had PC clones and the highly successful Commodore 64 to sell, but we always had one eye on the star in the stable: the Amiga.

It was at about this time – and excuse me if my chronology is a little out – that two major milestones were reached in the history of Commodore UK.

Firstly, there was a major shuffle of staff, with Chris Kaday leaving to pursue other interests and the charismatic and larger-than-life figure of Steve Franklin and his entourage from Granada Business Centres joining to take the helm.

Secondly, two new products were introduced into the market: the Amiga 500, with a design and price point aimed unashamedly at the video games market; and its big brother, the Amiga 2000, an expandable desktop ideal for developers and applications that could take full advantage of the Amiga coprocessors.

At the same time, the UK video game market started to get behind the Amiga 500, attracted by the opportunity to bundle their products in packs such as the Batman Pack. Meanwhile, a growing band of geeks, nerds, visionaries – call them what you will – saw the power and potential of the Amiga as a superb graphics delivery station, both for productivity and for developing niche applications.

Soon the Amiga 500 was seen as an amazing gaming machine, and started its rise to dominance as the UK's number one games computer, with a cult following that would be the envy of other manufacturers, including Atari.

On the other side of the business, the Amiga 2000 had established the platform as a serious contender for specialist applications, including wireframe animation, weather forecasting, titling, presentations, music, imaging, ANPR (yes, you can thank a couple of guys at Guildford University and their Amiga for the Automatic Number Plate Recognition system in use today) and a host of other vertical applications.

As a result, Commodore UK, led by Steve Franklin, changed its structure to a Consumer Division, whose primary role was to create and maintain a channel to market that included retail, mail order and distributors serving independent retailers; and a Business Division that had a similar remit, but with additional focus recruiting value-added resellers and LGEM (local government, education and medical) dealers.

Both had one goal – to sell volume product – and while the Consumer Division did this with creative marketing and strategic alliances with major video games houses like EA, Ocean, Activision, US Gold, Core Design and others, the Business Division's job was oceans apart. While we had no shortage of clever and exciting business applications being developed, they were generally very specific and did not sell much hardware. Commodore USA wanted volume and they really did not care where it came from or how we achieved it. And so, while my colleagues in the Business Division, such as Barry Thurston, worked on some very clever applications with organisations such as Scala, I stepped back and took a leaf out of the Consumer Division's book.

I had been told early on in a sales training course that you need to fulfil customers' needs, and frankly pushing the Amiga 2000 with no killer software was not going to fulfil anyone's 'needs'. So I started to talk to some of our distributors and retailers and asked how we could make this a product they would be happy to sell and which, more importantly, their customers would be attracted to buy.

After a while, I had a brainwave: reduce the price of the A2000 by removing the hard drive but still give them a medium to save files on in the form of an extra floppy disk drive. As it was effectively a reduced version of the A2000, it made perfect sense to name it the Amiga 1500, bridging the gap between the A500 and the A2000. The last job was to decide what we should put into the bundle, and after some planning and talking to software houses we came up with a great mix of gaming and productivity software.

The finishing touch was the full name: 'Amiga 1500 – Personal Home Computer'. This was a machine aimed at the home user that was both educational and fun, and designed to attract parents. It was not just a video games computer.

We had some amazing packaging and literature designed, and the result was a success with almost every retailer and mail-order company taking the product, and all of our loyal distribution partners.

The computer press began to talk about the product and wanted to know where it was designed. We all kept tight-lipped and said nothing, creating a little mystery around the whole project that ultimately helped drive sales. The UK was the only country that ever had the Amiga 1500, so some sources started rumours that it was produced exclusively for the UK, which of course it was.

*

On the other side of the Business Division we still had the unenviable task of trying to sell the PC clones, which were a little overpriced and under-specified, and had to contend with the amazing success of Alan Sugar's Amstrad PCs.

We had a few small wins but really we were second fiddle to the other PC brands, and with the Amiga 500s recent successes we were mocked by our PC resellers as being merely a 'games computer' manufacturer.

Of course, we were, and a bloody good one at that, but it would not help us sell PCs ... or would it?

We decided to segment our PC range and jazz it up a bit. With this in mind, I came up with three new brand names: KeyLine, SlimLine and ProLine. These mirrored the look and capability of our product

The Commodore PC-20

range at the time, but were based on the Intel processors used in the XT (8088), AT (80286) and 386 (80386).[1]

I wanted a piece of this market, so once again I talked to my key customers to see what we should do. With their feedback, the team came up with three Commodore PC starter packs: the PC-10, the PC-20 and the PC-30. These were distinguishable by the colour-coded end-strip on each pack (turquoise, purple and yellow, respectively) and the packaging for all matching peripherals were similarly colour-coded to make it easy for the dealer and the customer.

It was still early days in the home productivity market – before the release of Windows – so all users would see when they powered up their computers was an intimidating command prompt. We wanted to take away a lot of this fear, and so we worked with a software house to design a simple menu system and preloaded all of the software onto the hard drive so that when the customers turned the computer on they would simply have to select their required application – spread-sheet, database or word processor – from the menu.

---

1   Faster, newer chips were being introduced, but the XT was seen as the volume seller – particularly in the home market, which is where Amstrad was making major inroads.

This of course presumed that they would know how to put the computer together, so the next step was to script and produce a video explaining how to do it. With the help of our marketing agency and the Services Sound and Vision Corporation,[2] who donated the studio time, we put together a production team with the intention of making a humorous instructional video that would be both entertaining and educational.

We enlisted the acting talents of Tim Brooke-Taylor, who played the inept boss, and Joanne Campbell, who played the competent and long-suffering PA, and filmed our short instructional video.

Finally, as the computer industry was notorious for using jargon that totally baffled the average consumer – terms like RAM, ROM, FSS, BIOS and so on – I set about compiling a short A to Z of computer jargon.

We were almost there, and with the addition of retail packaging and some amazing marketing materials, the product was launched. The concept was simple and it worked to perfection, enabling us to sell volume and at last become accepted a serious supplier of PCs.

Because this was not a Consumer Division product, we had a relatively limited budget, so when it came to the retail packaging, which we had decided to illustrate with photographs representing different professions, we made the controversial decision to involve our own staff. So we had each person dress up as a nurse, an electrician, a builder, a professor, a secretary and so on. This was lots of fun and saved us loads of money!

Things went well for a while but storm clouds were gathering. But this didn't stop us planning ahead, and with the future of Commodore Inc. in the US and Canada looking decidedly gloomy, the UK operation, led by joint managing directors David Pleasance and Colin Proudfoot, led a bid to buy the global rights to Commodore and the Amiga. One facet of this plan was to ensure the future of the Amiga by producing a product nobody had seen that was not on the market – a tower-based Amiga designed to use previous Amiga

2   The SSVC were also our customers and ran shops in all the UK military bases overseas.

motherboards such as the A500, A600, A500+, A1200 and beyond, and expandable to incorporate the Motorola 68030 processor or even faster chips as they became available.

We worked with German company Mikronik on the design and fabrication, and arranged to meet with them at the CeBIT exhibition in Hanover, Germany.

A group of us from Commodore UK, including David Pleasance, John Smith and myself (apologies if I have not mentioned anyone else who was there) sat in a small coffee shop at the edge of the hall and met with the two designers. They walked in with a small trolley and our 'baby' covered in a blanket. When they uncovered it I remember thinking, 'If the customers walking past us only knew what we were looking at, they would be amazed.'

It was a fantastic product – beautifully simple – and now all we needed was a name. With my marketing head on, I came up with 'Amiga Infinity', as the product was infinitely expandable and gave the user infinite options. It was designed to be marketed and sold through our independent dealer network, who were perfectly equipped and capable of offering this long-term upgrade path to our very loyal Amiga user base.

Alas, this product would never see the light of day, as the UK's bid to purchase Commodore – which would have secured the future of the Amiga on a global basis – was scuppered by German company ESCOM. And the rest is history.

*

In the days leading up to the closure of Commodore UK, rather than being gloomy about the prospects of breaking up a great team of people, David Pleasance suggested we do something as a sort of last hurrah. So after talking with my colleagues and the great Peter Brameld, we came up with the idea of creating a company to hold an Amiga exhibition – there was certainly interest from the European community, as well as from the press.

And so World of Amiga was born, with myself and Peter as the two directors and main organisers. We hired Wembley Conference

Kieron Sumner, today

Centre, publicised the event in all the Amiga-related press (at a heavily discounted rate), and even purchased the bankrupt stock of Amiga products from retailer Rumbelows, who had just ceased trading.[3] With the help of the rest of the sales team we even refurbished the whole stock so exhibitors would have stock available to sell at the show.

3   The Rumbelows sites were also taken over by ESCOM, a move that proved to be one of the reasons why ESCOM ultimately went out of business, taking with them the Amiga.

After a few days of building the stands and preparing for the big moment, the morning of the show arrived, and we turned up early at Wembley hoping that all of our planning had not gone to waste.

As Peter, David, myself and the rest of the team turned the corner, we could not believe our eyes. The queues of customers waiting for the exhibition to open was around the block. The show had completely sold out, and both exhibitors and customers left the weekend-long event happy and wanting more.

Sadly, it was only a very short time later that the bid to buy Commodore fell through at the last hurdle, and the doors closed for the last time.

*

My time at Commodore was probably the most fun I have ever had in a job, with a great product, great colleagues, amazing contacts in the software and publishing industry, and customers who were open to new ideas and opportunities. Sure, it was hard work and frustrating as hell at times – particularly with a couple of personalities in Commodore head office – but I feel privileged to have worked with such a great team and to have had the opportunity to be creative and in some small part carve my name in the Commodore history. And given the chance, I would do it all over again tomorrow.

12

A LOVE LETTER TO AROS

STEPHEN JONES

Author's disclaimer: I have tried to ensure the information in this chapter is accurate to the best of my abilities, but as it's a long time ago now some dates may be a bit off.

It all started in 1986. I had been a roofer for 12 years by that time and was working on a job over in Twickenham, just outside of London. I had given up computing at school as I wanted to go off and earn some money – mainly to buy a motorcycle and impress the girls, which of course didn't really work.

On a lunch break one day, I went down the road and came across a small computer shop that just happened to have an Amiga 1000 in the window playing the *Juggler* demo. I was transfixed – I could not believe what I was seeing. At that time I was still using the comparatively simple Amstrad PCW 8256, with a ZX Spectrum long-since consigned to the cupboard. The PCW was fine for my purposes – it did my accounts and letters and I could experiment on it, plus I was not really into games anyway so didn't need the horsepower – but nevertheless, I wanted the A1000. But I knew I could not afford it, and put it to the back of my mind.

A short while later I was at a computer show in London and saw the A1000 being demoed again. I was in awe as I saw the Workbench of AmigaOS in action and listened to the mysterious bouncing noise. When the Workbench screen was pulled down to reveal the boing ball my reaction was quite emotional, as this was amazing for the time. By that point I was totally hooked, but still I could not afford one as I had a young family to consider. Fortunately for me, the more affordable Amiga 500 was released not much later, so I quickly got my hands on one.

A couple of months later, a software developer in the local shop I purchased the A500 from offered me his A1000, knowing I had always wanted one. We made a deal and I bought it from him along with a 40MB SCSI drive – I have that same A1000 to this day. The A500 would end up being used to promote one of my products and was lost in time ...

CHECKMATE DIGITAL AND THE CHECKMATE A1500, 1989–1990

The developer who sold me the A1000 introduced me to a man named James Campbell. They were working together on a 16-bit sampler for the high-end Amiga market and James needed a partner to help launch it. Around this time, my doctor told me I needed knee surgery and would have to stop my roofing job for at least six months – and in that way, fate decided that I quit the roofing game and finally move into my first love since school: computers. I didn't need too much persuading.

James had an office in Stoke Newington, and though sadly the 16-bit sampler did not make it to market, we began development on a new product that would become the Checkmate A1500, a case for the Amiga 500 that would allow for internal expansion. Though I did not design the case, I talked James into creating a Zorro II and video slot because the original designer had just made an adaptor for the A590 that prevented accelerators from being fitted. We added a left-mounted Zorro II slot for the A2000-HC8+ RAM/SCSI card, which we would actually cut in half to get it to fit inside.

A video slot was provided on the right that connected to the Denise chip so you could fit a flicker fixer, and a Mega-Midget Racer 030 card was installed so that what you were left with was an incredibly

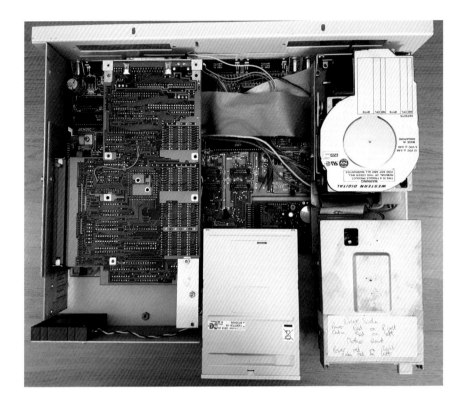

Inside the Checkmate A1500,
complete with two floppy disk
drives and A590 adapter board

powerful upgrade for the humble A500. In the end, the system had
a 33mhz 68030 CPU/8882 maths coprocessor Amiga 500 with 16MB
RAM, a 512MB SCSI drive, a flicker fixer and two floppy drives, and
included a boosted power supply based on a PC power supply unit. As
you can see, this was *the* Amiga to have until the A3000 came along.

AMIGA PRODUCTS SOLD UNDER CHECKMATE DIGITAL
Though we sold a lot of Amiga products, we also acted as distributors
for a number of groundbreaking third-party products as well.

CANDO FROM INNOVATRONICS
CanDo was essentially *Visual Basic* long before Microsoft knew what
that meant, and it was an incredible piece of software. It grew out of a

developer tool and allowed you to lay out windows and then generate all the source code for you. It was an amazing self-contained programming tool. It's a shame they went bust before the introduction of AGA (Amiga Advanced Graphics Architecture), because if it had supported that and Workbench 3.0 it would probably still be the ultimate development platform for beginners all the way up to serious programmers.

HAM-E FROM BLACK BELT SYSTEMS
This amazing device gave Amiga users 24-bit colour HAM8 modes long before AGA arrived. It worked like a DCTV video digitizer, but instead of outputting just composite video, it had true RGB video output that could be genlocked (a form of picture synchronisation). It worked by converting two hi-res interlaced 16-colour images that were encoded in a special way to give you 8-bit planes instead of the usual 4. They had some great software to go with it as well.

ARCHOS AVIDEO 12/24-BIT GRAPHICS CARDS
These days, Archos is a big France-based company, but we used to distribute some of their great early Amiga products. They had a fantastic hard drive system for the Amiga 1200 called the Archos OverDrive, but more importantly they developed these amazing 12 and 24-bit graphics cards that fit onto the Denise chip in the Amiga. Later on, these would fit in the video slot and give a genlocked hi-res 4096 colour mode animation, or a full 24-bit frame buffer with 12-bit animation. They were great products that sadly did not find a big audience in the UK as most users at the time were just playing games. (As a side note, I saw the first ever Amiga 3500 at Archos with an early version of the AGA chip set.)

These products were well-received and we would try to sell them into the professional CAD, graphics and animation markets, among others. But the problem was always the same: as soon as people discovered that the Checkmate A1500 had an A500 inside, the usual refrain of 'Oh, that's just a games machine' would surface – it is ironic to think back on, as these days most office machines are just as capable of playing video games.

The good news is that we sold plenty of Checkmate A1500s to Amiga 500 owners who wanted a neat way to upgrade and make their computer look like a big box machine. So much so that it caught some unwanted attention.

COMMODORE MEETING, 1990
I had accrued a lot of good PR from thriving Amiga magazines like *Amiga User International* (with the wonderful Anthony Jacobson), *CU Amiga*, *Amiga Future* and so on. People liked what we were trying to do – so much so that we received an invite to meet Commodore at their Maidenhead offices.

We wanted to make a good impression at the meeting so I bought a new suit and, to help set the right tone, James insured his black Porsche Turbo in my name for the day so I could turn up in style and look more impressive than we actually were (and obviously I would make a little noise on arrival!).

I was invited into the office by Kieron Sumner and told in a very short meeting that what I was doing was hurting Commodore and that they were going to wipe us out, accompanied by a few unrepeatable words to emphasise the point.

'Oh,' I thought as I sat back in the Porsche. 'That could have gone better.' It would not be the last time somebody at Commodore had disappointed me.

A couple of months later, Commodore released the 'official' Amiga 1500 – essentially an A2000 with two floppy disk drives and a tacky 'A1500' sticker on the front of the case. More importantly – and most damaging to us – they slashed the price.

The rest is history, and they made good on their threat. So begins the history of Commodore being their own worst enemy.

HIQ A500 TOWER, CIRCA 1991
Stinging from defeat, James and I decided to go more high-end and developed the HiQ Amiga 500 Tower with an added bus board. This had six slot lines that could be a mixture of CPU, Zorro II, ISA and video. It was to be distributed by Innovatronics in the US for the Video Toaster, but sadly Innovatronics went bust shortly before the

product was due to be shipped.

This was very sad as we had already made about five prototypes that all worked brilliantly. Even worse, this final straw ended my fruitful partnership with James (though he did create one more thing for me – more on that below).

I took the HiQ A500 to a New York show with a Video Toaster installed and it went down very well, so much so that NewTek's Tim Jenison gave me a free copy of their 3D-rendering software, *LightWave 3D* (in fact we still keep in touch occasionally to this day).

But that was not the most memorable part.

We had spent ages preparing the machine for the show. The case was huge, so we boxed it up and I decided to take it with me on the flight to New York as cargo hold luggage. On arrival, I was told by security to go into a room and wait – suffice to say, I was a little nervous.

When the cop walked in snapping on a pair of surgical rubber gloves ... well, I thought the worst, but luckily they were only for examining the system! I looked on and begged them to be careful as they took the machine to pieces, telling them repeatedly it was a prototype. Once they were happy there were no drugs hidden inside it (bombs were not the issue back then), they told me why there was a problem.

Apparently I should have filled in a special import form for the computer, and me saying it was an Amiga made them trust me even less: this was scary, new-fangled tech from outer space!

But despite my uncomfortable journey, the show went great. Those were the heady days of the Amiga, and all the greats were there: NewTek, Digital Creations and so on. I even went to one of the fabled NewTek parties – which was amazing, but I was very shy and sat in the corner like a lonely nerd (though Kiki Stockhammer did look amazing, of course).

HIQ POWERSTATION, CIRCA 1993

As a hardware and software developer, I was now working pretty much on my own. Thinking towards my next pay cheque, I came up with the Amiga 1200 PowerStation, a simple idea based around an OEM PC desktop or tower case.

Inside the HiQ
A500 Tower

I get hold of a bunch of Amiga power connectors and used them to custom-wire PC power units to power the Amiga. And as they were off-the-shelf cases, I could fit SCSI CD-ROM drives, hard drives and so on.

It was great business – people would order a SCSI controller, some RAM and a PowerStation to upgrade their A500, A1200 or A600. It carried on happily for a while, but the A1200 had more potential for the next product owing to the inclusion of the great Amiga OS3.

SIAMESE SYSTEM, 1996

As I was selling these systems I had been thinking about ways of putting a PC motherboard into the Powerstation that could share components with the Amiga. Windows 95 PCs were becoming a serious threat, and this meant we could give users the best of all worlds:

Amiga, Windows and even Macintosh platforms.[1] James kindly returned to develop a video switcher card that could be controlled by the serial port and plugged into the PC, and I contacted Paul Nolan of Photogenics to develop things like control software for drive sharing and so on.

The software would switch between the separate video outputs of the Amiga and the PC using a keyboard combination so that the PC display ultimately acted as another Amiga screen. We supplied a parallel cable that enabled the PC drives to mount on the Amiga, which made file transfer very simple, and code was written to enable the sharing of mouse and keyboard, and to allow sound to be routed to the PC's 16-bit sound card.

The product sold really well, especially through our German distributors, Eagle Computers. But as usual, I wanted more.

SIAMESE SYSTEM RTG, 1997

I asked Paul if it was possible to create Amiga windows on the PC to display Amiga programs over the serial cable. Paul went so much further than I could ever have hoped for, coming up with a retargetable graphics (RTG) solution that could interface with AmigaOS using the available hardware. Over the next few months, we managed to get the new SiSys RTG to market as a Siamese 2.5 upgrade, which again sold very well. It was quite possibly the first efficient remote desktop software ever, and worked by getting the PC graphics card to act like an Amiga graphics card. It was so efficient it even worked using serial interface speeds. As it was TCP/IP-based it could be run over a network too, so with an ethernet card we were getting speeds comparable with the best Amiga graphics card on a Zorro II bus.

MICK TINKER'S INSIDEOUT, 1997–1998

Around the time of the Gateway buyout – maybe just before – I visited an Amiga show (I think it was the Cologne Computer Show '96)

---

1   The Macintosh operating system was possible on all Amigas (with enough RAM) via the use of emulation software and an official ROM, as the Amiga shared the same 68000 processor. (The retargetable graphics needed Kickstart 3 to achieve 256 colour mode, however.)

Packaging for the
Siamese System

and met up with Mick Tinker[2] of Index Information at a developer meeting. He told me he had something to show me, opened his brief-case and pulled out a PCI card with a Motorola 68040 on board.

Instantly I knew that if we put this into a Windows PC with our Siamese RTG and custom software we would have the makings of a next-generation Amiga project. This iteration may not have had the AGA chipset, but the serious market was moving to RTG-based applications with 24-bit graphics anyway, and we knew that was the future for the Amiga.

This card was essential for running Windows 95, Amiga and Macintosh software on the same computer – but I knew that for the Amiga to survive as a platform, its OS would need to be ported over to the x86 architecture (although as this was before Amiga emulation you would still need separate hardware to run classic Amiga software

2   Mick is perhaps best known for his BoXeR motherboard.

that relied on the original chipset). Once ported to an x86 system the Amiga would be free again, but on a far more cost-effective performance platform (if not the most elegant).

I knew this as far back as then, but it would not be an Amiga company who realised my vision ...

It was at around this time that I had the second disappointment in my decade-long Amiga career.

I was at a conference in Stockholm. Petro Tyschtschenko had just finished a speech about how things were great at the company and had segued into trying to sell to the crowd a boing ball mouse mat and music CD. I got on stage and explained he was talking rubbish, showing people the PCI Amiga card and explaining the potential with Siamese RTG. The crowd loved the concept, especially as some were already Siamese System owners – and yet Petro had no interest in progressing the Amiga through this route. He did not even want to discuss its potential. Such a shame.

PCI AMIGA CARD AND THE GATEWAY 2000 PURCHASE OF AMIGA, 1998

Some time in 1998, Paul Nolan, Mick Tinker and I were invited by Gateway 2000, who now owned the Amiga, to visit their headquarters in South Dakota. They entertained us at a local lap dance bar (of all places), which I recall we got to by passing a very smelly meat processing plant in the middle of nowhere. (Suffice to say, they were very pretty girls and Paul got his first lap dance!)

The next day, discussions were had with the heads of Gateway 2000's new Amiga team, who were planning on putting the PCI Amiga card into their high-end Gateway PCs. Remember, by this point Amiga was nowhere in the business world (it arguably never was), so to get it included on all of Gateway's machines would have been amazing.

At that time, you could still emulate the Macintosh legally as the ROMs were readily available, and Gateway knew we were doing this with the Siamese RTG system. By putting a fast 040 – maybe later an 060 – into the PC and running our Siamese RTG custom software, the PCs would outperform the latest Macintosh 040 machines due to the greater speed of Windows 2D graphics cards of the time, and would allow for cutting and pasting between the platforms as you did with the Siamese System. And obviously they would be able to run the whole Amiga software library.

I stated that over time I believed we could fully port the Amiga operating system over to x86 architecture and so get access to all of this great low-cost commodity PC hardware. We signed a letter of intent with Gateway 2000, received tens of thousands of dollars between us, and returned to the UK feeling triumphant.

Over the following weeks we waited and waited, and looked forward to working with this big American backer – but in the end all we got was a cancellation letter saying the project was no longer going to happen.

Running multiple operating systems on one machine that can share data is commonplace these days, but at the time it was a novel concept, and the Amiga could have been the driving force behind it. So many missed opportunities.

This marked the end of my 12-year Amiga adventure – they had been some of the happiest days of my life.

THE BIGGEST MISTAKE OF MY LIFE

With Gateway's letter of intent I thought we had a solid contract and began investing all of my time and a significant amount of my own money into the project. I made the regrettable decision to start taking £50 pre-orders to ensure demand, but having received around 25 of these that I put safely away in a company savings account, it became clear things were not happening as planned. But by the time I had stopped accepting deposits, the damage was done.

In the end I lost my house, my company went bust and – perhaps inevitably – my marriage collapsed.

In the midst of this I lost all the pre-order money when the auditors stepped in. Over time I have managed to track down a handful of these early investors and personally refund them, but there are still 10-15 outstanding. (If you are reading this and can prove you were one of them, I will gladly honour the refund, for double the amount to account for inflation.)

I suffered depression for a while and threw most of my Amigas out, including an Amiga 4000T tower (which, looking back, was such a shame). The only model I kept was my A1000, but that was put in a box and locked in the garage for over a decade.

After a while, a good friend of mine in the Amiga business, Tony Ianierie of Power Computing, talked sense into me and told me to go out and get a proper job – some of the best advice I have ever been given. I got myself together, walked into an internet system developer job (a role I still do to this day), sorted out my financial problems, bought my own place and secured equal shared custody of my wonderful kids.

AROS, 2008

But my love for the Amiga would resurface when I found out that while I had been away, my dream of running an Amiga on x86 architecture had become a reality. I had thankfully skipped the Power PC wars – it had been obvious to me and others all along that the x86 would win the CPU battle (although I now believe the Amiga community should focus on ARM as its future platform).

I came across the open-source Amiga operating system Amiga Research Operating System (AROS) running on x86, and though it was far from perfect, I was amazed. I still had terrible guilt over the PCI Amiga card pre-orders, and believing in karma, I saw this as an opportunity to try and balance things in some way.

I could see that what was needed was a low-cost AROS computer that could run on Intel Atom processors at a cost of a couple of hundred pounds, and decided to look into making these as a viable business project.

ALL AMIGA DEVELOPERS ARE ANGELS

I knew I would need custom drivers written for my project, so I decided to contact the Amiga community: Nick 'Kalamatee' Andrews wrote the network driver; David Wentzler wrote the AHI sound driver for the HDAudio chips (and actually over-delivered, expanding on the brief to cover most of the Intel HD Audio subsystems of the time); Neil Cafferky wrote a driver for the Atheros 5000 Wi-Fi network chip; and the great Michal Schulz wrote an amazing graphics driver from scratch for the Intel GMA 950 chipset, a massive undertaking that took him quite a few months. Because AROS is based on an OpenGL system, Michal's driver meant that Intel GMA chips were now 3D ready.

Armed with this toolbox, I launched the iMica computer. It only sold a few dozen units, but anybody who purchased an Atom board or netbook with these chipsets could build and run an AROS experience and use the great Amiga emulator that was built in. A good example is the Acer Aspire ONE D150 netbook that is fully supported and works beautifully even now with the latest version of Icaros (a modern operating system based on AROS).

With all this work done, I went to the launch of the original Raspberry Pi and got talking to its founder Eben Upton, an amazing guy and secretly a huge Amiga fan who owned an Amiga 600 back in the day. He wanted to get an Amiga emulator onto the Pi so that it could run Amiga games and was fully prepared to fund the development, even back then. I saw another great opportunity for the Amiga community.

I contacted Cloanto (makers of *Amiga Forever*, the official Amiga emulator) and Hyperion (current developers of AmigaOS) to see if they were interested in working together to get an Amiga emulator onto the Pi. Unfortunately the project never went any further.

Since then, the *UAE4ARM* emulator and a Linux distribution called *Amibian* have both emerged – both create an amazing Amiga experience on a Pi3 that is faster than even my 68060 and Cybergraphics 3D-upgraded Amiga 2000. A happy ending at last.

ANOTHER BREAK FROM AROS

After this let down – and perhaps still sore from the catastrophes before – I decided to just let it all go and concentrate on my new marriage, and in the end I took a break of about three years.

But I am back again and I have been doing another round of developer support and video promotion to get more modern drivers created for AROS to bring it up to date with the latest high-end components. Exciting times.

The Icaros desktop environment,
created by Paolo Besser and
based on AROS

WHY AROS?

While others have had the complete AmigaOS source code to work
from over the past 15 years, AROS development is a complete rewrite
of AmigaOS3.1, which was the final official version of Commodore's
iconic operating system. As such, AROS is probably the most
advanced version: it has had a standards-based OpenGL 3D engine
since 2010; 64-bit SMP (for CPU multi-core) that allows for greater
than 4GB ram; a large library of driver and software support; and is
available on x86, 68k, PPC and ARM platforms. With the acquisition
and integration of Directory Opus 5 source code, the file-handling
system is also amazing with easy FTP access and other benefits.
Porting Amiga and Linux applications is made easy with a full development tool kit, there is SDL support for 2D graphics, AHI retargeting
sound implementation, a USB stack and a Linux-hosted version of
AROS to help Linux developers get started. And on top of all this, it is
open source!

In the old days you had UNIX and it was controlled by a big company, AT&T, with all the problems associated. Then along comes Linux,
a complete rewrite of UNIX, just as AROS is to the Amiga OS. Now

The new Checkmate A1500 Plus, a modern re-
imagining of the original Checkmate A1500.
See www.amigasystems.com for more details

Linux is the dominant force in the computing world and an amazing system in its own right, and I think AROS has the same potential.

SO HERE'S A CONTROVERSIAL IDEA...

AROS becomes a central repository for all Amiga x86, ARM and 68k software. Hyperion and MorphOS continue with their excellent PPC OSs but also create their own distributions of AROS on these other platforms (x86 and ARM), just like Icaros on x86 and now Vampire with AROS 68k. All platforms dip into the AROS source code library, as has been done before, and help improve and add features to the AROS source. People can then run any Amiga brand on any platform and we all benefit.

There are some issues to overcome for us to get there, but if it works for the biggest companies in the world using Linux, surely it is possible in our little pond.

WHAT IS AN AMIGAN?

An Amigan is somebody who fell in love with the Amiga back in the day but has a spirit in them that makes them want to create, push their Amiga to the limit and stretch the boundaries of what is possible.

Stephen Jones today, sat next
to the Checkmate A1500

In the old days, it meant developing bits of hardware to capture images or sound, bouncing videos around a screen in hardware, writing software that could render ray-traced images, animating in paint software or making music. It meant being in awe of demo writers and game creators who could amaze us all with what they could wring out of the chipset, and of the coders who simply wrote useful utilities to backup disks. Amiga is about creation, and to my mind an Amigan creates.

We are lucky in this community to have such a diverse group of users and developers, and those in control of the great Amiga IP need to give back and work towards the bigger picture.

We are a small community, but if we work together, we can make Amiga great again.

13

THE STORY OF THE COMMODORE 65

CARLO PASTORE

My passion for Commodore machines started with the Commodore 64.

I was given my C64 when I was 14 years old. At the time, all my school friends had personal computers – computer science was a big thing among us teenagers. And the C64 was undoubtedly our favourite machine.

One afternoon, when I got back from school, I saw on my parents' bed the computer with its cassette player and joystick. I remember clearly the sunlight reflecting off the immaculate box.

I spent hours and hours trying to understand what could be done with that object. It could play games, certainly – but you could also program your own. Computer science at that time was already full of creativity, fantasy and beyond. I remember fondly how the descriptions and images of video games in magazines at the time were many times more complicated than their simple representation on screen. But all it took was imagination to fill in the gaps.

Now you may ask, 'Why a chapter on the Commodore 65?' Well, many prototypes at Commodore never saw the light of day – but this one was meant to be the successor to the best-selling computer of all time. So what happened?

THE HISTORY

In January 1982, Commodore Business Machines introduced the world to what would become the best-selling personal computer of all time, the Commodore 64, which went on to sell over 20 million units.

Trusty independent home-computer shopkeepers were still a thing back then – back before the larger retailers came along and took over. These small neighbourhood businesses would also be interested in the larger world of electronics. The owner of one such small retailer in Rome, an 80-year-old man called Antonio, once told me a touching moment from his career selling electronics.

The launch of a new Commodore product was a tantalising prospect for computer lovers back then – the same people who today would covet the newest mobile phone and excitedly anticipate the latest technology coming to market – and Antonio was always on the lookout for the latest electronics.

He remembers clearly, that December in 1982, the contagious excitement he felt when a customer held the Commodore 64 in their hands for the first time. Commodore had warned distributors months earlier that a new computer was coming in time for Christmas. They'd said it was amazing – and so it was.

The C64 represented a prodigious leap forward compared to its predecessor, the VIC-20, which itself had been no slouch at market – it was the first computer to exceed 1 million pieces sold.

And the C64? Well. High-resolution graphics, text mode, a dedicated sound chip, expansion slots, RAM that could expand quite some way (at a time when even 1k of RAM came at considerable cost), movable sprites and a competitive launch price of $595.

There is, to my mind, no human activity for which an application on Commodore 64 has not been designed – from software that monitors the growth of plants to a program that adjusts the angle of an antenna to better receive television broadcasts.

With such great versatility and near endless possibilities for designing video game and work applications, the Commodore 64 developed a broad base of dedicated programmers and end users. It was so easy to code for and so prevalent that every Commodore 64 had the potential to produce software for distribution – indeed, many software houses at the time would comprise a single person working form their bedroom. Its large user base and a sudden increased interest in software development made the machine a resounding success – and Commodore along with it.

The history of this gloriously flawed company in fact runs parallel to the sales of the Commodore 64. For many years, profits from the runaway sales of this computer would fill in gaps in the company's balance-sheet that would result from the production and marketing of machines that, even from their outset, had a whiff of failure.

In 1985, Commodore launched the Commodore 128. The C128 was actually three systems in one, and on the same motherboard featured a CSG 8502 processor with BASIC 7 and 128k RAM, a CP/M system with a Z80 processor and a Commodore 64. It should have been the successor to the Commodore 64, but in the end it was not.

The reasons as to why the system's features were never fully utilised have never been clearly outlined. Perhaps given the wide range of applications already developed for the C64 there was no real incentive to make new software on the newer hardware. A more drastic change was needed, something to stimulate the imagination of programmers and development houses.

By 1987, Commodore 64 sales were not in any kind of crisis, and the revolutionary 16-bit Amiga was already on the market. But there was still room for what could be considered an entry-level machine – something suitable for everyone that was cheap and had a wide range of software. But how long could the C64's success have lasted in the light of increasingly fierce competition? A powerful and efficient successor was required.

So, the company conceived of the Commodore 65.

A small group of engineers and technicians were asked to design a worthy successor to the Commodore 64. Bill Gardei, an eclectic engineer and expert in video, was appointed project manager; CPU design was given to Victor Andrade (a true talent, he later went on to create the AMD Athlon (K7) line); memory controller work was assigned to Paul Lassa; and system software was the responsibility of Fred Bowen (considered in Commodore a software wizard, who had already written the Basic 7.0 program that came with the C128,

The Commodore 65 (prototype)

as well as several other operating systems for the company's various computers).

First they changed the operating system. The C64's BASIC 2.0 used PEEK and POKE[1] to manage audio and video by reading and writing into certain memory locations, but had no specific instructions for managing dedicated hardware. Moreover, the slow execution of the BASIC interpreter meant the language was unusable for commercial and professional applications. In order to get decent BASIC programming language on the C64, you needed *Simons' BASIC*,[2] which was achieved by purchasing an external cartridge and sacrificing kilobytes of memory to set up the interpreter. BASIC Version 10 for the Commodore 65 was therefore designed from scratch.[3]

The CPU was the CSG 4510 (codenamed 'Victor'), and was a custom processor that underwent a number of revisions (the most common being 3) and had a clock of 3.54 MHz. Based on the 6502 core, it was

1   PEEK and POKE are commands used to access the contents of a specific memory cell referenced by its memory address.
2   *Simons' BASIC* was an extension to BASIC 2.0 for the Commodore 64 written by 16-year-old British programmer David Simons in 1983.
3   Development of BASIC continued in an unofficial capacity by engineer Fred Bowen, who went on to complete the instruction set in November 1991 after the project had been abandoned for many months.

COMMODORE 65
TECHNICAL SPECIFICATIONS

- CSG 4510 R3 CPU with a clock frequency of 3.54 MHz
- CSG 4567 graphics chip (aka VIC-III) capable of producing 256 colours from a palette of 4096 (supports all VIC-II video modes)
- A text mode with 40/80 × 25 characters
- Genlock synchronisation with external video source
- An integrated DMA Controller (DMAgic custom chip)
- Two CSG 8580R5 SID chips for stereo sound, and separate control (left/right) for volume, filter and modulation
- 128 kB RAM, expandable up to 8 MB using a RAM expansion port
- 128 kB ROM
- BASIC 10.0
- A 3½-inch DSDD floppy disk drive

The Victor (top) and Bill (bottom) chips

a significant step up while maintaining compatibility with the 6502's instruction set.

Video was to be handled by a powerful CSG 4567 chip (also known as 'Bill' or the 'VIC-III'), which could achieve a resolution of 1280x400 pixels. Fully compatible with the C64's VIC-II, it would have represented a significant evolution.

Audio was entrusted to two 8580 SID chips (the C64 only had one) and would have outputted in stereo.

The computer also included a programmable logic array (PLA), which was ELMER in some board revisions and IGOR in version 2b, and dealt with communication between CPU and GPU.

Board revision 2b

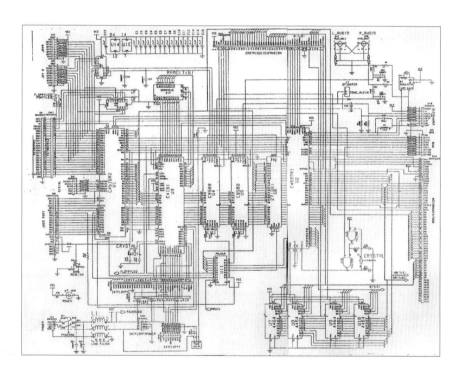

Schematics for
board revision 1

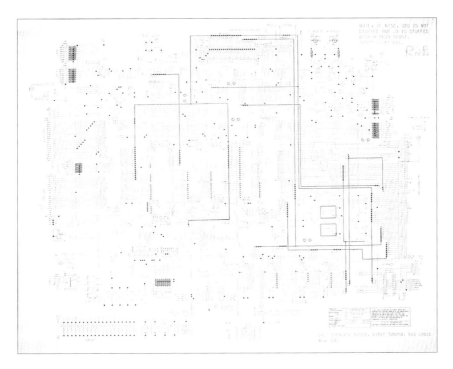

Schematics for
board revision 2b

Another change of direction was the idea to integrate the logic for the control of disk peripherals (handled by a CSG 4165 chip) into the motherboard. This meant that a peripheral was no longer necessary to do the task, just a few circuits handled by the computer. A 3½-inch floppy disk drive was to be integrated into the machine, although a cheaper model would have excluded this with the option to purchase it separately as an external drive called the Commodore 1565.

There was also an expansion port underneath the computer at the back, as with the Amiga 500, which could hold an enormous 8MB of memory.

So as not to lose the large user base of the Commodore 64, the C65 maintained minimum compatibility with its forbearer. As such, the C65 could run around 70 per cent of the C64's software – 100 per cent compatibility would not have been possible and was not sought after as it would have limited the new features of the machine.

If you held down the Commodore key as the machine was turned on, you could directly access the Commodore 64 emulation portion of the computers main ROM. Or, if you needed to access it during a C65-mode work session, you were able to using a GO64 instruction in BASIC 10.[4]

The project also recalled by name the Commodore 64: on the motherboard the words 'Commodore 64 DX' were imprinted, alongside the initials of all the participants in the project.

SO EVERYTHING WAS PERFECT! WELL, NOT REALLY...

The development team's small size, combined with economic difficulties around that time due to the flop of the Commodore 264 series, meant that development time increased significantly. The machine, which was conceived in 1987, was not ready for Christmas 1990, the proposed date for which it was scheduled to appear on the market. Only 205 prototypes were built, equipped with the incomplete 2b revision card, and were dispatched to various Commodore locations around the world as test stations. But by that point in 1991, 8-bit computers were seen as outdated, and the project was cancelled.

This was not an insignificant expense for Commodore. Years of development, resources spent on the development of custom chips and PCBs, as well as on plastic housing, further impoverished the company's coffers. And ultimately, what was an excellent idea for the last few years of the 1980s turned into yet another financial disaster for the company.

All that could be salvaged from the project was the CPU (the CSG 4510), which went on to be used as the display manager of the Commodore CDTV CR, the successor to the CDTV. But was this commercialised? No.

---

4   This command was also available to owners of the Commodore 128 in the computer's BASIC 7. It was commonly used as owners often had to resort to C64 programs due to the lack of original software on the machine.

Carlo Pastore is the owner of
www.retrocommodore.com
and an avid Amiga fan

COMMODORE 65 IN 2017

Although development of the Commodore 65 ended in 1991, revision 5 of the motherboard could be considered almost definitive, and BASIC 10 was completed a short while after the project was been terminated.

In recent years, prototypes of this machine have emerged on the web, and some autonomous groups have thought to exhume the project and follow it up. The most advanced outcome in terms of development towards a modern version of the Commodore 65 is the MEGA65.

Housed in an case that is identical to the original Commodore design, the MEGA65 aims to be perfectly compatible with the C65, albeit with a CPU that can far outperform the CSG 4510 and a GPU capable of higher resolutions than the VIC-III (CSG 4567). It also comes equipped with Ethernet, HDMI and a Super VGA port.[5]

5   As at the time of writing the project has made significant headway, and progress can be monitored on their website at mega65.org.

A RAM expansion board for the Commodore 65 has also appeared on the web, although obviously there are only a small number of prototypes available that can benefit from it.

Commodore 65 prototypes appeared for sale on auction websites several times in 2017. One such prototype that came equipped with the original memory expansion sold for over £70,000, while another prototype featuring the 2b revision motherboard, but without the memory expansion, sold for a smaller but equally impressive sum of around £21,000.

CONCLUDING CONSIDERATIONS

Commodore developed some wonderful machines that were often ahead of time – but the company also created some great failures. And what of the Commodore 65? It was the beauty that wasn't. A machine equipped with a 3.54 Mhz processor, stereo sound, advanced graphics capable of video resolutions even higher than those of the Commodore Amiga, it was an excellent piece of hardware that perhaps should never have been marketed as a Commodore 65. In my opinion, it would undoubtedly have had a great impact on the public regardless.

But the Commodore 65 is not dead, and its ardent fans hold out for hope of its completion by the modern groups who have taken up the torch.[6]

---

6   The Commodore 65 is just another example of a product where considerable investment had been made by Commodore management without ever conducting any meaningful market research. Sadly, there was no appetite for the product from consumers or from the Commodore subsidiaries around the globe.

PART 3
APPENDIX

QUOTES

GARY BRACEY
DIRECTOR, OCEAN SOFTWARE

I have extremely fond memories of dealing with Commodore over the Amiga Batman Pack. Working with David Pleasance was an absolute joy as it was clear the passion and enthusiasm for the project was equal on both sides regarding the Commodore–Ocean collaboration – we all knew we were putting together something special for the avid games players and that belief was certainly borne out by the success of the Pack. In terms of OEM partnerships, it was 'the perfect storm' in every regard!

MARTYN BROWN
CREATIVE AND FOUNDING DIRECTOR, TEAM17

Perhaps one of my favourite memories of this very exciting time back in the early nineties was being invited down to Commodore UK HQ.

We were in the boardroom when the discussion turned to the soon-to-launch CD32. The controller prototype for the machine was brought out and we were asked what we thought of it – but before we could answer the tea lady came in and it was it was quickly hidden away so she couldn't see!

It was my first experience of prototype hardware and one I will always fondly remember. Commodore felt very much like a family back then (tea lady aside!).

MARK CALE
FOUNDER AND MANAGING DIRECTOR,
SYSTEM 3

Commodore and its computers made it possible for System 3 to prove to the world that it could create great games. With our *Last Ninja* series selling over 23 million copies worldwide (which at the time made it the best-selling home computer series ever made), the Commodore 64 proved to be the right machine to showcase that global ambition.

With an operating system one could use royalty-free and management that engaged with publishers, Commodore opened up the world of gaming to many companies that had started in people's bedrooms. It had great people like David Pleasance who understood how to sell and could bundle excellent value into a package that became the world's most successful home computer.

Many of our games were bundled into its packs – games like *Super Putty, Flimbo's Quest, Myth* and many more – and as a result, David and his team helped open doors and new ways to sell products. System 3 went on to be recognised as one of the leading games companies on Commodore systems, with classic games like *International Karate, International Karate Plus* and the aforementioned *Last Ninja* and *Myth*, as well as many others.

Commodore and its team were the catalyst for the UK gaming industry – something neither the Spectrum nor the Amstrad could claim due to their limited global reach and restricted computing and graphics power. Nor could Atari with their distant management and overpriced machines.

David Pleasance and his team didn't just build and sell computers – they helped create an industry.

DAVID GARDNER
DIRECTOR, EUROPEAN SALES & MARKETING,
ELECTRONIC ARTS

The Amiga marked the beginning of a key growth stage for Electronic Arts and our relationship with Commodore in Europe was pivotal to EA's longer-term success.

   We had an incredible situation where an early internal artist's tool called *Deluxe Paint* became a must-have piece of software on the Amiga. We were really nowhere yet in terms of setting up EA across Europe, but through our relationship with Commodore we were guaranteed a bundle where you could buy an Amiga with *Deluxe Paint* included in the box. I will always remember the nervous start of a new selling season where we would wonder if *Deluxe Paint* would be in the Christmas bundle once again. There was always a silly negotiation over the price, but it seemed to be good for both parties and we both needed it to work.

   That recurring revenue allowed EA to build itself up into a major force in the games business in years to come.

JON HARE
CO-FOUNDER, SENSIBLE SOFTWARE

For Sensible Software, Commodore was the most important of all the hardware manufacturers. We moved from being kings of the Commodore 64 to being kings of the Amiga, so the importance of this company to us cannot be understated. We were also very grateful to be involved in the discussion with Commodore UK towards the end of the Amiga's life, and greatly appreciated their acknowledgement that the leading developers were an important part of the Commodore ecosystem. I cannot think of any other hardware manufacturers that would offer us developers that much respect.

RANDELL JESUP
DEVELOPER, COMMODORE

When I joined Commodore in April 1988 (around the same time as Bryce Nesbitt, author of Workbench 2.0) it was a place where an engineer could swing for the fences and try something new. Lots of projects and products would come up from the bottom from line engineers who simply had an idea. Far from all saw the light of day, but it produced a culture of innovation and cross-pollination as people kibitzed on each other's personal pet projects.

Rarely did major direction come down from above (although that's partly because the execs generally weren't often computer people). There was the CDTV, the Commodore 65, Ed Hepler's RISC-based chipset design, the Amiga 1000+, the A4091 SCSI controller, some of the object-oriented stuff Peter Cherna did for UI elements, an A2024/ Moniterm-like hi-res colour graphics board and many others I've forgotten (or never knew about).

We were well aware that Apple probably had 10, 20 or perhaps 50 times the engineering resources we had – and IBM/Microsoft had even more. But we were keeping up with them and even at times surpassing them with a fraction of their resources.

Working under Andy Finkel, I programmed the original hard drive partitioning software; rewrote AmigaDOS from BCPL to C/assembler (including the Ram Disk and other bits); rewrote the trackdisk device (the floppy disk driver) to greatly speed it up and help it recover from disk errors much better; worked on SCSI drivers included for the A4091/ A4000T; worked on the peer-to-peer network filesystem and other Ethernet stuff; redid the CDFS for the CDTV-CR and the CD32 to add read-ahead and caching; did all the IDE drivers; and much more. By the end, I was the team lead for the operating system, but mostly because everyone else had gone – if I recall correctly, Darren Greenwald took over from Bryce then went to Scala, at which point I took over.

Most of us were there because we were passionate about the work we did. We often worked crazy hours – we literally slept on cots in a dark meeting room (which had a pile of video games in there too, such as *Asteroids*) trying to get Workbench 2.04 out the door. I saw quite a few sunsets at Commodore – often as I was arriving at work – and more than a few sunrises. That passion was on display by everyone at the 'Deathbed Vigil' party held at my house the day after Commodore's bankruptcy was announced.

I remember George Robbins – who was a core engineer, owner of cbmvax and our connection to mail/news and later the internet, and designer of many things (most notably the A500) – essentially lived at the office. He, Bryce Nesbitt and I frequently went out for pizza and pinball (before heading back to the office to work some more). Once every few weeks he would cycle 20-ish miles home to the former rail station he owned to wash his clothes and pick up his mail – on week-ends if you came in at the wrong time you would find wet footprints leading from the bathrooms back to his office from ad-hoc showers. Accounting eventually forced him to cash his drawer full of pay cheques and sign up for direct deposit. Sadly, though not surprisingly, some years after Commodore he died of a heart attack late one night in his office.

When I left Commodore, I was offered a job at DEC working on SCSI (I had been working with DEC people on a ANSI SCSI subcommittee), but I decided to join Scala instead, along with Jeff Porter. A bunch of other Commodore people were already there including Peter Cherna, and Dave Haynie joined us shortly after. That was probably in April or May 1994.

While at Scala, I did a contract job via Andy Finkel to add ATAPI CD-ROM support to the Amiga OS/A1200 for a Chinese company using Amiga technologies. I asked if I could release it (and charge them less), but they said no.

I was at Scala until September 1998, when I joined WorldGate Communications to work on internet browsing over cable boxes. I was recruited by company founders Joe Augenbraun, a former hardware engineer on the A2091 and A1000+ (among other things); Hal Krisbergh, the former CEO of General Instruments; and Randy Gort, Commodore's main lawyer in West Chester. A few other Commodore people were there at times.

WorldGate went public in 1999 and was for a time valued at over $1 billion, with around 330 employees. After a few years, however, we couldn't force the cable companies to follow through on deployment promises, and in 2003 we sold our patents to them for a few million dollars, shrunk the company to around 25 people and switched to building consumer videophones, such as the Ojo PVP-1000.

We built a videophone from scratch in under six months and showed it at CES 2004, attracting a ton of attention from the likes of Steve Wozniak and Paul Allen, and ultimately made a deal with Motorola to market it for us. We stayed in that business and were finally bought by a company that sold videophones in around 2009.

They were a multi-level marketing company and in bed with Donald Trump, who used one of our phones as the focus of an episode of *Celebrity Apprentice*. In the end they laid off everyone but the engineering team and tried to sell us. The entire engineering team quit a few weeks later in May 2011.

I then joined Mozilla. At WorldGate I led the browser team and had switched us from *Spyglass* (which Microsoft licensed to build Internet Explorer 2.0) to a pre-release version of *Mozilla*. (This was in the days before *Firefox, when* Mozilla was an open-source project at Netscape to replace *Navigator*). The company hired me to lead the WebRTC team, since I knew both browsers and video communication.

My current position is as a senior staff engineer at Mozilla, working on browser architecture, performance, security and development tools.

PETRI LEHMUSKOSKI
EX-MANAGING DIRECTOR, TOPTRONICS OY

Commodore was great fun to work with. We always focused on action, not on form, and that was the norm from the moment we started working with them. David was the energetic driver of our relationship and 'kicked our butt' many times to get things done quicker.

Towards the end of Commodore's reign you could feel the 'corporate' creeping in – they began to focus more on form than real action.

I have had the great opportunity to work with most leading companies in this industry – Amstrad, Commodore, Microsoft, Apple, Electronic Arts (from back when they were just 12 people), Activision (from before their first bailout!) and many more – but Commodore and particularly David were one of the most memorable of them all.

MIKE WEST
DIRECTOR, SDL

The early days of computer games were exciting times with significant innovation and growth and lots of great memories. David Pleasance, with his enthusiasm and single-minded commitment, signed up SDL as a Commodore distributor and by 1993, thanks to the work of Tony Deane, we were a top distributor selling 72,500 units. David was very driven in achieving results, and through packs and promotions, ensured the only gamble we made was a bet at the annual Prix de l'Arc de Triomphe races in Paris.

Commodore hospitality was always first class. In 1989, David proposed an inspired marketing sponsorship of dealer conferences arranged by the distributor. These soon became a sought after annual event, which was no surprise as they were held in Hamilton Island, Mauritius and Beverley Hills. They were great times to drive sales, talk about the future and understand dealer viewpoints. What an impressive idea!

David is also remembered for some hard bargaining and negotiation – but then that was all part of the fun!

ACKNOWLEDGEMENTS

I owe immense gratitude to the following people for their mentoring, guidance and support in putting this book together (in no particular order):

- Simon Busby (simon.busby@gmail.com) – for his editing, layout and design, chapter sequencing and general project management.
- Chris Wilkins (chris@fusionretrobooks.com) – for his Kickstarter management and 'master mentor' all things book-related.
- Dan Wood (dw@friendup.cloud) – for producing quality video updates (as well as the Blu-ray), and being a superb all-round adviser and friend.
- Trevor Dickinson (rtd@enterprise.net) – a huge Commodore and Amiga aficionado and investor in next generation Amigas, as well as a great friend, for writing the Foreword.
- Marcel Franquinet (marcel@franquinet.eu) – for being an absolute stickler for detail (thankfully), and his dynamic ideas for the book cover.
- Paul Kitching (thetekken@ntworld.com) – a creative master of 3D illustrations and rendering, for his genius with the book cover.
- Wayne Ashworth (wayneashworthartist@outlook.com) – another master of graphic design, for his work on the book cover.
- Ravi Abbot (ravi.abbott@gmail.com) – for advising on all things IT and especially on the FriendUP project, and being a good friend.
- Mike Battilana (m@cloanto.com) – the founder of Cloanto, for being a huge supporter of Commodore and Amiga, and a good friend.
- Steven Fletcher (steve@wavemstudios.com) – producer of the documentary *The Commodore Story – Changing the world 8-bits at a time*, for his help with the Blu-ray and being a very good friend.

- Kim Justice (elmyrdehory@gmail.com) – retro documentarian, for kindly allowing me to include her film *The Last Stand of Jack Tramiel: The Atari ST vs The Commodore Amiga* on the Blu-ray.

I must also pay homage to the many people who have influenced my life in innumerable ways and at completely different moments. Each has left an indelible memory on my not-so-young brain, and I owe them all a huge debt of gratitude for shaping my life and my career:

- Peter Williamson, who introduced me to and taught me how to play the ultimate guitar playing style called flamenco.
- David Beresford, a fellow musician, great friend and flatmate (remember the insanity of 'The Davey Brothers'? Haha!).
- Michael Bourne, a friend and mentor of all things classical guitar-related (and at one time my landlord).
- Leo and Sonja Avellaneda, brother and sister guitarist and dancer, and my fellow performers in our flamenco outfit Jaleo Flamenco with whom I did many television appearances and concerts in Australia.
- John Smith, my work colleague first at Practical Credit Services in Sheffield and then at to Commodore – a great friend.
- Colin Stokes and Paul Patterson, sales director and sales manager respectively at Ocean Software, who helped immensely with ideas and concepts for some of the bundles CBM UK developed – very memorable laughter.
- Simon Wilson, managing director at Design Directions, who, with his superb team, created all the designs for our packaging and marketing brochures – simply the best in the business.
- Sally Costerton, director at Quentin Bell, our PR agency at Commodore – exceptionally skilled and well connected.
- Jennifer Laing, managing director at Laing Henry, advertising agency par excellence (and later acquired by Saachi & Saachi).
- Ed Fermor, a sublime musician, good friend and my business partner in Tangent Music Design (you can hear his talent on our concept album 'Everybody's Girlfriend', a celebration in music of 10 years of the Amiga that I have just re-released in support of the launch of this book.

- Hogne Titlestad, founder and chief architect of the Friend Unifying Platform.
- Arne Peder Blix, joint founder and CEO of Friend Unifying Platform.

Apologies if I have left any of my many wonderful friends off of this list – I have been truly blessed that you have been in my life, and you are all incredibly special to me.

PHOTO CREDITS